TO PIXAR AND BEYOND

TO
PIXAR
AND
BEYOND

MY UNLIKELY JOURNEY WITH STEVE JOBS
TO MAKE ENTERTAINMENT HISTORY

—

LAWRENCE
LEVY

HOUGHTON MIFFLIN HARCOURT
BOSTON   NEW YORK
2016

For information about permission to reproduce selections from this book, write to trade.permissions@hmhco.com or to Permissions, Houghton Mifflin Harcourt Publishing Company, 3 Park Avenue, 19th Floor, New York, New York 10016.

WWW.HMHCO.COM

Library of Congress Cataloging-in-Publication Data
Names: Levy, Lawrence (Lawrence B.), author.
Title: To Pixar and beyond : my unlikely journey with Steve Jobs to make entertainment history / Lawrence Levy.
Description: Boston : Houghton Mifflin Harcourt, 2016.
Identifiers: LCCN 2016020541 (print) | LCCN 2016023332 (ebook) | ISBN 9780544734142 (hardback) | ISBN 9780544734197 (ebook)
Subjects: LCSH: Levy, Lawrence (Lawrence B.) | Executives— United States—Biography. | Pixar (Firm)—History. | BISAC: BUSINESS & ECONOMICS / Management. | BUSINESS & ECONOMICS / Entrepreneurship.
Classification: LCC PN1998.3.L4673 A3 2016 (print) | LCC PN1998.3.L4673 (ebook) | DDC 791.4302/3092—dc23
LC record available at https://lccn.loc.gov/2016020541

BOOK DESIGN BY MARK R. ROBINSON

Printed in the United States of America
DOC 10 9 8 7 6 5 4 3 2 1

For Hillary, Jason, Sarah, and Jenna

CONTENTS

PROLOGUE

"HEY, STEVE, YOU UP FOR A WALK?" I ASKED OVER THE phone.

It was the fall of 2005. Steve Jobs and I had asked each other that question countless times over the past ten years. But this time was different. Steve had turned fifty earlier that year and the burden of cancer and surgery was taking its toll. For a while now we had kept our talks and walks light. Steve had enough on his hands at Apple. In the past year he had introduced a new line of iPods, including the brand-new iPod shuffle and iPod nano that continued to usher in a new era of music listening.

Today, though, I had something specific on my mind. I was on Pixar's board of directors, having previously served as Pixar's chief financial officer and a member of its Office of the President. I had been considering this particular matter for a while, and I felt it was time to broach it. Steve had been feeling a little better lately. This was as good a moment as any.

"Sure," he said. "Come on over. I'm around."

We lived in Old Palo Alto, a neighborhood just a mile or two east of Stanford University in California's Bay Area. Steve's house was just a few minutes' walk from mine. It sat on a corner lot, a beautiful, Tudor-style country cottage, brick walled, with a steep-sloped slate roof. I entered from the back gate and went through the kitchen door where, as was usual, an array of delicious-looking fruits and snacks sat on the long, rustic wood table. I said hello to the family chef, who was warm and welcoming, and made my way through the kitchen, down the hall, to Steve's office.

"Hi, Lawrence," Steve said with a smile, as he looked up and saw me.

"Still up for that walk?" I asked him. "We can sit if you like."

"Let's go for it," he said. "Be nice to get some fresh air."

Walking the streets of Palo Alto was a tonic for Steve. He loved the air, the architecture, the climate. The weather was clear and warm as we strolled down the flat streets lined with oak, magnolia, and ash trees, past the variety of architectures, from small ranch houses reminiscent of an earlier era to large remodeled estates that reflected Silicon Valley's growth. After we caught up for a few minutes, I brought up what I wanted to discuss.

"I'd like to talk about Pixar's stock price," I said.

"What's on your mind?" Steve asked.

"I think Pixar's at a crossroads," I said. "Its valuation is too high to stay still. If we have any miss, any miss at all, even a small one, Pixar's value could be cut in half overnight, and half of your wealth will go with it." I paused and then added, "We're flying too close to the sun."

We had enjoyed an incredible run: ten years of one blockbuster after another.

"Either Pixar uses its sky-high valuation to diversify into other businesses," I went on, "just like Disney did, or . . ."

"Or we sell to Disney," Steve finished my sentence.

"Yes, or we sell to Disney, or anyone else that offers the same opportunity for diversifying and protecting Pixar as Disney does."

But we both knew no other company did.

"Let me give it some thought," Steve replied. "I hear what you're saying."

A few months later, on January 25, 2006, Pixar and the Walt Disney Company announced that Disney would acquire Pixar for a price of $7.6 billion. At that time, Steve owned the majority of Pixar's stock, making his share of Pixar worth several billion dollars. Ten years later, due to the precipitous rise in Disney's value, those Disney shares almost quadrupled in value.

When I first started talking to Steve about Pixar, a little more than ten years earlier in late 1994, the company had burned through almost $50 million of his money, with little to show for it. The value assigned to Pixar's stockholders on its financial statements at that time was negative $50 million. Now, Steve's investment in Pixar had made him one of the wealthiest individuals in the world.

My tenure at Pixar lasted from my first conversations with Steve in 1994 until the sale to Disney in 2006. This opportunity was one of the great privileges of my life. Although much has been written about Pixar's legendary creative and production processes, my side of the story looks at Pixar from a different angle. It is about the strategic and business imperatives that enabled Pixar to flourish.

It is perhaps easy to look at Pixar's film accomplishments and imagine that they emerged in a blaze of creative glory, that Pixar was created as a storytelling, artistic utopia. This wasn't my experience of it. The making of Pixar was more akin to the high-pressure grinding of tectonic plates pushing up new mountains. One of those plates carried the intense pressures of innovation: the drive for artistic and creative excellence in storytelling and the invention of a new medium, computer animation, through which to express it. The other of those plates carried the real-world pressures of survival: raising money, selling movie tickets, increasing the pace of production. These two forces ground ceaselessly against each other, causing many quakes and aftershocks.

This is the story of how the little company that made the world fall in love with toys, bugs, fish, monsters, cars, superheroes, chefs, robots, and emotions emerged from the forces at work beneath it. It is about the choices and the absurd bets and risks that made it possible. It is about the tension between creative integrity and real-world necessities, and how that tension shaped those involved with it—Steve Jobs; Pixar's creative, technical, and production teams; and me. It is a story about what it means to put the creative impulse first, and why that is so very hard to do.

This is also a story about how, through the eyes of a two-thousand-year-old Buddhist philosophy called the Middle Way, I came to see Pixar in a larger context. How I learned that the tensions at Pixar were the very same forces that lie at the heart not just of making great films, but of living great lives, building great organizations, and freeing our inner capacities and creativity.

If I learned anything at Pixar, it is that story comes first. Pixar's creative leader, John Lasseter, used to say, "Great graphics will keep us entertained for a couple of minutes; it is story that holds us in our seats."

This one began with a phone call.

Lawrence Levy
March 2016

PART I

1

WHY WOULD YOU DO THAT?

ONE AFTERNOON IN NOVEMBER 1994, THE PHONE IN MY office rang. I was the chief financial officer and vice chairman of the board at Electronics for Imaging, a Silicon Valley company developing products for the burgeoning field of color desktop publishing. It was a clear and cool fall day in San Bruno, California, near the San Francisco airport. I picked up the phone, not knowing who it might be. The last thing I expected was to speak to a celebrity.

"Hi, is this Lawrence?"

"Yes, it's me."

"This is Steve Jobs," the voice on the other end of the line said. "I saw your picture in a magazine a few years ago and thought we'd work together someday."

Even in those days, when the downfall of Steve Jobs was a favorite topic around Silicon Valley eateries, a call from him was enough to stop me in my tracks. Maybe he wasn't as hot as he had been before his unceremonious departure from Apple ten years earlier, but our industry had never had a more charismatic figure. I couldn't help but feel a spurt of excitement at realizing not only that he knew who I was, but that he had actually called me.

"I have a company I'd like to tell you about," he said.

NeXT, I immediately thought. He wants to talk about NeXT Computer. Jobs's latest venture, supposedly his long-awaited second act, had been famous for its eye-catching cube-shaped workstations, but it was also rumored to be on shaky ground, especially after it was forced to close its hardware business not too long before. My mind raced: he wants to turn NeXT around; that could be an exciting challenge. But what he said next caught me off guard.

"The company is called Pixar."

Not NeXT. Pixar. What in the world was Pixar?

"That sounds great," I said, not wanting to reveal how little I knew about Pixar. "I'd love to hear more."

We agreed to meet.

As I put the phone down, my first reaction was shock. A call from Steve Jobs out of the blue? That was startling. But the initial thrill faded rapidly; rudimentary research revealed that Pixar had a decidedly checkered history. Steve had acquired ownership of Pixar when George Lucas spun it off from Lucasfilm eight years earlier. He then apparently poured millions of dollars into the company in the hope of developing a high-end imaging computer and accompanying software. The result: not much. Pixar had long abandoned the quest to develop an imaging computer, and it was not clear to anyone I talked to what was sustaining Pixar now.

Moreover, Steve Jobs may have been Silicon Valley's most visible celebrity, but that made it all the more glaring that he had not had a hit in a long time—a very long time. His last two products before being stripped of all responsibilities at Apple in 1985—the Lisa and the original Macintosh computers—had both been commercial disasters, and the NeXT Computer was regarded by many observers as the triumph of hubris over practicality. It had been heralded as a technological marvel, but it had been unable to compete with the likes of Sun Microsystems and Silicon Graphics that sold less expensive, more compatible machines. More and more, Jobs was looking like yesterday's news. When I told friends and colleagues that I was meeting Steve Jobs about Pixar, the most common response was "Why would you want to do that?" Still, I was intrigued, and there would be no harm in a meeting. I followed up by calling Steve's office to arrange a time.

Despite his reputation, I was excited to meet Steve in person, although I really didn't know what to expect. Would I encounter the mercurial tyrant Silicon Valley loved to vilify, or the brilliant genius who led the personal computer revolution? Our meeting was in NeXT Computer's ostentatious headquarters in Redwood City, California, where, upon arrival, I was ushered into Steve's office. Rising from behind a commanding, book-strewn desk, wearing his trademark blue jeans, black turtleneck, and sneakers, Steve, a few years my senior, greeted me like he had been waiting to see me for years.

"Come in, come in," he said excitedly. "I have so much to tell you."

The conversation needed no warm-up. Steve jumped in, exuberantly telling me about Pixar—its history, its technology, and the production of its first full-length film.

"Only a few minutes of the film is finished," he said, "but you have to see it. You've never seen anything like it."

We hit it off immediately. For almost an hour I sat in a chair on the other side of his desk, listening carefully as Steve sketched out the role he hoped I would play. He explained how he wanted someone on the ground at Pixar while he was at NeXT, someone to run the business, to hone the strategy, to take it public. He described how Pixar had revolutionized the field of high-end computer graphics and was now focused on producing its first feature film.

Steve quizzed me about my background, my family, and my career. He seemed impressed that I'd studied law at Harvard; had been a partner at Wilson, Sonsini, Goodrich & Rosati, Silicon Valley's largest law firm, which had taken Apple public many years earlier; and that I had created a new technology transactions department there, the first of its kind as far as I knew. He also liked that I had personal experience taking a company public. I felt he was testing my pedigree; it seemed important to him that I be a solid citizen. I was glad that he seemed to like what he heard.

The conversation proceeded effortlessly. But even while we were clearly hitting it off, a gnawing unease was growing within me. If Jobs had in mind taking Pixar public, he must have some serious notions about Pixar's business and strategic plans. He never mentioned them, though. I thought about whether to ask if he had numbers or a business projection I could see, but he was driving the agenda, and I decided this wasn't the time to interrupt. He was sizing me up to see if he wanted to meet again. When Steve eventually asked, "Can you visit Pixar soon? I'd love it if you could," I felt pleased. I thought it would be fascinating to at least see what Pixar was all about.

By the time I was halfway home, though, my mind was back on the business issues; he should have mentioned them, and I should have pushed to hear about them. We had made a personal connection —better than I could have imagined—but how did I know Steve wasn't putting up another "reality distortion field" for which he was notorious? That phrase had long been associated with Steve's ability to make others believe almost anything, regardless of the business or market realities. Maybe he was weaving another fantasy, this time about Pixar. If I took this job and Pixar flamed out, as everyone I had spoken to seemed to think it would, the career I had so carefully built, along with my reputation, would take a huge blow.

Worse still, the more I looked, the more there seemed to be no end of individuals who felt burned by Jobs's excesses. A year earlier, there had even been a book published, *Steve Jobs and the NeXT Big Thing* by Randall Stross, a scathing critique of Steve's behavior and business practices at NeXT. I didn't want to risk being a Steve Jobs fall guy. But I decided it was better to be patient. This wasn't the time for decisions. The next step was in sight: a visit to Pixar.

Pixar was located in Point Richmond, California. I had never been to Point Richmond, never even heard of it. I had to look on a map to find where it was. Point Richmond was a tiny town between Berkeley and San Rafael. My heart sank as I mapped out how to get there. From Palo Alto, it was a ride up 101 north to San Francisco, then onto the Bay Bridge via 80 east, then 80 veered north and went past Berkeley, then onto 580 west to Cutting Boulevard where Pixar was located. I tried to tell myself that this was manageable, that it wouldn't be too bad. Inside, however, I was full of doubt. These highways were among the most clogged in California. Driving to Pixar would not be fun.

I had always worked hard to be home for my family. I had two children—Jason, who was nine, and Sarah, who was six—and my wife, Hillary, was pregnant with our third. The demands of my career hadn't made it easy to be home at the right times, but I had done my best to pull it off. I was part of my children's lives, read to them at night, helped with homework, drove them to school. I knew how much discipline that took. I didn't think I could take a job that might put this in jeopardy.

I was pretty dejected when I put down the map.

"I don't know about this," I said to Hillary one evening. "It's too far away. I don't see how we can pull it off and remain living here. And it makes no sense to move. It's far too risky for that. Who knows how long this might last? If it flames out, I think we'd want to be here."

Hillary and I had met as undergraduates at Indiana University. I started there at seventeen, a year after my family immigrated to Indianapolis from London, England, where I'd grown up. Hillary was petite, with blue eyes, wavy brown hair, and a pretty face with a cute, pointy chin. She was sweet-natured, grounded, and insightful. We had married while we were both in graduate school. We liked to say we grew up together because our twenties were a time of much change.

We had both attended graduate school in Boston, after which we worked in Florida for a little while, where my family then lived. After a couple of years there, we moved to Silicon Valley so I could try my hand at practicing law in the emerging world of high tech. With our one-year-old son in tow, we went west on our own. Hillary had a Master of Science degree in speech pathology and worked at Stanford Medical Center, where she specialized in rehabilitating stroke and head trauma patients who had language deficits. We talked through all our major decisions together.

"Don't worry about Pixar's location yet," she suggested. "I wouldn't dismiss the opportunity out of hand. Check it out. It's not time for a decision yet."

I arranged a meeting at Pixar and a few days later set out for my visit. As I approached San Francisco on Highway 101, I could see its impressive skyline appear before me: the rolling hills densely filled with homes, the broad cluster of shining office buildings in the financial district, the low clouds on the coast side that would burn off later in the day. It was a dramatic and stunning approach. As the highway split into two directions, one leading through the city toward the Golden Gate Bridge, the other heading onto the Bay Bridge toward Berkeley on the other side of the bay, I moved to the right lanes for the Bay Bridge.

The beauty of the city suddenly gave way to the reality of the clogged lanes merging onto the Bay Bridge. As I drove over the aging spans, I couldn't help but think of the Loma Prieta earthquake that five years earlier, in 1989, had caused part of the bridge to collapse, killing one person among the almost sixty who died in that earthquake. The surreal images of the slice of road that had fallen down from the top part of the bridge became alarmingly fresh as I thought about crossing that bridge every day. Once across, I could see the traffic build up on the other side of the road as the cars coming into San Francisco stopped at the long line of tollbooths. The backup seemed to last for miles. This would be my drive home. My worst fears were confirmed. How could I take a job with a commute this horrendous?

It was small consolation that if I did this drive every day, I'd certainly have time to listen to the radio. Bill Clinton was president and the Democratic Party had just lost control of Congress in the midterm elections. The news was abuzz about a coming showdown between Congress and the president. There was also plenty of good music to hear. My car radio had been playing Whitney Houston, Boyz II Men, Mariah Carey, and Céline Dion. Elton John's "Can You Feel the Love Tonight" from the past summer's smash film *The*

Lion King was also a hit. But no matter how much I was interested in the news, or enjoyed pop music, my plan was not to sit in the car listening to them for two or three hours a day.

Even worse, as out of the way as Point Richmond was, there was nothing to make up for it in terms of scenery. When arranging the interview, I had heard Pixar's after-hours answering machine proudly proclaim that Pixar was "across the street from the refinery." That was no understatement. Pixar was literally across the street from a Chevron oil refinery. I could see the tall smokestacks and mass of machinery and pipes.

Things did not appear much better as I pulled into Pixar's parking lot, in which spaces were scant. Pixar was in a one-story, ordinary office building with no remarkable features. Its lobby was equally unremarkable, small, poorly lit, with a display case against one wall that showcased some of Pixar's awards. It could not have been more of a contrast from the contemporary, sleek offices where Steve worked at NeXT. As I entered the main door, I thought to myself, "This is it? This is Pixar?"

My host for the day was Ed Catmull, cofounder of Pixar. Pixar's other cofounder, Alvy Ray Smith, had left the company a few years earlier. Ed had been recruited by George Lucas in 1979 to start the computer division of Lucasfilm that would eventually be spun off as Pixar. As Ed's assistant walked me back to his office, I noticed how dreary the place seemed: a worn carpet, plain walls, and poor lighting. Ed's office was a good size, with a wall of windows on one side and a large bookcase on the other. I glanced at books on math, physics, animation, and computer graphics. Ed had a desk at the far end of the office, and a couch at the other. He invited me to sit on the couch, and he pulled up a chair to sit across from me.

Ed was a little shy of fifty, with a slight build and a thin beard. He had a quiet, even demeanor, authoritative and inquisitive at the same time. He asked me about my background and experience, told me a little of Pixar's history, then the conversation turned to Pixar's present situation.

"As you know," Ed said, "we're making a feature film due out in November. We're also selling RenderMan software and making commercials. But we don't really have a business plan for building the company. We could really use some help sorting that out."

"How does Pixar fund its business now?" I asked.

Ed explained how it was very much just month to month. Disney paid for film production costs while sales of RenderMan software and animated commercials brought in some revenues. That wasn't enough to cover Pixar's expenses, though.

"How do you cover the shortfall?" I asked.

"Steve," Ed explained. "Every month we go to Steve and tell him the amount of the shortfall, and he writes us a check."

That caught me by surprise. I understood that Steve was funding Pixar, but I hadn't expected it to be in the form of a personal check each month. Normally an investor puts in enough money to last six months, a year, or even more. Going to an investor every month for money was unusual, and probably not much fun, judging from my knowledge of investors in companies that were running out of cash.

Ed shifted just a bit in his chair and added, "It's not an easy conversation to have with Steve."

"Not an easy conversation" was an understatement. Ed explained that getting Steve to approve Pixar's spending could be torturous. I got the sense that Ed had grown to dread it.

"Why is it so hard?" I asked.

"When Pixar was spun out from Lucasfilm, Steve wanted to invest in a hardware company," Ed explained. "We were developing a high-end imaging computer. Animation was merely a way to showcase the technology. In 1991, we shut down Pixar's hardware division."

This was my first real glimpse into the details of Pixar's history. My meeting with Steve had focused more on the future than the past.

"Steve never had his heart set on a company that was telling stories," Ed went on. "He's resisted it. It's been a struggle to keep investing in story and animation."

I had not realized that Pixar had morphed so drastically away from

Steve's initial vision. Pixar's history was starting to look a lot more checkered than I had imagined.

"So, he doesn't support what you're doing?" I asked.

"He does now," Ed said. "Steve was on board when we negotiated with Disney to make a feature film. He was a big help in making it happen. But he still gets frustrated at having to keep funding the rest of Pixar."

"How much has he invested in the company?" I asked.

"Close to fifty million," Ed said.

Fifty million! That was a huge number by Silicon Valley start-up standards. No wonder Steve griped when he had to put in more.

I enjoyed talking to Ed. He wasn't pulling any punches with me on our first meeting, even though what he was saying wasn't making me feel great about this opportunity. Pixar felt like a company that had meandered from here to there but never found its way. Why would I join a company that had been struggling for sixteen years and whose payroll was paid every month out of the personal checkbook of its owner? If I became CFO, it would be me going to Steve for that money every month. That didn't seem like a lot of fun.

I found Ed to be thoughtful, smart, and easy to talk to. His reputation in the computer graphics industry was stellar; he was definitely someone from whom I could learn, and with whom I'd enjoy working. But that wouldn't be enough. I had not realized how dire Pixar's financial situation was. It had no cash, no reserves, and it depended for its funds on the whim of a person whose reputation for volatility was legendary. True, I didn't yet have an offer for this job, so it wasn't as if I even had a choice to make. But I felt myself less and less certain that if I did, it would make any sense to take it.

It was also becoming clear that even if Steve had embraced Pixar's moves into doing more stories and content, he hadn't set out to do that. I knew that his well-publicized efforts to make a new computer at NeXT had failed. I hadn't known that his original vision for Pixar had also floundered. This meant that both of Steve's bold attempts to make computers after his departure from Apple had gone nowhere.

It felt like he had two strikes against him. One more and he might be out for good.

We were interrupted by Ed's assistant, who put her head in the doorway.

"The screening room is ready," she said.

"Let's head over there," Ed said. "We'll show you what we've been doing."

2

GOOD SOLDIERS

THE ENTRANCE TO PIXAR'S SCREENING ROOM WAS AN UN-remarkable door in one of the main hallways that ran through Pixar's offices. Behind it was a windowless, darkened auditorium. The room was about the size of a small theater, like one might find at the back end of a local cinema multiplex. At one end, to the right, was a big screen. At the other end, to the left, was a room with a window, behind which I imagined was a film projector. It was what was in between that was surprising. Instead of traditional rows of viewing seats, the room was filled with rows of old couches and armchairs. It looked like someone had picked up furniture left at the end of driveways to be given away and had dumped it all in this room. It seemed comfortable, the kind of place where you might take an afternoon nap, but was this the mission central of a studio doing serious work?

"This is our screening room," Ed noted. "Every day the animators gather here with John Lasseter to review their latest work on our film."

Ed invited me to take a seat and said he'd like to show me some of Pixar's earlier work first. The lights went down and two of Pixar's short films were played on the big screen, *Luxo Jr.* and *Tin Toy*. *Luxo Jr.* was about the relationship between two lamps, a parent and a child. *Tin Toy* was about a one-man-band toy trying to escape from a baby. It had won an Academy Award for Best Animated Short Film in 1988. Both of these films were a marvel of computer graphics and whimsy. They illustrated the beginnings and the evolution of computer animation. They had elements that were simple about them, even crude, but I found myself drawn into the plot, actually rooting for a lamp and a toy.

Next up was the main event, a screening of a few minutes from the beginning of Pixar's first feature-length film project. Ed explained that it didn't have a final name yet but went by its working title, *Toy Story*. There were many caveats.

"Keep in mind that not all the scenes you will see are completed," Ed cautioned. "Some of the animation isn't done, so you'll see a few characters moving across the scene as solid blocks. The lighting isn't complete, so you'll see dark or awkwardly lit spots. And not all the voices are final; some are makeshift stand-ins by Pixar employees."

With that, the lights in the room went black, I settled into my armchair, and the film began to roll.

"Pull my string. The birthday party's today," were Woody's first words. Woody, a computer-animated cowboy doll sitting on the computer-animated bed of his computer-animated owner, Andy.

In the next few minutes, in this ramshackle theater, in this unremarkable building across from an oil refinery, in this company that was hanging by a shoestring, I witnessed a level of creative and technical wizardry that I could never have imagined.

The beginning of the film takes place in the bedroom of a little boy named Andy whose birthday party is that day. The bedroom is a typical boy's room, with blue wallpaper dotted with white clouds and toys strewn all around. Except for one detail. When the humans aren't around, the toys come alive. And today they are in a panic over being replaced by Andy's new birthday presents.

Woody, Andy's favorite toy, is the ringleader, trying to calm everyone down. There is a moment when Woody sends a troop of little green army men to scout out Andy's birthday presents. In this sequence, the army men are approaching the door of Andy's kitchen when they hear Andy's mom coming and must freeze in place so she does not see they are alive. Andy's mom opens the door, notices that Andy has carelessly left his now-lifeless plastic army men strewn all about, accidentally steps on one of them, and kicks the rest aside. In that moment, when she steps on that soldier . . . in that moment as I sat in that theater . . . in that moment something happened that I would never have imagined. *I cared about that plastic soldier.*

I cringed at seeing the soldier injured, and I needed to know if it was okay. A few seconds later, the toy army men are up and about again. The stepped-on soldier is wounded but okay. He tells the others to go on without him, only to hear his comrade say, "A good soldier never leaves a man behind," and he carries him to safety.

"My goodness!" I thought to myself. "What is this?"

The clip ends when the toys first meet Buzz Lightyear. Andy brushes aside Woody from the prime spot on Andy's bed and puts Buzz there instead. Woody is trying to act as if everything is fine, telling the other toys that they just have to make friends with the new toy. As Woody approaches Buzz, we see Buzz come alive for the first time.

Buzz blinks his eyes and says, "Buzz Lightyear to Star Command. Come in, Star Command." Buzz believes he is an astronaut on a mission. Now, here I am sitting in my armchair as the audience. I have just bought into the delusion that these toys are real. And now I'm believing that this one toy, Buzz Lightyear, is himself delusional for not realizing he is just a toy.

This was insane.

As the clip came to an end, Ed looked over at me. "What do you think?" he asked.

"Ed, I hardly know what to say. This is extraordinary. I've never seen anything like it. The leap from the short films to here is remarkable."

"Thank you," Ed replied. "We've got a very long way to go to finish the film but you can begin to see what it might look like."

"This is going to amaze audiences," I added excitedly. "They'll have no idea what to expect. It's fantastic."

"I hope so," said Ed. "We've got a lot riding on it."

The lights went up and I found myself back in the makeshift screening room, still sitting in an old beat-up armchair. But for ten minutes I'd been transported somewhere else. Andy's room. A world where toys lived. Had feelings. Had problems. I had no idea who was behind it all, but somewhere in this building there were magicians at work.

"Can I show you around?" Ed asked.

"Of course," I replied. I didn't know if I'd be working here or not, but I certainly didn't want to pass up the chance to see how this magic was done.

The first stop was Pixar's animation department. We walked into a large open space filled with cubicles, each of which had been built and designed by its occupant to reflect his or her artistic sensibility. The area looked like a cross between a college dorm and a Halloween theme park. It was littered with old furniture, artwork, and odd collections of toys, balls, colored lights, anime, models, posters, comic books, and all manner of paraphernalia. Each animator sat in a space of his or her own design, in front of one or sometimes two large computer monitors. Some of the animators had full-length mirrors on the wall nearby.

"Why the mirrors?" I asked Ed.

"Animation is really all about acting," Ed explained. "Before the animators animate a character on screen, they will often act out the part in front of a mirror so they fully understand the movements they need to create on screen."

Ed walked me to Pixar's storyboard department where rows upon rows of large cork boards were filled with index cards on which appeared hand-drawn scenes from the movie. Each storyboard represented a sequence from the film, and there seemed to be an endless number of them stacked against every wall, and every spare scrap of space. The quality of each drawing was remarkable, and there were thousands of them, all drawn by hand, all telling a little piece of the film's story.

Then we visited the film lab, a darkroom almost filled from wall to wall by a mysterious machine that sat in the middle. The machine looked like a flat, metallic table with a large microscope type of device on it. It was an imposing machine, something you'd expect to see in a big university or government lab. I couldn't quite understand its purpose, something to do with transferring images to film. Apparently it had been hand-built by Pixar.

I was then taken to a room called the renderfarm, whatever that meant. It was a huge bank of computers whose function, apparently, was to draw the computer-generated images that made up each frame of the film.

"Just one of these images can take hours to render," Ed explained, "and we have to do over a hundred thousand of them for the film."

The scale and detail of what I was observing were staggering.

Ed then brought me back to the animation area, and we sat down at a table that had been set up in one corner. Here I was to meet John Lasseter, Pixar's creative lead. John had directed Pixar's short films, and he was the director of *Toy Story*.

John was maybe a couple of years older than me. I was struck by his bright and boyish sensibility. He wore jeans and a Hawaiian shirt, was a little stocky, with short, slightly receding hair. He had a twinkle in his eye, as if he were perpetually at the ready to play a prank.

"Thank you for coming to visit," John started, graciously. "Steve seems excited that you might be a great fit. I'd love to hear about what you've been doing."

And with that John listened attentively as I described my career so far. I told him about my law practice, and how I'd left to join one of my clients. John was interested in why I left.

"I enjoyed practicing law," I explained, "but it could be a grind, and I didn't love billing my time in six-minute increments. I looked at my start-up clients and to me they were on an adventure. One, Echelon Corporation, was developing sensors to make buildings smart. It was exciting technology; I yearned for the kind of adventure they were on."

Soon, the conversation turned to Pixar.

"John, the film clip I saw is extraordinary," I gushed. "I had no idea this was going on at Pixar."

"Not many really get what we're doing yet," John said. "We have this rare blend of the technology and the creative sides of filmmaking. I'm directing a film that's breaking ground technically, but I'm not a technology person. It's a partnership. I tell our technology team what I'd like creatively, and we go back and forth to try to make it happen. I don't get everything I want, but we work it out. Our technical team is brilliant, amazing. It's like a marriage."

"It sure shows in that clip that I saw," I replied. "I can't wait to see more. And what about Pixar as a company? How do you see its future?"

John thought for a moment. His countenance shifted slightly; he became just a bit more serious, as if what he was about to tell me wasn't easy to say.

"I'll tell you," he started. "The effort that our people have put into this company is beyond extraordinary. It's not been easy. Not easy at all. People have hung in there year after year, doing work that amazes me every single day, sacrificing for this company, and not asking much for doing it."

John had become really passionate about what he was telling me.

"These are brilliant, creative, dedicated people, from the top to the bottom of Pixar," he continued. "I want to see them gain the recognition and reward that they deserve. It has always been a struggle. But I want Pixar to succeed for them, for all of us."

By this point, John's voice was all but quivering with emotion. It was as if he were the flag bearer for a deep injustice that needed to be corrected.

We talked a little more about *Toy Story*. John explained how the idea had emerged from his earlier short films, how excited he was that Tom Hanks and Tim Allen had signed on to be the voices of Woody and Buzz, and that Randy Newman was doing the music.

These were some big names. Tom Hanks had just come off a string of successes that was making him one of the world's biggest stars — *Sleepless in Seattle, Philadelphia, Forrest Gump* — and the coming summer he was slated to star in a film with a lot of buzz, *Apollo 13*.

Tim Allen had a hit TV show, *Home Improvement,* that was in its third season and experiencing great ratings. Randy Newman had enjoyed a stellar career as a recording artist and a composer of film scores.

"They are a coup!" I said. "You must be ecstatic."

"I am," John said. "And they are so amazing to work with. And the rest of the voice cast is amazing too. We've been very lucky."

As we were wrapping up, it was hard for a Silicon Valley guy like me not to feel a little starstruck. The movie business was light-years away from anything I'd done. And here I was having a conversation about how great the voice casting was for a company I might join. It felt a bit surreal, like I was on a Hollywood studio tour rather than interviewing for a job.

As I sat there with John and Ed, my experience of the day was suddenly giving birth to a new feeling. These two leaders had dedicated themselves for years to their crafts, with almost no commercial success and recognition. I had no idea how, when, or where they might succeed, but one thing was becoming clear to me. They were winners. I might not know how that victory would come, but I was quite confident that, for them, somehow it would.

Ed then introduced me to Pam Kerwin, Bill Reeves, Ralph Guggenheim, and a few others on Pixar's leadership team, and before I knew it my visit was over. As I left the building, however, it didn't take long for my starstruck bubble to burst. I was now back in Pixar's dreary parking lot, with a view of the oil refinery across the street and a long, traffic-filled drive ahead of me.

There wasn't much point in jumping to conclusions yet; after all, I didn't know if I would even receive an offer. It certainly depended on how Ed, John, and others I had met felt about me. At the personal level, I felt it would be an honor if they did want me to join the team. But at the professional level, Pixar remained an enigma. There was so much that was great about it, but there was an even greater number of red flags. No matter how impressed I was with Steve, Ed, John, and what Pixar was doing, my job would be to build its business, make it a commercial success, maybe even take it public. This would require much, much more than my watching a few amazing minutes of a film.

Moreover, I didn't have a feeling for this business. Filmmaking was foreign to me. It was alluring to see Pixar's work, but I was no closer to wrapping my head around it than I had been when Steve first called me. In my head, a great film, great technology, even great acting talent, did not translate into a business strategy. No one had articulated what business Pixar was in, and Ed had hinted at resentments with Steve from Pixar's past. I wasn't at all sure if it would be a good idea to get in the middle of that. And I certainly didn't want to join a company simply because I felt a little starstruck.

The next day Steve called me on the phone.

"Your meetings at Pixar went great," he said. "They liked you and really thought they could work with you. I'm really happy about that. How did you feel about it?"

"Thanks, Steve," I replied. "I'm thrilled to hear that. It was an excellent visit. I was very impressed, blown away actually."

I wasn't sure how much or how many of my doubts to reveal to Steve. It seemed he was working his way toward making me an offer, which I didn't want to jeopardize even if I wasn't sure what to do. But I had to say something about it.

"I still have questions about Pixar's business," I said. "The products, technology, and team seem amazing. But I'm not certain where the business growth comes from."

"That's what we have to figure out," said Steve. "Pixar has this amazing collection of talent, doing work that no one has seen before. Now it's time to turn that into a business. I think you would be great for this. How about we get together and discuss you coming on board?"

I was excited to hear this. No matter what I thought about Pixar's business potential, I felt more than a little flattered that they wanted me to join the team. Steve and I met a couple more times, including at a dinner at his home with Hillary and Steve's wife, Laurene. The time for a decision was not far off. I needed to get closer to figuring out what I would do.

I turned for advice to my old friend and mentor Efi Arazi, founder and CEO of Electronics for Imaging, where I was still CFO. It was Efi who had given me my big break in business.

Efi was just shy of sixty, an Israeli-born entrepreneur who was heralded as one of the fathers of Israel's high-tech industry. The company he had founded in Israel, Scitex Corporation, revolutionized the field of color printing and graphic design. Ironically, Efi was often described as the Steve Jobs of Israel, partly due to his pioneering efforts in the Israeli high-tech field, partly due to his flamboyant and larger-than-life character, and partly because, in 1988, he had abruptly left the company he founded because it lost its way after its early successes.

Efi then moved to Silicon Valley with dreams of founding a new company that would continue the revolution in digital color printing. That company, Electronics for Imaging, was located in San Bruno, California. Shortly after its founding, Efi had contacted my firm's senior partner, Larry Sonsini, in search of a lawyer. Efi needed someone with experience crafting complex technology deals. Larry asked me to take the assignment. We first encountered Efi when we drove to the offices of his new company, about a half-hour drive north from my office in Palo Alto.

Efi greeted us in the lobby. He was tall and strikingly handsome, with deep blue eyes and curly hair that was heavily receding. He was immaculately dressed in tailored pants and a perfectly fitting silk shirt, and he had a distinguished, almost regal walk. Despite a somewhat thick Israeli accent, he was also very well spoken in English.

"Greetings," Efi said. "May I offer you some libation?"

"Who says 'libation'?" I thought to myself.

So began a collaboration that would take Efi and me all over the world making deals with the titans of the office automation industry, companies like Canon, Xerox, Ricoh, and Kodak. Developing fair arrangements with these enormous companies was no small task for tiny Silicon Valley start-ups. In fact, my entire law practice was built around doing this. The habit of corporate giants like these was to try to tie up the start-ups every which way they could, often blocking their freedom to become independent, thriving companies. The large corporations often had impenetrable walls of bureaucracy that were stifling to the far nimbler start-ups. My job was to make sure these little start-ups got fair deals.

As Efi and I spent more and more time together, a friendship blossomed that extended beyond business. Efi, who was over twenty years my senior, became like a favorite uncle in my family. He loved to fly sport kites, two- or four-string kites that could be made to fly exquisite patterns, and he would sometimes take my family kite flying at San Francisco's beautiful Marina Green where views of the Golden Gate Bridge and San Francisco formed a stunning backdrop.

When I began to question whether I wanted to continue to practice as a lawyer, it was Efi who gave me my first opportunity.

"You could come work for us," Efi said.

"In what capacity?" I asked.

"Whatever you want," he said. "We'll find something that works."

"It's intriguing," I replied. "But I don't think I'd want to do so in the capacity of your lawyer. If I'm going to practice law, I'm in a great place to do it. If I come on board, I'd like to expand what I do."

"You can expand as much as you want," Efi said. "I'll give you the chance to develop yourself in business, and as long as you can handle it, you can keep growing."

It was a most intriguing opportunity, a chance to see a start-up from the inside, with someone I trusted. I felt this was as good a chance as I might have to gain that experience. With the full support of my law firm, I took the job.

Efi proved to be a magnificent partner. He loved military history, and he saw business strategy as its modern-day equivalent. He could also be very stubborn and intransigent, habits that often got us into trouble. With Efi I cut my teeth quickly on standing my ground when it felt like we were heading in the wrong direction. Together with Dan Avida, the brilliant engineer Efi hired from Israel to run the company's hardware division, we built Electronics for Imaging into a powerhouse in the field of color publishing. Along the way, we took the company public and I became its chief financial officer and vice chairman of the board. In Efi I came to see that beneath his outer flamboyance was a scholar, a deep thinker, and a big heart, and I could hardly have asked for a better mentor in business, not to mention a great friend.

In 1994, Efi retired. He still visited quite often, though, and when he did he would saunter over to my office and stand in my doorway to say hello, always impeccably dressed, with his black ballistic nylon bag slung over his shoulder. Now, toward the end of 1994, I had something specific to ask him.

"Efi," I began, "my talks with Pixar have been going well. I think Steve will make me an offer."

Efi paused. He knew I'd been talking to Steve and understood I might leave Electronics for Imaging. He had met Steve a couple of times and had been an avid follower of his career and reputation.

"And what are you thinking?" he asked.

"I don't know," I said. "I'm torn. I think I have a great connection with Steve, but who knows what would happen once we started working together? The team at Pixar is extraordinary. But I can't wrap my head around their business. They've blown through a lot of capital. A lot. They don't have a clear business direction. Steve's talking about taking the company public, but it's not ready, not even close. It's like I'd be going in blind."

"And what do you make of this film they're producing?" asked Efi.

"The few minutes I've seen look fantastic," I said. "Brilliant, groundbreaking, but that doesn't make it a business. How do I know I'm not simply falling for the allure of a high-tech company making a film?"

"Lawrence, you have enough experience now to trust your instincts," Efi said. "If you can't make it work with Steve, or can't get done what you think you should, you'll leave."

And with that, Efi, the brilliant thinker and strategist, who of all people I would have expected to fully tear apart the idea of a tech company going into film, turned to discussing his latest escapades.

Efi's comment really struck me, though. Maybe I had needed some sort of tacit permission to work with Steve. People were hardly lining up to join him. If anything, they were running in the other direction. NeXT had downsized, and I didn't know of any new executive who had joined Pixar in a while. I understood that Pixar was fraught with business risk; this came with the territory. But Steve brought another layer of uncertainty. I felt like I'd be the only person heading in his direction. Efi's advice helped me with this. He essentially gave me the confidence that if I thought something was too far off, I could trust myself to fight for it, or I would have to leave.

A few days later Steve made me an offer to become Pixar's executive vice president and chief financial officer, and a member of an Office of the President that he would create with himself as CEO, Ed Catmull as chief technology officer, and me as CFO. I asked Steve if I could have a day to think about it.

I had a habit of walking when I had to think through hard decisions. On that day, I must have worn down the pavement in my neighborhood.

Rationally, it just didn't add up. I had worked my way up into an enviable position as chief financial officer of a public company in Silicon Valley. I was about to give it up to go work for a little company owned by the notorious Steve Jobs, whose record for success had gone off the tracks, and the record of Pixar itself had fared no better. My friends and colleagues were hardly going to give me a hero's sendoff.

But there was just enough intrigue about the opportunity that I couldn't get it out of my head. I didn't know what it would be like to work with Steve, but did I want to turn down the opportunity to find out, especially after we had connected in person so well? I also had to admit there was an allure to joining a company making a movie, a family one to boot. My children would love that.

I talked it over with Hillary.

"I can't help you much with evaluating Pixar," she said—like most people we knew, Hillary had never heard of Pixar before Steve called —"so I trust you on that. But I believe Steve is genuine. He really wants to work with you. You're ready to leave Electronics for Imaging anyway, so maybe this is worth a shot."

Maybe it was.

A couple of days later, still not fully certain if it was the right move, I took the leap and accepted Steve's offer.

3

PLANET PIXAR

I ARRIVED AT PIXAR IN FEBRUARY 1995. STEVE DIDN'T GIVE me any specific instruction for what to do first. Ed greeted me and, over the first couple of days, walked me around Pixar, introducing me to the key players and describing my role.

Everyone was friendly, welcoming, and greeted me with polite gestures like "Glad you're here, let me know if I can help." Something was missing, though. For as much as people were friendly and polite, I also felt they were a bit distant and aloof. There didn't seem to be a lot of excitement that Pixar had a new chief financial officer. I felt that little effort was made to include me. Not many invites to lunch, or events put on my calendar. I didn't expect a parade, but I thought this was a little muted. When I'd joined my last company, my calendar was quickly filled with meetings; they'd wanted to integrate me as soon as possible. I had the deep sense that Pixar's guard was up, and I didn't know why.

But it didn't take me long to find out. It started with Pam Kerwin, a Pixar vice president who was general manager of various business operations within Pixar. Pam was warm, gracious, and sharp. She was a little older than me, in her early forties, with striking red hair and a sweet demeanor that quickly made others feel at ease around her. Pam was also fiercely loyal to and protective of Pixar. Her office was just down the hallway from mine, and she was one of the few people who offered to meet and to give me the lay of the land.

"I don't envy you," Pam jumped in after some pleasantries, "but I don't think you really get what you're up against."

"Up against?" I asked.

"You're Steve's guy."

I must have given Pam a terribly puzzled look, because I wasn't sure what she meant.

"Pixar and Steve have a long history," she went on. "Not a good one. You don't know it yet but Pixar lives in fear of Steve."

"How so?"

"Steve doesn't get Pixar," Pam went on. "We're artsy and creative. We're like a family. We hug. And we're not a top-down organization; everyone here has a voice."

I liked hearing about Pixar's culture, but it was the strength of Pam's emotions about Steve that caught my attention.

"Steve is the guy who owns us—but he's never been one of us," Pam explained. "We've long felt unvalued, unappreciated. People worry that if he gets too close, he'll ruin Pixar and destroy our culture. And now, you're the guy he has sent to whip us into shape."

That much was true. My mission was to transform Pixar into a thriving enterprise. I was supposed to be an agent of change.

"Plus," Pam added, "he's broken promises. And people are angry about that."

"What promises?" I asked.

"Stock options. He promised them to us, and they've never materialized. Perhaps part of your job is to fix that, but every day that passes without a solution, people grow more cynical. Many here have been waiting for years to own a little piece of Pixar. All their friends at other companies have been rewarded, and now they're frustrated. They feel used. It's not going to be easy for you to win their trust."

This was a lot to take in. It certainly explained why my arrival hadn't been accompanied by much fanfare.

Pam's admonition was, if anything, understated. In my first days at Pixar I encountered animosity directed toward Steve throughout the company, especially from those who had been there since the early days. One person said to me point-blank, "Keep that man away from us." Those words really stuck in my head. How had Steve become "that man"?

This was an unwelcome surprise, to say the least. I began to fear that my concerns about Steve were coming true. I had accepted the job at Pixar with a considerable amount of skepticism. Although Steve and I were getting along great so far, his mercurial reputation had made most people I knew caution me against working with him. Even more problematic was the company itself. Pixar had been in business for ten years and had made almost no impact, and even worse, not even Steve could clearly articulate what he wanted the company to be—only that he didn't want to keep underwriting the millions of dollars it lost each year.

These were the risks I had known. Now it seemed I had the extra burden of being "Steve's guy," suspected of possessing some sort of hidden agenda. That wasn't true. I didn't have any preconceived biases at all. But that didn't matter. I was going to be more alone than I expected. Pixar began to feel to me like it was even further away from Silicon Valley than I'd thought, more like an alien planet. While the locals were cordial, they weren't going to treat me like I was one of them. At best I'd simply be left alone, at worst eyed with suspicion.

After the initial shock wore off a bit, my instinct was to figure out how to try to use this to my advantage. I determined that the best way to avert the gaze of skepticism was to do nothing that validated it. If people were going to leave me alone, I'd have a window of opportunity during which no one would expect much of me. That gave me a chance to quietly explore Planet Pixar.

I called Steve and told him I did not want to make any quick decisions, that my plan was to take a month or two to understand the company. Steve, however, didn't want me to waste time. He was still covering Pixar's monthly cash shortfall and he could not put an end to that soon enough.

"I'm focused on fixing that as soon as I can," I told him, "but I need some time to figure it out." Somewhat impatiently, Steve went along with my plan.

I asked each member of Pixar's senior team if I could follow them around for a while, literally shadow them, sit in meetings without participating, and ask them questions about what they did. I also asked for their permission to talk to the various individuals on their teams. Managers generally don't like other managers snooping around their domains; my newness absolved me from that, at least temporarily. They all went along.

I started simply by wandering around, with no agenda. I would stop randomly and talk to people, asking what they did: software engineers, production accountants, technical directors, storyboard artists, anyone who worked at Pixar.

It did not take long for me to observe the enormous complexity involved in computer animation. I would sit by the animators and watch the painstaking way they brought to life the inert, wireframe computer models of each character in *Toy Story*. It took an almost mind-numbing attention to detail for the animators to move each part of a character frame by frame, twenty-four frames per second. Imagine how many movements our own bodies have to make to walk, eat, talk, or play even for one second—each body part moving through time and space in unison. Animators have to breathe life into their characters in just this way. I watched their artistry with amazement. By adding a simple flourish to the movement of the eyes or the mouth, they could change the emotional tone of a scene entirely.

I also sat in lots of meetings. Production meetings. Sales meetings. Technical meetings. I was the proverbial fly on the wall, except that I carried around a yellow legal pad on which I wrote down questions about the things I didn't understand, which was a lot. The world of computer animation has its own jargon. I needed to learn it, along with Pixar's other endeavors.

Eventually my efforts became more systematic. Pixar had four primary areas of focus: RenderMan software, animated commercials, animated short films, and a feature film, still code-named *Toy Story*. Pixar also owned some patents, and it had tried but failed to launch an imaging computer, an effort it had abandoned a few years earlier, in 1991. If there was to be a commercially viable strategy for Pixar, it was going to exist in one or more of these areas. I needed to understand each one. I started with RenderMan, a software package Pixar had been selling for a number of years, and an enormous source of pride within Pixar.

RenderMan was a software program for generating computer images that were photorealistic. It had solved one of the peskiest problems at the heart of high-quality computer animation, namely, the ability to depict color, light, and shadow in the same quality and detail as photographic or filmed images. RenderMan had earned a fantastic reputation within the industry, having been used to draw some of the most famous visual effects in modern film, including the dinosaurs in *Jurassic Park*, the cyborg in *Terminator 2*, and the special effects in *Forrest Gump* and many other films.

In 1993, RenderMan had won its development team an Academy Award for Scientific and Engineering Achievement. This was one of Pixar's proudest achievements, and the Oscar was displayed in Pixar's lobby for all visitors to see. Ed Catmull, Loren Carpenter, Tom Porter, Tony Apodaca, and Darwyn Peachey, all members of that development team, were still at Pixar. These were luminaries in the computer graphics world, respected not just at Pixar but throughout the field.

RenderMan had another distinction: it actually made some money. Pam Kerwin, who had earlier given me those first warnings about Steve, ran the RenderMan division.

"It's not a product for consumers," Pam explained. "It's for special effects houses, advertising agencies, production studios, and film studios, places where professionals are using computer animation to create high-end special effects."

"About how many customers are there?" I asked.

"I'd say there are maybe fifty or so significant studios doing regular work at that level," she said.

Fifty! I was shocked by her answer. Just fifty significant customers —that made it a very small market.

"When studios are making films with special effects, they need lots of RenderMan," Pam explained. "Otherwise, they don't need it at all. Some years sales are up; some down. The software is really for big-budget films and a few commercials that really want to make a statement. Otherwise they don't use us, because of the expense."

"What's the average sales price?" I asked.

"About three thousand dollars," she responded.

I did some quick calculations. In a very good year, Pixar could sell a thousand copies of RenderMan. At $3,000 per copy, that was $3 million. To a company whose weekly payroll was being paid out of its owner's pocket, that was a lot of money. But to a company with aspirations for growth and a public offering, it was insignificant. To make a difference, RenderMan's business would not just need to grow. It would need to scale by a factor of ten.

And that, simply put, was impossible. There were not enough customers. It's not that Pixar hadn't tried to expand this market; under Pam's leadership it most certainly had. It's just that the demand wasn't there. At best, RenderMan looked like it would roll along at about the same rate, up a bit some years, down a bit in others. I'd seen this before. At my last company, we had launched groundbreaking, award-winning image-processing software, only to find its market much smaller than we thought. It had been my role to convince Efi, the CEO, that we had to shut it down, something it now looked like I might have to repeat at Pixar. RenderMan might be an Academy Award–winning industry leader, but from a strategic point of view, it wasn't a business; it was a sideshow.

This, of course, was not the conclusion I was looking for. I had been hired to stem the tide of red ink, and the first thing I'm thinking is maybe we should abandon the one product that was making any money. I wasn't in a rush to tell Steve the news.

Steve and I had gotten into a habit of regularly talking on the phone, usually every day, often several times a day; no hour was off limits. I had a dedicated line for business calls in my house, in the kitchen by the fax machine. Rarely did a night go by when it didn't ring. Although Steve had an almost permanent intensity about him —like he was always in top gear—there was an ease and fluidity to our talks. We could easily pick up a conversation where we had left off. If one of us was busy or tied up with family, we'd just call back a bit later. Whenever we did talk, it was like shifting from zero to a hundred miles per hour in an instant.

On the weekends, Steve would often saunter over to my house, about a five-minute walk from his. "Hey, Lawrence," he'd say. "Have time for a walk?" Then we'd meander through the streets of Palo Alto. For a person who had the means to go anywhere, Steve seemed most content in his own neighborhood. We would stop every now and again to admire one of the grand old oak trees or the features of an old house, or Steve might question the style of a new one. Sometimes we made it as far as University Avenue and had a slice of Margherita pizza.

The talks on these walks were more unhurried and relaxed, and not all business. We chatted about our families, politics, movies, and favorite TV shows. We could move easily from idle musing to Pixar's vision and strategy.

It was on one of these walks that I brought up RenderMan.

"So what you're saying," Steve said, "is that we're hooked on the small amount of money RenderMan brings in, but it's not helping us grow."

"That's exactly what I'm saying," I replied.

Steve wanted to know more.

"If RenderMan is the industry leader," he asked, "and if studios need it so badly every time they make a film, why don't we raise the price? Instead of three thousand dollars per copy, we'll make it six thousand, or ten thousand. If they need it, they'll pay."

That might be true if the studios needed RenderMan, but the problem was that, at least for most projects, they didn't.

"RenderMan might be the best software of its kind," I replied, "but there are other options. They are radically inferior, but they are still options. Production budgets for computer-animated special effects are extremely tight. Unless it's Steven Spielberg making dinosaurs for *Jurassic Park,* or James Cameron making cyborgs for *Terminator,* producers will simply live with lower quality."

Steve leaped ahead.

"Are you suggesting we stop selling RenderMan?" he asked.

"Maybe," I said tentatively.

It was a big decision, and an idea I didn't want to push too hard right now. "My fear is that it's a distraction. We use some of our best engineers to support customers. Maybe there are better things they can be doing."

The idea was to keep RenderMan for Pixar's use and to drop the considerable effort Pixar put into selling RenderMan and supporting its customers.

"Whatever we do with RenderMan, it's not going to be relevant in any sort of growth strategy or public offering."

Steve took it all in. He showed no signs of disappointment. This is a discussion we'd continue down the road. For now, it had gone well.

During my weeks of exploration of Pixar, I frequently met with Ed. Because his office was next to mine, it was easy to talk informally, which we did often. From Ed I learned a lot about Pixar's history, culture, and technology. In fact, through these talks and discussions with others at Pixar, I was beginning to discover that Pixar was, in actuality, a very warm and pleasant place. Ed, Pam, and the other executives had set an open and familial tone, and despite the initial leeriness over a new CFO, it was becoming much easier to talk to people.

In one conversation with Ed, he described the patents Pixar owned that covered some of the basic features in RenderMan. RenderMan's central breakthrough was a feature called motion blur. This gave computer-generated images the same feeling as live-action film. Without this feature, computer-generated images would look too crisp and perfect when compared to what we normally see in film. Solving this problem made it possible to blend computer graphics with live-action film, thus ushering in a new era of computer-generated special effects.

Anyone developing rendering technology would need to implement this feature, and it was hard to do so without violating Pixar's patent. Two companies in particular had been infringing our technology: Microsoft and Silicon Graphics, which was the leading supplier of workstations for the computer graphics industry.

Here at last, I thought, was an opportunity to make Pixar some money. If Pixar's patent was really fundamental, these companies might well pay significantly to license it. That would take the funding burden off Steve, at least for a while, although it wouldn't be easy to pull off. We could not just call up Microsoft and say, "Hey, you're infringing our patents; you owe us millions of dollars." To begin that conversation, we had to be prepared to sue them, which meant we needed lawyers ready to make our accusation of patent infringement have teeth. It was like preparing for battle. If they didn't see us amassing troops on the border, they'd ignore us.

Ed and I talked over the risks of asserting patent infringement claims against Microsoft and Silicon Graphics. "We might drag Pixar and especially our engineers into a long lawsuit," I said. "That could be a huge distraction."

This prospect did not discourage Ed. "They are infringing," he said emphatically. "We invented this technology, and I see no reason why others should use it for free, especially while Pixar is struggling financially. If the lawyers think we have a good case, I'm behind it."

The next step was to discuss it with Steve.

"You're saying that Microsoft and Silicon Graphics are infringing Pixar's patents," he said, "and we have a solid case to demand license fees from them?"

"Yes," I replied. "And neither of these companies can really hurt Pixar. We do use Silicon Graphics computers, but there are alternatives. And I doubt they'll sacrifice sales over this. The downside is the cost of preparing our lawyers and the time it will take to engage Microsoft and Silicon Graphics in a legal battle when we need our focus elsewhere."

Microsoft was an old nemesis of Steve, harking back to Apple days when they were fighting over dominance in the PC industry. The prospect of asserting infringement of Pixar's patents against Microsoft seemed to fire Steve up.

"We should go for it," he said. "Pixar worked years to develop this technology. Why should they use it for free? We should shut down their infringing products."

"We'd be better off charging license fees than trying to shut them down," I suggested. "Those products are not really threatening Pixar's business."

"How much can we get from licensing?" Steve wondered. "These are huge companies and our patents are central to their graphics businesses. It's worth fifty million at least."

"I don't disagree," I said.

It was true; we might have been able to earn license fees of that magnitude. But my years as a lawyer told me that Microsoft and Silicon Graphics wouldn't pay those kinds of numbers without a big court battle. That could take years and cost millions.

"We're better off making it easier for them to make a deal than to go to war for every penny that we think we're entitled to," I told Steve. "The biggest benefit to Pixar is to make this quick and to gain a cash infusion now, when we need it the most."

Steve didn't like the idea of going for less than he thought we were entitled to earn. He felt this would be too much of a bargain for Microsoft and Silicon Graphics. Five million, or even $10 million, was nothing to them if they needed these patents.

Steve wasn't wrong; I just didn't think going for too much was pragmatic. I was nervous about locking Pixar up in a protracted legal battle, even if we liked our chances of winning it. Patent licensing was not a business strategy for Pixar. It was a financing strategy, something we would do once or twice to bring in cash, but no more. It would buy Pixar time, not guarantee long-term success.

Steve could easily have told me to ask Microsoft and Silicon Graphics for $25 million each, the amount he wanted. He didn't. He wanted us to keep talking until we agreed. We ended up deciding to ask for an amount somewhere between what I thought and what Steve wanted.

The strategy ended up working. It took three months to conclude the Microsoft license and about a year to conclude the Silicon Graphics license. Microsoft paid $6.5 million and Silicon Graphics a bit more, plus it gave credits for Pixar to acquire the Silicon Graphics computers it needed to make films. Pixar got just the shot of cash it needed, and Steve was happy. It meant that, for the first time, he would not have to pay Pixar's cash shortfalls out of his own pocket for a while. It wouldn't last forever, but it gave us room to figure out our long-term strategy.

This was the first example of a pattern I would experience often with Steve. He would debate with intensity over any issue we were discussing, big or small. Sometimes we agreed; sometimes we didn't. When we didn't, I would find myself having to stand resilient, steadily holding to my position, yielding not to his intensity but to the merits of the matter. Time and again, I saw how Steve preferred that we come to a mutual resolution, marching forward together, rather than acting on an outcome that he imposed. Years later Steve told me he felt the business and strategic choices we made at Pixar were neither his nor mine but the product of just this process.

Next I turned to Pixar's animated commercials group, a team of half a dozen or so who occupied a small space at the end of one of Pixar's hallways. The group enjoyed a lot of success using Pixar's tools to make small segments of animation for commercials. They had won coveted Clio awards for computer-animated commercials for Life Savers and Listerine and had gained admiration for the dancing chocolate chip cookies in a series of Chips Ahoy commercials.

A young, warm, no-nonsense producer named Darla Anderson ran the group. She was only too happy to share the ups and downs of producing computer-animated commercials. Darla was endearing, with an infectious smile and a quick wit. She came across as being in control, even in the midst of chaos around her. Darla educated me on the commercials business—how it was not only sporadic and difficult to predict but required almost impossibly tight budgets. A job for thirty seconds of animation might cost $125,000 and take a small team of three or four about three months to complete. That would be just enough to cover costs and would make a tiny profit. If the estimate was wrong, or if unforeseen problems cropped up, the profit was wiped out.

"Everyone I know in this business struggles to make ends meet," Darla explained. "And many don't make it. Clients trust Pixar because we have a great reputation and they love our work, but we're also expensive. They like that we have the highest-quality animation, but our prices are often too high to win jobs."

So higher prices were not in the offing, nor was a higher volume of work. It was a shame, Darla lamented.

"We do excellent work," she said. "Everyone on the team puts their heart and soul in whatever we do. But the clients don't always care about our quality."

Pixar's revenues from animated commercials were small, and profits almost nonexistent. The division would have to scale by a huge factor, and become much more profitable, to make a meaningful contribution to the company's bottom line. Based on what I'd learned, this was all but impossible. Once again, Pixar was committing its talent to an endeavor that would never go anywhere. It might keep a small, talented group busy, but as a strategy for growing a company, animated commercials was another dead end. With little promise in RenderMan and animated commercials, the options for growing Pixar's business were diminishing, and my level of worry was on the rise.

Next to probe: short films.

One of Pixar's claims to fame was its beloved, award-winning short films. Known throughout the graphics and film industries as creatively and technically groundbreaking as well as brilliant, Pixar's short films had literally ushered in the field of computer-animated entertainment. The first one produced at Pixar had been *Luxo Jr.*, in 1986. I had first seen it during my interview with Ed.

Luxo Jr. is about two lamps, one small, one large. In the two-min-utc film, the small lamp is exuberantly playing with a ball that it accidentally deflates. Watching the film, it doesn't take long to believe that the two computer-animated lamps represent a wise and knowing parent watching a gleeful child accidentally break his toy. In no time, we are in the world of both parent and child as they navigate the small disaster. The film had been nominated for an Academy Award for Best Animated Short Film.

"*Luxo Jr.* was the first time Pixar demonstrated how computer animation could successfully convey story, character, and emotion," Ed told me. "It was a huge breakthrough, for Pixar and the industry, a jaw-dropping hit wherever we showed it."

Luxo Jr. had been the first of a series of beloved Pixar short films. It had been followed by *Red's Dream* in 1987, *Tin Toy* in 1988, and *Knick Knack* in 1989. *Tin Toy* won the Academy Award for Best Animated Short Film in what had been one of the high points of Pixar's history to date.

There was just one problem: animated short films had no commercial value. They were either done purely as a labor of love, or in Pixar's case as a way to test and develop its technologies and story development process. They were shown at trade shows, film festivals, and sometimes at the beginning of feature films in movie theaters, but they didn't make a dime. And in fact, they were very expensive to make. I didn't even need to analyze the economics of the animated short film market. There was no market.

It seemed that the more I looked for possible profit centers, the less I found. Sometimes a doctor has to give a patient a grievous diagnosis, but I didn't think I had been hired to tell Steve Jobs that his company was a hopeless case. He wanted positive answers, and I wasn't finding any.

"Pixar's an enigma," I shared with Hillary one night after dinner. "I don't think I've ever seen so much talent under one roof. Their efforts have been nothing short of heroic, but every business it has tried has either failed or has such limited potential it's hardly worth the effort. It's just running in place."

"If nothing's worked, how did it survive this long?" Hillary wondered.

"I suppose it comes down to Steve's stubbornness," I replied. "I don't know any other investor who'd have stuck it out this long. But I know even he's had his doubts. He's got nearly fifty million in Pixar and very little to show for it."

"Have you looked at everything?"

"I've still got more to learn about *Toy Story*."

"I'd keep going," Hillary said, trying to be encouraging. "Maybe you'll find better news there."

But in my exploration of Planet Pixar, somehow I felt I was now about to enter its murkiest terrain.

4

STARVING ARTIST

MY PREVIOUS EXPERIENCES HAD PREPARED ME FOR UNDER-
standing the aspects of Pixar's business that I had examined so far.
Nothing I had done, however, prepared me for understanding *Toy
Story*'s business potential. Getting my head around that was no small
task. Pixar had never released a computer-animated feature film. No
one had. There was no way to predict the market for it. No way to
gauge the public's taste for ninety minutes of computer animation. It
didn't help that I knew nothing about the film business.

The obvious place to start was Pixar's original production agreement with Disney, signed almost four years earlier on September 6,
1991. The agreement would at least tell me what Pixar might earn on
Toy Story, and the terms that would apply to future films that would
fall under the same agreement.

The agreement itself was surprisingly short: only twelve and a half
pages. I'd seen seventy-page agreements covering less complicated
matters. Though brief, however, it was impenetrable, written in in-
decipherable Hollywood jargon. One clause said, "AGR shall be defined, computed, accounted for and paid in accordance with WDC's
Exhibits GRP and NP and the Riders attached thereto." What did
any of that mean?

To decipher the agreement, I contacted Sam Fischer, Pixar's lawyer for negotiating that agreement. Sam was the newest partner in
one of Hollywood's elite entertainment law firms, Ziffren, Brittenham, Branca & Fischer. I visited Sam at his firm's spacious and taste-
ful offices in an upscale Los Angeles business district not too far

from Beverly Hills. Sam was sharply dressed, with a short beard and glasses. He was immediately warm, welcoming, and eager to help. He listened attentively and made me feel like what I said mattered. He came across as very natural and at ease in the arcane world of Hollywood and entertainment law.

Sam spent a couple of hours walking me through the details of the terms, exhibits, and riders of Pixar's contract with Disney. We started with the agreement's term. It was a three-picture agreement that would end six months after the release of the last of the three pictures. That sounded simple enough, but how long would it be exactly?

The first picture, *Toy Story,* was targeted for release in November 1995, just over four years after the agreement was signed. The second picture, as yet unnamed, had barely been started. It was ostensibly a story about bugs trying to save an ant colony. Everything I had learned so far about Pixar told me it would take at least the same amount of time to produce the second picture as it did to produce *Toy Story.* That meant the release of the second picture would be four years later, around 1999. The third picture would then take another four years after that because Pixar had the resources to work on only one film at a time. That would be November 2003. This meant that on our present track, the overall production agreement would end six months later, in May 2004. It was now May 1995. In sum, Pixar would potentially be living under the terms of this agreement for nine more years, a very, very long time in the world of start-ups. I started to grow nervous.

Another provision relating to the term of the agreement had also caught my eye. Tacked onto the end of a paragraph, it said that until the end of the agreement, Pixar would not submit to any other company any new film ideas it had presented to Disney, even if Disney had rejected these ideas.

"This can't be right," I suggested to Sam. "If Disney rejects Pixar's film ideas in 1995 and doesn't even have the slightest interest in those ideas, Pixar can't even talk to another studio about them for ten years. But we have to share film ideas with potential distribution partners years before films based on those ideas are released. This means film ideas we might love are completely off the table just because Disney doesn't like them."

"That is exactly what it means," Sam confirmed. "Disney wants Pixar focused on films for Disney, not other studios. That's why it's willing to put so much money into funding Pixar's films."

All right, I thought. The clause that prohibits Pixar from sharing ideas with other studios applied only to ideas Pixar presented to Disney and Disney rejected. But perhaps there was a loophole?

"That leaves us free to develop ideas that we *don't* present to Disney, right? In that case the clause would not apply and Pixar would be free to discuss those ideas with another distribution partner whenever it wanted."

"No, Pixar can't do that either," explained Sam.

He pointed to another paragraph called the "Exclusivity" clause. It said that the services of Pixar's animation division, including Pixar's key creative talent, would be exclusive to Disney during the term of the agreement.

I was aghast.

"This means John Lasseter and Pixar's entire team of animation and story artists can work only for Disney for the next ten years. We can't develop any film ideas, not one, for distribution by other studios."

"That's true," Sam replied. "This kind of clause is standard for unproven talent."

"But Pixar is not like a music group or TV actor; it's an entire company," I protested. "We could hire a thousand new people for our animation division and under this agreement they would have to spend all their time working for Disney. How can an entire company be tied up like that?"

"I hear where you're coming from," Sam said, "but look at it from Disney's side. When they entered this agreement, Pixar had never made a film. This was a risky bet on a totally unproven type of animation and an unproven director. They wanted to make sure Pixar was strictly focused on the films Disney was funding."

Sam felt Pixar had been fortunate to get a deal that funded all its production costs when Pixar had no track record, and that these exclusivity provisions were the price Pixar had to pay for Disney to take that risk.

But regardless of the reasons for these provisions, their combined effect was devastating. They meant that for the term of the agreement, which was likely to last from 1991 to 2004, Pixar could do film, TV, or video projects *only* for Disney and could not even discuss, think about, or work on projects with someone else. And since a film's development time averaged four years, that meant Pixar wouldn't be able to complete a fourth film under new terms until 2008, thirteen years in the future. I was stupefied at how long Pixar's hands were shackled.

Okay, I thought to myself, perhaps these severe limitations might, just might, be palatable if Pixar stood to make a great financial return on its films.

The terms by which Disney compensated Pixar took me the longest to understand. They were steeped in the peculiar world of Hollywood accounting. They began by saying that Disney would pay the production costs of each film, up to certain limits. Pixar would then receive a percentage of the film's revenues. Seven tiers of compensation were defined.

Sam slowly walked me through the provisions by which revenues from our films made their way to Pixar. As he did so, the nervousness I had felt before escalated into pure dread. Pixar did indeed have a share of the profits on its films, but by the time all the calculations were made, and Disney's costs and fees taken off the top, Pixar's ultimate share would be tiny, under 10 percent.

To help me understand the reality of these provisions, I decided to see how Pixar would have fared if we had produced one of Disney's most recent film successes, the acclaimed *Beauty and the Beast,* released in 1991. *Beauty and the Beast* was the third-highest-grossing animated film of all time, behind two more recent Disney releases, *Aladdin* and *The Lion King.* The film had earned $146 million in the domestic box office, and $200 million in the foreign box office. This was at least three or four times the revenues of an average animated film.

Under Pixar's agreement with Disney, I estimated that if we had made *Beauty and the Beast* for Disney, our share of the profits would have been around $17 million. Because it takes four years to make a film, this would amount to a little over $4 million of profits per year. I also guessed Disney would likely have made ten times that much. These were just educated guesses, because I didn't have access to the details of *Beauty and the Beast*'s financial performance, but even if I was off by 50 percent, it wouldn't change the impact on Pixar very much.

Four million dollars of profits per year may sound like a lot, but it really isn't close to enough to build a growing company, especially when those profits require success at the almost impossibly high levels of *Beauty and the Beast.* If Pixar's films earned $100 million in the domestic box office, a level still considered a smash hit but far less than *Beauty and the Beast,* Pixar's share of the profits under the agreement would be all but nonexistent.

The impact of all these contractual provisions was crushing: until Pixar could release a film outside of the Disney contract, the most we could expect to earn from our first three films would be a few million dollars a year — and even then, only if those films ranked with Disney's most profitable films ever. No one would invest in a company that had to perform at those levels in order to eke out a small profit.

"Sam, did no one at Pixar understand these calculations?"

"I'm quite sure Steve did," Sam told me. "We walked him through all the terms and what they meant."

I couldn't wrap my head around it. If Steve understood what Sam was telling me, why didn't he have someone run the numbers to see what it meant for Pixar as a company? Moreover, even if these profit provisions were standard for live-action film, Pixar was an *animated* filmmaker. It takes a year or two to make a live-action film, four or five to make an animated film. This meant that profits per year for an animated filmmaker would be much less. These numbers didn't make sense for animation. I just didn't understand why these differences were not taken into account.

As the reality of these provisions sank in, I began to feel a hopelessness I don't think I'd felt anytime in my career. And even worse, I still didn't fully understand the Disney contract. There were important provisions in the agreement covering sequels that I needed to dissect.

The agreement said that Pixar would have an option to make sequels of its own films only under limited conditions that included making the original film, on which the sequel would be based, within its agreed-upon budget, and agreeing on terms for the sequel that fit within Disney's standard parameters. If these conditions were unmet, Disney was free to make sequels of Pixar's films without any involvement by Pixar. Disney could literally take Woody and Buzz, characters lovingly crafted over years at Pixar, and make its own film with them. Once again, I asked Sam about these provisions.

"Sam," I asserted, "the only reason Disney would want to make a sequel is if the original film is a hit. These provisions say that unless Pixar meets all the conditions specified, Disney could do whatever it wants with Pixar's characters."

"Yes, but that's not unusual," Sam explained. "Disney is investing tens of millions of dollars to create these characters. They want to make sure that investment will yield returns, including making sequels. I'm sure they would prefer Pixar to make the sequels, but they need to be able to move forward if Pixar cannot."

"So we'd have to go to John Lasseter, *Toy Story*'s director, for whom Woody and Buzz are like children, and tell him, 'Thanks for the work; Disney will take over from here.'"

"I hope it wouldn't come to that," Sam replied. "Presumably Disney would prefer that John and his team make the sequels."

Which might be fine, except for one other issue: sequels wouldn't count as one of the three original films Pixar owed Disney under the agreement. If we made a sequel, it would be tacked onto the existing agreement, potentially extending it several more years.

"We lose either way," I told Sam. "Either Disney makes the sequel and Pixar loses control over its creations, or Pixar makes the sequel and the terms of this agreement continue."

I was left feeling very frustrated. I couldn't blame Sam; he was simply educating me in the ways of Hollywood deal making. In that world, he felt Pixar had fared quite well in this negotiation, especially for a company with no track record. He told me it was rare for Disney to give any profit share at all in an animated film, and that it had done so only because Pixar had invested so much in technology. Nevertheless, the size of that profit share was small, too small for building a robust company, and Sam acknowledged that Steve had yielded on how that profit share was calculated in ways that favored Disney. All told, the overall impact on turning Pixar into a substantial business, which was my focus, was devastating.

I read and reread the provisions of the Disney agreement, looking, trying to find some gap, some loophole, something missing. There was nothing. Fifty years of Hollywood lawyering had made it all crystal clear: Pixar could work only for Disney. Disney had to approve the films Pixar made. It chose whether to make sequels of those films. It had creative control over the films. It prohibited Pixar from working with anyone else. It kept the lion's share of the profits.

By tying up the company so completely in exchange for funding up to three films, it was as if Disney owned Pixar without ever buying it. And all this turned out to be just the standard way that Hollywood deals with new talent. Sam told me it was no different in music or other parts of the entertainment industry.

One evening at home, after the children had gone to sleep, I shared my frustration with Hillary.

"I'm not sure how to say this," I said. "I don't think I knew what I was getting myself into. I think I blew this one."

"What do you mean?"

"I've turned over every stone at Pixar. There's nowhere to take it. Disney has closed every door. The best we can hope for is a tiny profit, and that's only if our films are among the most popular animated films ever made."

"Pixar has to be as successful as Disney is at animation?" Hillary asked.

"More successful! Disney keeps the lion's share of the profits on its own films. That means the hits can make up for the flops. But Pixar has such a small share of the profits that it wouldn't even have this luxury. They all have to be hits. I don't know what Steve was thinking when Pixar signed that contract."

"So what are you thinking about doing?" Hillary asked.

I didn't know.

"If I had known what I know now," I said, "I can't imagine I would have taken this job. Taking this company public seems like a crazy notion. No investor I know would come near this. Fifty million in losses, no profits, no growth, Disney holding all the cards. I'm not sure Pixar even needs a CFO."

"I think you have to understand where Steve's at with all this," said Hillary.

But as frustrated as I felt, I waited. I needed to be in a better frame of mind for a discussion I didn't expect would be easy. If I called out Steve on entering what I thought was an insane agreement with Disney, I expected he would dig in and defend it. It must have seemed like a good idea to him at the time.

One Saturday afternoon about a week later, I headed over to Steve's house. We took a seat on the back porch, and I went through what I had learned.

"Steve," I concluded, "this contract ties our hands for the better part of a decade. We can't talk to other studios. We can't make much money. And it doesn't even make sense to make sequels."

"Do we even want to make sequels?" Steve asked.

"We might. Disney's having a lot of success with direct-to-video sequels. We might want to make those."

"Can't we get through the contract faster if we speed up how long it takes us to make our films?" Steve asked.

"I've discussed this with Ed," I said. "He's very skeptical about making films quicker. He's open to looking at it, but he's doubtful."

"Well" — Steve shrugged — "if *Toy Story* and the other two films are hits, we'll make some money. Then we'll be free to do whatever we want."

That was certainly a true statement, but it wasn't the answer I was looking for. Of course we'd be free after the three films, but that was still years away. I wanted to ask Steve why he let Pixar enter such a one-sided contract, why he didn't tell me it was so constraining, and why he seemed so nonchalant about it.

But I didn't. As we sat there talking, I realized Steve had no interest in looking back. He didn't defend the contract. He didn't justify it. He listened carefully to everything I had to say about it, taking it all in. That was pretty much it.

Instead of pressing Steve, I was left to draw my own conclusions. I pieced together a scenario that made sense of what had happened, at least to me. I never verified it with Steve; it was simply my own way of understanding things.

I reasoned that around 1991, Steve was ready to let go of Pixar. He had never set out to build an animation company. In 1986, when he took control of Pixar, Steve dreamed of building a technology company, a graphics powerhouse that would stun the world with machines that could do computer imagery like no other. Storytelling was an afterthought, a way to demonstrate the technology. The hopes of that graphics company had rested in part on the Pixar Image Computer, which had failed. By 1991, that division of Pixar had been shut down completely.

At that moment, I concluded, Steve was ready to give up on Pixar.

He must have wanted out. The burden was simply too great, and the dream dashed. He was in a very tough spot, however. It was five years since his departure from Apple, and he had not had a hit since. If he couldn't chalk Pixar up as a win, he badly wanted to avoid another highly public loss. That was the instant when the Disney opportunity came along. To Steve, the deal with Disney was a way to stop the financial bleeding. Steve's guard was down, and in that negotiation with Disney he had been bested by Jeffrey Katzenberg, chairman of Walt Disney Studios, who handled the deal on behalf of Disney. Steve had signed up for terms the implications of which he either didn't fully understand, or to which he had simply yielded in order to get the deal done.

None of this changed our current situation, however. We had no long-range hope in RenderMan software. No hope in animated commercials. No hope in short films. No hope in animated feature films. One of the world's richest and most powerful companies controlled our future and our fortunes. And on top of everything else, a terribly strained relationship between Pixar and its owner, Steve. That was the hand we were dealt.

Early in my career I had learned the wisdom of not griping over the hand I was dealt. I had a mentor who taught me lessons about business and life that served me for many years. He looked at business the way a grand master might look at a chessboard.

"There's nothing you can do about where the pieces are," he'd say. "It's only your next move that matters."

I had worked at training myself in this way of thinking. It was a lot more productive than getting emotional about things that were out of my control. Business can be harsh, but the stakes are rarely a matter of life and death. It was not going to help me to fret over the reasons why Pixar may or may not have entered a one-sided contract a few years earlier. I simply had to remain focused on the task at hand: find a way for Pixar to flourish.

I also found one silver lining to keep me going. Somewhere out of the fog of those first two months, one more important conclusion struck me. Hillary and I discussed it as we were sitting in the living room after dinner one night.

"You know," I said, "in all my conversations with Steve these past two months, I've never found him defensive. I've critiqued and dismantled every aspect of Pixar's business and he had every reason to justify and defend it. But he didn't. Not once. It's as if he's taking this journey with me, learning it at the same time I am."

"He hasn't given you a reason to distrust him," Hillary said. "You two are in this together. You have to work it out together."

That's how it felt. Whatever mess we were in, we were in it together. What mattered was our next move.

5

MY BIG BREAK

BY THE END OF APRIL 1995, I FELT MY HONEYMOON PERIOD at Pixar should be coming to an end. I had walked and talked around its hallways and offices for long enough. I wanted to move forward, to find a toehold somewhere. But I was having a hard time doing so. It felt like I was meandering around the base of the mountain instead of actually climbing it.

It didn't help that there was a growing fear within the company that its first film, now officially named *Toy Story*, would not be finished on time. People worried about whether we were too far behind in the animation, lighting, rendering, and other myriad details required to finish the film. For as much as I wanted to move forward, I had to finish my homework. I needed to understand the risks surrounding the completion of *Toy Story*, and I had far more to learn about how films make money.

Toy Story's release date was set for November 22, 1995. That triggered a whole set of must-hit dates for the delivery of the film: completion of the songs and music, development of the marketing campaign, and many other details involved in preparing the film for release. Pixar was marching into a place no company had ever been. This was the first computer-animated feature film ever attempted, and, as I was beginning to realize, the challenges were staggering.

One of those challenges involved the need to create every single detail that the audience sees, literally everything. For example, in live-action filmmaking you don't have to think about where the sky will come from. Shoot any outdoor scene with a camera, and the sky will be there. Background buildings and trees will be there. The leaves on the trees will be there. The wind rustling the leaves on the trees will be there. Live-action filmmakers don't have to think about the leaves on the background trees. But in animation, there is no sky, no trees, no leaves, and certainly no gentle breeze rustling those leaves. There is just a blank screen on a computer. If you want anything on that screen, you have to give the computer instructions to draw it.

There are challenges even more daunting than these. We take for granted elements in our reality like light and shadow. We never think to ourselves, "How did that shadow get there?" or "How come that part of the fence is sunlit and that part isn't?" But if lighting and shadow are off, even a tiny bit, in a photo or portrait, we notice it immediately. It looks weird to us. In computer animation there is no light, no shadow. It all has to be created.

Even this pales in comparison to something as seemingly innocuous as skin. A live-action filmmaker never has to worry about skin. Touch it up with a little makeup perhaps, but it will be there. Yet skin is one of the most complex things to create artistically. It is full of details — color, hair, blemishes, folds, and texture — and it is very difficult to capture the way light interacts with skin. These are nuances we never think about, but they are glaringly obvious when they are missing. Ed told me that without these careful details, skin would look like "painted rubber."

Pixar had set up entire departments dedicated to these challenges. There was a lighting department, a team whose sole function was to get the computer to generate lighting and shadows correctly. There were technical directors who were dedicated to projects like leaves and sky and skin.

Bill Reeves was the company's top technical leader and the supervising technical director on *Toy Story*. Many of the trickiest challenges landed on his desk. Bill had been with the team all the way back to its days at Lucasfilm. He had red hair, thin-rimmed glasses, and a quiet demeanor. I sat in his office one day to see how he felt about finishing the film. His office was plain, a big computer screen on his desk, and not terribly well lit.

"I don't know if we can do it," he told me flat out. "The number of details we have to complete is enormous. But we're going for it. We've had tough challenges before." Bill conveyed a sense of calm confidence. He was worried, but not panicking.

"How would you assess the risk?" I asked.

"That's hard to say," he said. "There's risk. Our best people are working night and day. Animation is a few weeks behind. Lighting too. And we're trying to finish the humans, Andy and his mom. The skin, clothes, and facial features are challenging. But we're on it."

I began to fathom how these technical challenges imposed enormous constraints on the film. I learned that there was a reason the film was specifically about toys, and not about animals or people. Toys are made of plastic. They have uniform surfaces. No variation. No skin. No clothing that needs to wrinkle with every movement. Toys have geometries that are much easier to create with computers. For similar reasons, the opening scenes of the film take place inside Andy's bedroom. The bedroom is a square box. Its features—bed, dresser, fan, window, door—are more geometric than outdoor features. Easier to draw. Much easier to light.

Audiences would be in the last ten minutes of *Toy Story* before they saw the scenes that were far more technically challenging. There was a big outdoor chase scene at the end of the film in which Woody and Buzz are in a toy car trying to catch a moving truck. Imagine if that scene took place in streets with leafless trees, or carless roads. It turned out that part of the genius of *Toy Story* was not just the brilliance of the story and characters; it was crafting them amid almost impossible constraints. This built up more and more pressure on finishing the film. The hardest elements were being saved for last. Was it possible to get them done at all?

Some of the challenges were so technical that I would never have thought to even ask about them. For example, Pixar had a tiny department run by David deFrancisco, a brilliant graphics and film pioneer whose office consisted of two small, windowless rooms. One of those rooms looked like a high school lab, the other a photography darkroom. This was Pixar's photoscience department. I had never heard the term *photoscience*, but people at Pixar were worried about it.

To understand what all the fuss was about, I went to visit David. He was about ten years older than me, soft-spoken and understated, with a beard, glasses, and a professorial manner. David explained that the task of the department was to solve the problem of transferring computer images to film.

Pixar did computer animation. There were no cameras. No film. Just images on computer screens. But the only way to watch a film in a movie theater was to play it on a film projector. Pixar's computer images had to find their way onto celluloid if they were to be seen by the public. That was David's job. In order to accomplish it, he invented a machine to transfer computer images to film. This was the mystery machine I had seen during my first interview. It sat in the middle of a darkroom and looked like a huge slab of metal on which sat a giant microscope-like device. Into that machine came every single computer image of a Pixar project, where it was painstakingly recorded onto film.

David and I sat in this small, darkened room, with this huge machine in the middle. "So," I asked, like the slowest student in class who was finally beginning to catch on, "this one machine has to record over a hundred thousand frames of *Toy Story* onto film?"

"Exactly," David replied.

"And it all has to happen in the right sequence, and with the right color and tone so it looks consistent?"

"Right again."

"And this is the only one?" I asked. "If this breaks down or a part fails, there's no backup?"

"Yes, that's right. This is the only one in the world. We have almost enough spare parts to make a backup, but we haven't really focused on that. It would take a while to assemble."

"What happens if this one breaks during production?"

"It can't," David blurted, then paused to correct himself. "Obviously, it could. But that would be a disaster. There would be no film that would be delivered and shown in the theaters. It's not an option."

The more I learned, the more the magnitude of what Pixar was attempting to do dawned on me. Making *Toy Story* was not just finishing another film. It was more like climbing Everest or landing on the moon for the first time. Computers had never been pushed to this level of artistry before. Pixar had more than one hundred of the most powerful computer workstations available just to draw the final images that would appear in the film. Each frame of the film took anything from forty-five minutes to thirty hours to draw, and there were around 114,000 of them. Pixar was embarked on a lonely, courageous quest through terrain into which neither it nor anyone else had ever ventured. The summit was just beginning to poke out from behind the distant clouds, and no one was certain how thin the air would get. This was hardly a fertile environment in which to raise money to finance Pixar.

The more I understood the challenges with finishing *Toy Story*, the more I wondered where my toehold for moving Pixar forward might come.

"I'm starting to wonder if Pixar will get *Toy Story* finished," I mentioned one night at dinner, thinking aloud.

"Why is it so hard?" Jason, my nine-year-old, wanted to know.

"Getting the story right has taken a long time," I explained. "*Toy Story* was almost shut down because Disney didn't like it. It's also very hard to finish all the animation, colors, and details of each frame in the film."

"Why didn't Disney like it?" Jason asked.

"They thought Woody was too mean," I said. "So Pixar made a

lot of changes. They turned the film into an adventure story. Those changes really delayed the film, though."

"Who's your favorite character?" Sarah, my seven-year-old, asked.

"Buzz Lightyear is really funny," I said. "So is Rex, the dinosaur."

"I like Slinky," declared Sarah, who had seen the first part of the film.

A cute slinky dog. Of course. Judging from my children's interest in the film, if Pixar did get this finished, kids everywhere were going to fall in love with it.

In the meantime, while the company bent under the pressures of finishing *Toy Story*, I had to understand the financial implications of *Toy Story*'s release. I had done some back-of-the-envelope calculations based on the Disney contract, but they were only educated guesses. To even think about the viability of animated feature films as a business strategy, I needed to understand precisely how those films would generate revenues. The questions were simple enough: How do films make money and who gets it? Put another way, if I buy a movie ticket and popcorn, who gets the dollars? The movie theater? The film studio distributing the movie? The people who made the movie? As a chief financial officer, it was almost embarrassing not to know these basics.

To learn more about this, I called Tim Engel, who was in charge of finance at Walt Disney Animation Studios. He was part of the management team that had created Disney's recent successes, including *Beauty and the Beast, Aladdin,* and *The Lion King.* I had been introduced to Tim recently and he seemed very open and helpful.

"I'm trying to understand the financial details of how these films work," I explained to Tim. "Would you have someone at Disney who might be able to help me with that?"

"I'd love to help you," he replied. "But our financial models for films are proprietary. We don't share them."

I wasn't completely surprised by Tim's answer. I well knew that companies were protective of their business models. I was hoping I might get Disney to make an exception.

"But we need to understand the way our films make money," I said. "That will also help us going forward as we map out the future films under our agreement."

"The royalty reports we provide you will show you where the revenues came from," Tim suggested.

Disney was obligated to provide these reports to Pixar to show how they calculated Pixar's share of the film revenues.

"That won't help us now, though," I went on. "We won't see those reports until long after *Toy Story* is released, at least a year from now. And my understanding is those reports won't contain nearly enough information."

I knew from my lawyer days that the information in royalty reports could be scant, and they often needed auditing to verify their accuracy.

"Is there anything you can do to give us more detail now?" I asked. "We'll agree not to share it with others. We just need a start to develop our own projections for how our films will perform."

"I'm sorry," Tim said. "We've just never given them out. I could give you a sample royalty report from another film if that's helpful."

It wasn't. It wouldn't be close to what we needed. This wasn't Tim's fault either. I thought about escalating the issue higher within Disney. But with the pressures of finishing *Toy Story*, I didn't want to start a skirmish over information Disney had no obligation to provide. I was stymied. The numbers mattered. Without them I would not find the foothold I wanted. I wouldn't even be able to do my job.

As I processed the risks of not finishing *Toy Story*, and worried about where I was going to get the numbers I needed to understand Pixar's business, one more challenge began to rear its head, this time having to do with Steve.

"I'd like to start coming up to Pixar more often," Steve said on the phone one evening. "Maybe once a week, or every two weeks."

Steve had spent almost no time at Pixar during the nine years he had owned it. He didn't even have an office there. He had founded NeXT in 1985, right after leaving Apple, and although he took over

Pixar in 1986, he had worked full time at NeXT all those years.

Steve didn't say why he wanted to spend more time at Pixar; he certainly didn't need a reason to spend more time at the company he owned. I figured he was sensing possibility, and wanted to be closer to it. With a film coming out, there was more action than there had been in a while. The problem was that after I had heard admonition after admonition to keep Steve away from Pixar, it wouldn't help my cause that shortly after I started, Steve now wanted to increase his presence there. I wasn't sure how to broach this issue, with Steve or Pixar.

None of this brought me much comfort in terms of what I had been hired to do. If *Toy Story* missed its deadline, I was certain that Pixar's chance of success, however minuscule it might be, would all but evaporate. I had no access to the financial information I needed to even create a rudimentary business projection. And the very person whom Pixar feared the most was now making noises about wanting to spend more time there. I felt like I needed something, some opening that I could grab onto, to create a little momentum. I'd been involved with a number of start-ups throughout my career, but this one carried more doubt and uncertainty than I had ever encountered.

Then, one day at the end of the first week of May 1995, a couple of months after I started, something happened that jolted me out of my doldrums in a way that I could never have imagined. I can't say if it made a difference in any of Pixar's challenges, but it sure made a difference in me.

"I'm taking the video back to the store," I casually told Hillary one Sunday afternoon. "I won't be long, maybe twenty minutes. I'll pick up another one for tonight."

Hillary was more than eight months pregnant with our third child. We'd spend the evening at home watching a film while she rested. There was a Blockbuster film rental store about a mile from our house.

I decided it would be fun to skate to Blockbuster. It would take only ten minutes and I'd get some exercise. So I laced up my Rollerblades, inline skates that were all the rage. I often went skating at the local playground with Jason. We liked to play our own version of roller hockey.

It was a pleasant spring day, warm and sunny. I was relaxed and skating down a neighborhood road I'd been on a thousand times before. All of a sudden, without the slightest warning, instead of going straight along the road, I felt myself rearing off to the side, picking up speed. I must have hit a pebble or something. All I knew was that my right leg was off the ground and I was spinning around on my left leg; only it was my body that was turning, not the leg. The amount of torque on my leg at that instant was far more than it could bear. As I headed toward the ground, I heard a nauseatingly loud pop, and then I was lying on the road reeling from the shock of what I knew instantly to be a badly broken bone, just where the skate touched my leg.

My leg was not so much in pain at that moment as feeling horribly weird, and I felt myself shaking. I kept thinking, "How are they going to get my skate off?"

Traffic began to stop and a woman came up to me to ask if I needed help.

"I don't know how I fell. I've broken my leg. I need to let my wife know. We live close by. Thank you."

"I'll wait here till someone comes," she said.

I later learned that someone drove to my house and knocked on the door. Hillary answered to hear the words that no woman who is eight months pregnant wants to hear.

"Your husband's been in an accident."

It didn't take long for Hillary to get to where I was lying in the road. "I'm okay," I told her. "My leg's broken. I don't know how they're going to get the skate off."

"I'm sure the paramedics will know how to do it," Hillary tried to comfort me.

The ambulance arrived and the paramedic took one look at my leg.

"We need to remove your skate," he said. He was insistent and told me it would be much harder to do it later. Somehow they took it off.

Soon I found myself in the emergency room having x-rays taken of my leg. The diagnosis was a jagged spiral fracture of the tibia, just above my left ankle. The orthopedist on call in the emergency room explained my options: a cast, or surgery to mend the bones. I was thinking a cast wouldn't be that bad, and it sounded a lot better than the surgery he was describing. But Hillary wanted another opinion. She had connections through her job at Stanford Medical Center, so she called for a recommendation for the best doctors in the area. It was a Sunday, and I couldn't see anyone that day, but she did find a surgeon we could see the next day. We headed home and I sprawled on the couch with a broken leg and a heavy dose of painkillers until the next day.

"A cast is out of the question," the surgeon said. "If we cast it, there's a real risk you'll have a permanent limp. The break is too jagged, and too close to your ankle. One leg will be longer than the other. Even surgery is a risk, but if it goes well your walk will be normal."

The surgery he was talking about involved screwing an eight-inch titanium rod into my bones to hold them together. If it went well, I could have the rod removed in a couple of years.

"I can do it tomorrow," the doctor said. "You won't be able to drive for three months, the recovery will be painful, and you'll need physical therapy to rehabilitate that leg. But try not to worry. We'll take care of it."

"Try not to worry!" I thought to myself. This was a disaster. We were having a baby in three weeks. I was less than three months into a new job, with a demanding boss and a company looking at me to figure out a strategy for success. How was I going to be able to do it all? I'd fail before I even started. But what options did I have?

The next day I was wheeled into the operating room at Stanford Medical Center in Palo Alto. I came out of it with a titanium rod knitting my bones together, and a morphine drip for the pain. The following few days were a fog. The pain from screwing the rod into the bone was searing, and the morphine was making me delirious.

The day after surgery, Steve was in my room. He just showed up at the hospital.

"How much pain are you in?" he wanted to know.

"It's not too bad." I tried to brave it. "These drugs are helping."

I felt embarrassed. Here I was just a few weeks into a new job and I was out of commission.

"I'm sorry about this," I said.

"Don't be!" Steve exclaimed. "Just get better. If there's anything you need, anything at all, let me know."

My room filled with flowers and cards, from family and friends, and also from the Jobs family, and from Ed and the Pixar team. When I got home, Steve brought his family over to visit several times. I'd known him less than six months at this point, and he was acting like an old friend.

The surgery had been a success. The rod had gone in just as the doctor planned, and it was doing its job of holding my bones in place so they could heal.

A week after the surgery, as I emerged from the fog of morphine and was practicing hobbling around on crutches with a big black boot on my left leg, I was ready to get back to Pixar. Only for the first time, something in my attitude had changed. For almost three months I had wandered around Pixar, feeling increasingly dejected about its prospects, questioning if I should even be there. Now I'd been away for ten days and I missed it.

Nothing had happened to change any of my conclusions. I still didn't have the toehold I needed. But I was feeling something else. Maybe it was the shock of the injury. Maybe it was the care and concern I had experienced from Steve and others at Pixar. Maybe it was my growing appreciation for the magnitude of what Pixar was attempting to do. But there was no question I was experiencing the first glimmer of pride about being on this ship. Pixar was becoming more than a job. What its people had been through, and what they were attempting to do now, was over-the-top extraordinary. It was crazy. I was itching to get back. I wished I had more answers than I did, but if I had a shot at figuring out what to do, I wanted to take it.

The first thing to fix was arranging an office for Steve. Steve was unaware how his frustrations with Pixar over the years, the failure to give employees stock options, not to mention his personal style, had instilled a real fear that he would ruin Pixar's familial culture. I didn't want to bring this up with him directly. There was no reason to be inflammatory, or even risk making relations worse, but I needed to address this issue somehow. I called him on the phone one night.

"Steve, I'll return to Pixar in a couple of days. It's also a good time to talk about getting you situated at Pixar."

"That sounds great," Steve said. "I'm glad to have you back. I only need an office. I plan to come up every week, or every two weeks, probably on Fridays."

"That's no problem," I said, "but we'll have to make it clear just exactly what your role and purpose is."

"Why do we have to do that?" Steve asked. I could feel him getting testy.

"As the owner of the company," I went on, "everyone will want to know why you're coming up more and what it means. It's a change for the company—a good change, but a change nevertheless. You're the CEO, so you hold a lot of power. People might think you want to change things, or start to do things differently."

"I don't want to change anything," Steve protested. "I want to hang around Pixar more. Be part of it. I also want to be closer to discussions around marketing our films. Disney does the marketing, but Pixar should have a strong say in it."

"I think it would be great to frame it just that way," I replied. "You're there not to change how Pixar operates but to be part of it, to be closer to it, and to be involved in the marketing aspects of the films."

I called Ed Catmull and Pam Kerwin to discuss all of this with them. If they bought into it, others would too. Ed told me that in the past he had talked to Steve about not interfering with Pixar's story process, and that Steve was okay with that. Pam also understood that we had to make this work.

"We know Steve owns the company and can be here anytime he wants," Pam said. "We just have to control the situation, get people used to it."

"I understand," I said. "He's on board with how we're going to position it. That's all we can ask for."

Two weeks later I was standing in the front hallway of my home one Friday morning, looking through the window at the road in front of my house. I was waiting for Steve to pull up. He'd be in his silver Mercedes, and he was picking me up to drive to Pixar where he had a new office. I had my crutches and a big boot on my left leg.

It felt more than a little odd waiting for my boss, Steve Jobs, to drive me to work. But that is how it was. For three months, until I could drive again, every time Steve went to Pixar, he drove me there, and he drove me back. On the other days, Sarah Staff, my newly hired right-hand person who had a similar commute to mine, very graciously picked me up.

Finding a way for Steve to spend more time at Pixar wasn't quite the toehold I had imagined, but at least it was a resolution to one issue we needed to address.

A week after that first ride with Steve, Hillary went into labor and we had our third child. I spent the event standing on one leg in the labor and delivery room. When we left the hospital, we were both pushed out in wheelchairs, Hillary holding our new baby, me holding my crutches.

At the end of the closing credits on *Toy Story* is a heading called "Production Babies," below which is a list of all the babies born to Pixar employees during the production of the film. I could not possibly have been prouder to say that my new daughter, Jenna, was among them.

6

WHAT'S AN ENTERTAINMENT COMPANY?

"STEVE," I NOTED ONE NIGHT IN EARLY JUNE 1995, "WE don't have precise data, but I'm looking at this home video market and it's huge. Disney is making a fortune on it."

"It's because people love these family films," Steve said. "They don't want to see them just once in the movie theater. They want to see them over and over again. They love those characters. And parents would rather their children watch *Aladdin* or *Beauty and the Beast* than a lot of garbage."

My own home was a great example of this. We owned all the recent Disney animated films, and Jason and Sarah had watched them many times. *Aladdin* was their favorite. They never seemed to tire of the Genie, masterfully voiced by Robin Williams. It was similar at Steve's house, where he had a shelf lined with the same films.

"People are paying thirty or forty dollars a film to own them," I continued. "Some are renting from Blockbuster, but with these animated feature films it looks like there's a strong preference for actually owning them."

"Do we know how much Disney makes on them?" Steve asked.

"Not precisely," I said. "I'm trying to get the exact numbers, hopefully soon. But remember the calculation that said if Pixar had released *Beauty and the Beast*, we'd make about seventeen million dollars? I think that's about ten percent of the actual profits. Even if

I'm off by a lot, that means their profits on the film are enormous, maybe a hundred fifty million or more. I think much of that is coming from home video."

Home video was turning animated feature films into big business, bigger than we had imagined. *Beauty and the Beast, Aladdin,* and *The Lion King* looked like they were among the most profitable films of all time. They had ushered in a new era of animated entertainment, and they were catapulting Disney's animation division to new levels of commercial success.

"Investors will love this," Steve said. "Pixar can be in a multibillion-dollar video market."

"I agree, but let's get the data first. Even then I'm not sure we can count on home video alone to take Pixar public."

Steve winced at this. He didn't like it when I made any suggestion that Pixar might not be ready to go public. He was itching to go public as soon as we could. I had one foot on the brake, though. Pixar was frantically trying to finish *Toy Story* for its launch in six months. I didn't want potential investors to see how precarious the project was. Worse, we didn't have a business plan to confidently share with them, and I knew from my talks with Sam Fischer that Pixar's share of the home video revenues under the agreement with Disney was very small, even if the market for home videos was big.

It was one thing to learn that animated feature films had more financial opportunity than we thought, quite another to bet the entire company on it. In the first place, under the Disney agreement, our share of the profits from our films would remain small for a long time, potentially ten years. Second, there was no modern precedent for taking an independent animation company public. Disney had first sold shares to the public in 1940, and by the time it listed on the New York Stock Exchange in 1957, it had expanded beyond animation. My hope had been to do the same, to balance the risks of animation with more stable businesses like RenderMan software sales.

"You don't believe any of Pixar's other technologies can scale?" Steve continued.

"You're right, I don't," I replied.

"That leaves animation," Steve said.

"Yes," I replied. "But getting Wall Street interested in a pure animation company that's never released a film will be close to impossible. It would mean we'd be raising our flag entirely as an entertainment company, a business we know little about."

Taking a company public meant selling its stock to investors through the public stock exchanges. It served the twin purposes of raising capital to finance a company's business and enabling anyone, including the company's founders, to freely sell their stock. In Silicon Valley this was an imprimatur of success like no other. From the time Steve and I had first met, Steve mused about taking Pixar public. It was one of the reasons he had hired me, and the idea was never far from his mind.

But taking a company public was a gargantuan task, exceedingly difficult to pull off. Most start-ups just ran out of money before they ever got to it. Steve's willingness to fund Pixar for close to ten years went beyond all the norms for keeping a start-up alive. By Silicon Valley standards, Pixar should have closed its doors years earlier. Now Steve was envisioning an endpoint, and he couldn't get there fast enough. Rushing wouldn't help us, though. We needed a crystal-clear vision for what Pixar was. That vision was not just important to taking Pixar public; it was the strategic direction that would guide the company for years. But so far, we didn't have one.

One of our challenges in developing that vision was that we were looking at a business Steve and I knew nothing about. We had no experience in the entertainment field. We had to learn it. On this front, Steve was all in. He may have been impatient about beginning the process of taking Pixar public, but he knew we had a lot to figure out first. We quickly threw ourselves into the challenge of learning the entertainment business, sharing what we learned, and piece by piece putting together a picture of what it was all about.

I began with reading all I could about the Disney company. Some of the parallels between Disney and Pixar were striking.

Walt Disney had long had an interest in newspaper cartoons. After returning from service as an ambulance driver in France in World War I, he encountered animated cartoons for the first time and quickly fell in love with the field. Ironically, he feared that he had entered the field too late, that there was no growth opportunity left in it. He ended up creating that opportunity by pushing the field into new territory, both creatively and technologically, just as Pixar was doing now.

In 1928 Disney released a short black-and-white cartoon that changed the course of animation. Called *Steamboat Willie*, it ushered in breakthroughs on two fronts. It introduced the world to the most fully formed cartoon personality audiences had ever seen: Mickey Mouse. It was also the first cartoon to use synchronized sound, meaning that the sounds were timed to the action, making the overall audience experience far more immersive than ever before.

After the success of Mickey Mouse, Disney set his sights on the first animated feature film. It took him until 1937 to release *Snow White and the Seven Dwarfs*, a virtuoso accomplishment that ushered in many more breakthroughs in story, character, color, sound, and the way animation displayed depth. The film also introduced the world to the Seven Dwarfs and quickly sealed their place as icons of American culture.

Other parallels between Disney and Pixar were less inspiring. Like Pixar, Disney had struggled financially for years. Walt Disney had bet it all on *Snow White and the Seven Dwarfs*, including mortgaging his house and a risky bank loan. The success of the film paid off financially, but it wasn't long before Disney was struggling once again. Animation was proving to be a very fickle business, and soon Disney was diversifying.

In 1953, he started a film distribution company, Buena Vista Distribution; in 1954, he went into television, with the acclaimed *Disneyland* television show that first appeared on ABC; in 1955, he opened Disneyland, a daring adventure to re-envision the theme park experience; he also went into live-action films, culminating with the breakthrough

Mary Poppins in 1964. The enormous degree to which Disney had diversified made the idea of a pure animation company seem even more doubtful. If the undisputed king of the animation world hadn't pulled it off, what was the likelihood that anyone else could?

Maybe the answer was for Pixar to diversify as well, just in the way Disney had. But two of Disney's businesses seemed out of the question for Pixar right off the bat. It would cost billions to open a theme park, and Disney had the rights to use Pixar's characters in its parks, so we wouldn't even be able to use our own characters. A film distribution business was also out of the question. Film distribution had been locked up by the major studios for decades, and we didn't even have the rights to distribute our own films. But what about live-action film? That might be worth exploring. Which is what led Steve and me to a meeting in the offices of Joe Roth one day.

Joe Roth was an A-list Hollywood executive and film producer. He had been chairman of 20th Century Fox and a year earlier had become chairman of Walt Disney Studios. All of Disney's live-action film business went through him. Steve and I felt fortunate to arrange a meeting with him. Our goal was to understand the business of live-action film so we could determine if Pixar should go into it.

Arriving at Joe Roth's office felt like we were entering the inner sanctum of Temple Hollywood. It was located at the Team Disney corporate headquarters in Burbank, California, built just a few years earlier, an imposing building on Disney's Hollywood lot. Towering above us on the building's facade were giant statues of the Seven Dwarfs. We stopped and ogled them on our way into the building, like kids going to Disneyland.

Beyond the giant dwarfs, the building emanated a quiet somberness. Few people were around; security guards kept a close watch. We were directed to Joe's office, in the executive suite. His office was large, plush, and imposing, a beautiful wooden desk on one end, by the window, with a couch at the opposite end where he invited us to sit.

Joe was immediately warm and friendly. He was a few years our senior, soft-spoken, casually but well dressed, with a warm and gracious smile and graying hair. We began by describing what we were up to at Pixar. After a few minutes, a phone rang in the corner of the room behind Joe's desk.

"Excuse me," Joe said, "I'm terribly sorry. I need to take that call, but it won't take long. Please stay and be comfortable here."

Joe spent a few minutes on the phone by the window at the other end of his office. Then he returned to us.

"So sorry to have to take that call," he said. "It was Robert Redford. He's not easy to reach. There won't be any more interruptions."

As soon as we left the building, Steve and I tried to keep our cool, but we both had one thing on our minds.

"Robert Redford!" Steve exclaimed. "*Butch Cassidy*! *The Sting*! I wouldn't have kept him waiting either. Wow!"

"I know," I said. "That's about all I could think about the rest of the meeting!"

"Me too," said Steve.

We were starstruck! It would be a few years yet before Steve had access to every celebrity in the world, but in this moment, we were more like teenagers glimpsing stars on the red carpet.

In that meeting we had also received our first lesson on live-action filmmaking.

"Think of it as a portfolio business," Joe had explained. "Each year a studio earmarks funds for a slate of films: low budget, medium budget, and big budget. Then we do the same with marketing, allocating amounts to market each film. We release the slate, hoping that we create enough hits to make up for the ones that don't perform."

"How many films are in the slate?" Steve asked.

"It depends," Joe said. "There's no magic number. It could be as few as a half a dozen, as many as fifteen or twenty. It depends on the year, the size of the studio, the sources of financing, and other factors."

"How do you know which might be the big films?" Steve asked.

"We don't know," Joe confessed. "We like to think we do but we really don't. It's hard to predict the films that will break out. Sometimes you know a big star will assure a big opening, but even that doesn't tell you how the film will ultimately perform."

"So it's as much a financing strategy as a creative strategy?" I asked.

"That's right," Joe said. "Of course, we try to make the best films we can creatively, but it's all about assembling the right slate."

This was all new to us. Disney and the other studios were spreading money across a slate of films, hoping that some would break out and become hits, to make up for the ones that didn't.

"Filmmaking is not a great business," Joe went on. "It's hard to succeed by releasing new films. The value often comes in the library."

"How does that work?" Steve asked.

"Once a film has enjoyed its theatrical run, both here and abroad, it becomes part of a studio's film library. If it's a good film, it stands to be watched again and again over the years. New technologies like home video make that even more likely. The major studios have built up enormous film libraries that continue to provide value to their film businesses."

Another revelation for us. I wanted to know how studios valued those libraries.

"It's not an exact science," Joe explained, "but look at the value of the major Hollywood studios and you'll see their library of films is really significant."

Steve and I continued the discussion on the way home. Steve had rented a private plane to fly us to Los Angeles and back. It was a small jet that could seat around six people in comfortable leather seats. We had flown commercial before but Steve didn't like the airport hassle. We sat across from each other, my first time in a private jet. Joe had been immensely open and helpful, so much so that our meeting turned out to be the start of a relationship that would culminate a few years later with him joining Pixar's board of directors.

"The big studios are really about providing capital and distribution," Steve said. "They don't focus on making one single great product. It's a different business model completely."

"In that model," I added, "even if a film does just okay in its theatrical release, it may have value for years in a film library. That's the opposite of tech products that become obsolete quickly.

"It means that if we go into live-action film," I went on, "we can't do it a little. We'd have to make a slate of films every year, hope for some hits, and build a library."

"But animation is different," Steve added. "Even Disney makes only one or two animated films a year. Why couldn't we apply the same model to animation? If Pixar pours itself into making one animated film a hit, couldn't we do the same for a live-action film?"

The discussion continued as we contemplated how Pixar might enter the live-action film business, whether it would be able to attract the right talent for filmmaking, need an office in Hollywood, and other details. As we considered it, I couldn't help but think that there I was on a private jet, talking with Steve Jobs about whether Pixar ought to go into the live-action film business. For a brief moment, I felt like a Hollywood mogul. We were not studio executives yet, but we were having fun learning about it.

A few days later, we took the topic up with Ed. We sat in his office and discussed whether we could make live-action films the same way we made animated films.

"It's about the way the films are made," Ed said. "In animation there is much more control. We iterate on the story over and over again, through storyboards, character modeling, animation tests, and other processes. If the story or a character isn't working, we can change it. Live action doesn't offer that flexibility. Once the film has been shot, you're locked into using the footage you have.

"This is why so many films don't quite hit the mark," Ed went on. "It's not that the filmmakers want to make films that fall short; it's that they have to make the film from the footage they shot, and sometimes it's not what they need."

"Wouldn't Pixar's approach to storyboarding help with making a live-action film?" Steve asked.

"It would help," said Ed, "but it wouldn't be a guarantee. In animation we still have the chance to iterate on a story even when we're into production of a film. That's a lot harder in live action when all the sets have been dismantled and the cast and crew have moved on."

On our way home, in Steve's car, we continued the discussion.

"I'm not sure if going into live-action film gives us any advantages," I said. "In animation we put all our eggs in one basket, and we watch it very closely. In live action we spread out the eggs over many baskets, hoping a few of them will hatch. Both businesses are risky. I'm not sure one balances or helps the other."

"It might even be the opposite," Steve said. "If we have to release a slate of live-action films, what's to stop the ones that flop from damaging our reputation in animation?"

"That's true," I agreed. "Walt Disney only went into live-action film after he was established in animation."

"I hate the idea of Pixar releasing products that might not be great," Steve added emphatically.

I felt the same way. Silicon Valley was built around changing the world with breakthrough products. It wasn't that releasing a slate of live-action films was a bad strategy; it just was not the way we thought about things. And besides, it looked like *both* animated films and live-action films were very risky businesses. One would not offset the risk of the other.

From that point on, it felt like we were talking ourselves out of going into live-action film rather than evaluating it as a serious option. There was no part of Steve that bought into the idea of making products that might not all have a shot at greatness. Live-action film was quickly losing lift as the risk-reducing strategy we had hoped it would be.

More and more, committing Pixar to animated entertainment alone was looming as Pixar's only option. I'd been fighting it ever since I'd come to Pixar because every stone I had turned over revealed just how hard that path would be. I'd thought it when I'd learned how onerous the Disney agreement was, and then again when I learned the risks of releasing blockbuster films, and then again when I learned there had pretty much never been an independent, animated feature film company without other businesses to diversify the risks.

I had never had the notion that I was being hired to build a pure entertainment company. But it was becoming clearer that I needed to understand what that meant. Steve was keeping up the pressure on taking Pixar public, and I didn't have the numbers to support it. That would take more than a few meetings in Hollywood. If this were to be a serious strategy, I would have to understand the economics of the business in detail. Where should I begin?

I started at the library.

At the Mitchell Park Library in Palo Alto, I discovered a book on the entertainment industry, Hal Vogel's *Entertainment Industry Economics*. First published in 1986, this book had become somewhat of an industry reference, cataloging in detail all the financial and economic principles driving the entertainment business. It was a dry read, populated with charts, formulas, and dense economic analysis. I read it cover to cover, and many sections I read repeatedly.

The book's section on filmed entertainment began with this ominous assessment:

> *Many people imagine that nothing could be more fun and potentially more lucrative than making movies. After all, in its first four years, Star Wars returned profits of over $150 million on an initial investment of $11 million. Nonetheless, ego gratification rather than money may often be the only return on an investment in film. As in other endeavors, what you see is not always what you get. In fact, of any ten major theatrical films produced, on the average, six or seven may be broadly characterized as unprofitable and one might break even.*[1]

— —

1. Hal Vogel, *Entertainment Industry Economics: A Guide for Financial Analysis* (Cambridge University Press, 1986–2011), p. 71.

Ouch! Ego gratification the only return on investment? Two out of ten films profitable? This was worse than baseball batting averages. Vogel's analysis made it clear that the likelihood of a hit was small, the likelihood of a blockbuster tiny.

It got worse.

Later, in the book's discussion of filmed entertainment, Vogel became even more foreboding:

> *As historical experience has shown, common stock–based offerings do not, on the average, stand out as a particularly easy method of raising production money for movies. Unless speculative fervor in the stock market is running high, movie-company start-ups usually encounter a long, torturous, and expensive obstacle course. . . .*
>
> *Strictly from the stock market investor's viewpoint, experience has shown that most of the small initial common-stock movie offerings have provided at least as many investment nightmares as tangible returns.*[2]

Vogel was talking about taking a film company public, exactly what we were hoping to accomplish. A "long, torturous, and expensive obstacle course" and "investment nightmares" were not the ideal scenario, to put it mildly. Steve was pressing for a public offering, and here Vogel was holding up a big, bright, neon warning sign. Now I worried even more if this was the right direction for Pixar, especially when we were struggling to finish our first film. I understood that a public offering was the path, and probably the only one, to raise the funds we would need to build Pixar. But a failed public offering would be a gigantic, possibly even fatal, blow for the company. I was caught between Steve's drive to go public and business realities that looked awful.

Vogel's book gave me a tremendous overview of the industry. I still needed something more granular, however, something that would show me the blow-by-blow detail of where every dollar went that was

— —
2. Ibid., p. 117.

associated with Pixar's films. We were still missing a detailed financial projection of how our films would make money. Without that information, we could not make headway in understanding and plotting the real business possibilities. It was like looking for buried treasure without a map.

By now it was June of 1995; *Toy Story* was coming out in November, Steve was antsy to start thinking about a public offering, and I still didn't have the basic information I needed to develop the numbers.

By this time, I had hired a new controller for Pixar, Sarah Staff. It was Sarah who so kindly picked me up on her way back and forth to Pixar while my leg was healing. She was my right-hand person in all the accounting and financial planning aspects of Pixar's business. Sarah was smart, thoughtful, and endearingly humble. She was polished and poised, tall, with straight blond hair, and consummately professional. Her office was in a corner of Pixar reserved for finance and administration. I was over there often.

"Sarah," I asked her one morning, "have you had any luck finding a film model we can use to build our projections?"

"No luck," Sarah replied. "I've talked to my old accounting firm, who checked in with their offices in LA, but they don't have one."

Another dead end. All we needed was a chart of numbers that all the studios had, and we couldn't get it.

"I have one more idea," I said. "How about calling Sam Fischer, our Hollywood lawyer? Ask if he knows where we can get this."

A couple of hours later, Sarah came over to my office.

"Good news, and not so good," she said. "I talked to Sam. Believe it or not, they have a film model. Only they don't give it out. They use it only internally, to advise their clients. He said they'd be happy to run the numbers for us but can't give us the model itself."

"Wow!" I thought to myself. "These financial models must be etched in gold plate. Why are they so secret?"

"That's not going to do it," I said. "We need our own model. Let me give Sam a try."

Sam explained that his firm's film projection model was confidential because it helped them counsel their clients and they didn't want others to have access to it. He also said that his model was only for live-action film and that animation would be different.

"I totally understand why you don't give out your model," I said, almost pleading, "but I'm really hitting a wall on this one. Every place I turn all I hear is that these film models are confidential, but Pixar has to have its own in order to move forward."

"I'm sympathetic," said Sam, "but we've never shared the information in our model."

But the truth was, I didn't want that particular information for live-action films. I wanted to build a model for animation, which would be different. I just needed a start.

I had an idea.

"Sam, you mentioned your model is only for live action. How about if Pixar agrees to use it only for animation? We'll evolve it. We won't need to use your original data because we'll tailor it to animation. Then we'll share the results with you and in the end, you'll have an animation model if you need it."

"Where will you get the data for animation?" Sam asked.

"Disney said they would help us; they just can't give us their model. With your model and their help, I think we can do it."

Sam thought for a moment.

"You know, I can go along with that," he said.

I felt like jumping through the phone and giving him a hug. I never thought I would be so thrilled over a spreadsheet. Sam's reticence to share the model was well founded. He had stretched himself to help us out. I felt truly grateful.

Sam's firm sent up the numbers. It was our first glimpse at the way films made money. At last, we could see how much studios kept from the box office revenues; what were reasonable assumptions for film marketing costs; when films were released in video, TV, and other markets; how much they made; the impact on profits of film production budgets and profit-sharing arrangements; as well as other details without which we'd never fully understand the business. To tailor the model to animation, we took up Disney's offer to answer our questions about how the business of animated feature films worked.

Before long we cobbled together our first model of how an animated feature film performed financially. It was rough and crude, at best. But it was ours. Over time we would learn how to perfect it. Right now, it was good enough to give us a start. Sarah and I were elated. It was one of those small, quiet victories that gave us far more satisfaction than one might expect. It may have seemed trivial to others, but it made us feel we could finally start talking the talk of the film business. There was a chance that one day we might even seem like we knew what we were doing.

As the numbers crystallized, however, I began to see why Hal Vogel had characterized raising capital through the stock markets as a torturous obstacle course for a film company. It was virtually impossible to make the numbers work in a way that generated the kind of smooth, even profit growth that investors liked. Worse, the numbers had tremendous risk in them. Just a small change in box office performance could wipe out the entire profitability of a film. There was also another issue that was unique to animation, a pesky detail that went under the title of "carrying costs."

Carrying costs are the costs of paying employees when they are not working on films. When animation finished on *Toy Story,* for example, Pixar still had to pay its animators even if it had nothing for them to do. I was learning that carrying costs could drain a little company like Pixar of all profitability. It was a problem that had dated all the way back to the time of Walt Disney, and one of the reasons it was so difficult to go into animation. This problem did not exist in live-action film because the crew making the film, from the producer and director to the film's stars, to the cameramen, extras, and everyone else, comes together for the sole purpose of making the film. They are paid only during the time they are involved. As soon as that ends, they all disperse and there is no further obligation to pay them.

Animation studios don't work this way. The artists and filmmakers are studio employees. They remain at the studio often for their entire careers. They are paid whether they are making a film or not. The cost of continuing to pay studio employees when the studio is not in the heat of producing a film could grow enormous. If Pixar didn't have well-planned solutions to keeping its people productive between films, even a hit film could be drained of its profits by the overall carrying costs.

"Steve," I said one night when we were on the phone, "I am worried about this carrying cost issue. The more we grow Pixar, the higher the carrying cost if we're not working on a film. We could literally have dozens of people sitting around with nothing to do and we'd still have to pay them."

"It's a pipeline issue," Steve said. "We have to have enough work in the pipeline to keep people busy."

"That isn't easy," I said. "It depends on story development, which is notoriously unpredictable. It would be better if we had more options than just a story pipeline."

We took it up with Ed.

"It's a big concern, I agree," Ed said. "But I think there are things we can do. We always have technical challenges to work on, problems like animated skin, water, wind, hair, human beings. We can move small teams of people to work on these. We also want to continue to make short films, as a way to develop talent, especially directors."

"So when film production is quiet, we basically do more research and development so that our future films are better?" said Steve.

"Yes," Ed said. "We obviously have to try to time our film production pipeline so that our employees remain busy. That's the main goal. But we have other options if that doesn't work."

"But that'll mess up our business plan," I said. "We still have to pay everyone. We're shifting the cost from filmmaking to research and development, but we're still incurring the cost. It would be much better if we could put people to work on products that could generate revenues."

"Pam's been thinking about video games," Ed said. "We have some people here interested in making games based on our films. We might be able to shift some people to that."

There were, at least, some options, but this carrying cost issue had the potential to be the Achilles heel that, even if our films did well, could eat away at Pixar's business viability.

It was now approaching the end of June 1995. The release of *Toy Story* was a few months off. I finally understood the business possibilities in animation. But even if I could make a case that an independent animated feature film company could work in theory, in Pixar's case we would remain for years under the vise grip of the Disney agreement, which gave Disney most of the profits. We also had to deal with the carrying cost issue.

My instincts said that animation as a stand-alone business, without anything to diversify its risks, was going to be very, very difficult to make stick with investors. Many would see it as a fool's errand. How could an upstart company with no experience in Hollywood credibly claim it would build an animated feature film studio that would rival Disney's? No studio had pulled it off in two generations, and Disney had long ago diversified.

Yet the pressure on me from Steve continued to intensify. He wanted to know when we'd take Pixar public. It felt like he thought going public was the endgame, that all would be magically okay if only we could do it. I didn't see it that way. The pressures that Pixar would feel once we went public would be monumental. The whole world would be watching for every single slip-up. Every misstep would be magnified. It could just as easily backfire as it could launch Pixar into a better future.

Moreover, if Pixar raised its flag as an entertainment company, we would take steps that would be hard to reverse. Things like: stop selling RenderMan software; shut down the commercials group; announce to the world, and particularly to Wall Street, that we were an entertainment company; assign more and more resources to filmmaking. Once we stepped into that world, there would be no turning back. No second chance. Pixar had to be ready for it, financially, strategically, psychologically. With the pressures of trying to finish *Toy Story*, I was not sure we were.

But I had examined this from every angle I could imagine. Fully committing Pixar to becoming an entertainment company focused on animated feature films was our only shot. Steve, Ed, and I were all on board with it. This was our mountain to climb, no matter how steep or far away the summit. With much weighing on my mind, it was time to begin the ascent.

7

FEW OPTIONS

MY LONG DAILY COMMUTES TO AND FROM PIXAR WERE worse than I'd imagined. The section on Interstate 80 between the 580 turnoff to Point Richmond and the Bay Bridge, which runs past Berkeley toward the east, was one of the worst traffic corridors in the area, maybe even in the country. The traffic backed up for miles every day as commuters, visitors, and tourists all drove to and from the Bay Bridge. On a good day the drive one way took me an hour and a quarter. On a bad day, almost two hours.

I often sat in that traffic and thought to myself how this landscape must have looked before we covered it with concrete. Spectacular, was my conclusion. I imagined the first humans to set eyes on this terrain, surely among the most beautiful and fertile on the planet.

To the east of Interstate 80 were the wooded, grass-filled, low peaks of the Berkeley Hills, exquisite rolling hills that spread for miles and enjoyed an almost perfectly temperate climate. To the west, and the view from those Berkeley Hills, was the San Francisco Bay, that spectacular body of water formed by two peninsulas, one from the north, ending at Sausalito and the Golden Gate National Recreation Area, the other from the south, ending in San Francisco. Between those two peninsulas was a small channel that linked the San Francisco Bay and the Pacific Ocean. The only way across that body of rough and frigid water was a boat or, for the past sixty years, the Golden Gate Bridge.

I imagined what life in this vicinity must have been like long before the area became a bastion for higher learning and innovation.

The Ohlone Tribe had lived in these regions for several thousand years. They had subsisted largely through hunting and gathering, building villages along the shores of the bay, traveling and fishing along the shallow waters in hand-crafted canoes, and moving inland in the spring to gather newly growing plants, nuts, and other edibles. The natural richness of the area must have been stunning to behold: tall grasses in tree-dotted meadows, herds of elk and antelope grazing, bald eagles overhead, abundant marshes and sea life near the shores of the bay. Ironically, like Pixar, story also mattered to the Ohlone. They lived by a rich mythology, full of spirit guides and shamanic rituals. Men spoke to the rising sun each morning; women sang in unison as they ground acorns and crafted exquisite baskets.[3]

I wondered whether, for all our modern conveniences, we really had it better than the Ohlone. We had done more to uproot the land in two hundred years than the Ohlone did in two thousand, decimating a way of life that seemed to have plenty going for it. Were we better off now, alone in our cars, waiting for the red brake lights of the car in front of us to turn off so we could edge a few feet forward?

Ever since modern man uprooted the Ohlone, we had been on an unrelenting march of technological progress, led in large measure by the start-ups that now occupied this terrain. The traditions that sustained a culture for two thousand years had been replaced by the relentless pace of innovation. Innovation had become our railroad into the future, ushering in sweeping changes to how and where we lived, what we did, and what we thought. Any company that could not keep up with the pace of change quickly became an artifact.

I had long been fascinated by why Silicon Valley existed at all. My work with new businesses left me mystified as to why giant companies with enormous resources and seasoned management teams allowed tiny start-ups to eat into their markets. Why hadn't IBM, which led the computing world for decades, or Xerox, which in-

---

3. One excellent source for the history of the Ohlone is Malcolm Margolin, *The Ohlone Way: Indian Life in the San Francisco-Monterey Bay Area* (Heyday Books, 1978).

vented the graphical user interface, not themselves become Microsoft and Apple? Years earlier, why hadn't the railroads become airlines? More important to my present task, today, why wouldn't Disney become Pixar? If Pixar succeeded at all, wouldn't Disney, the king of the animation hill for more than two generations, want to claim computer animation for itself? The answer was that it definitely would. What would stop it?

The answer, I believed, had to do with one thing: *culture.*

Culture is the invisible force on which innovation depends. We like to pin the mantle of invention on individuals, not circumstances. We anoint heroes and tell their stories. Yet innovation is a collective undertaking. It is as much the product of circumstance as of genius. There is a spirit to it. Preserving that culture and spirit at Pixar was very, very important.

Indeed, I had been brought into Pixar as a change agent. My job was to shake up the company and usher it into an era of commercial success and viability that it had never experienced. How could I know that the changes I was sent to make wouldn't end up destroying the culture on which Pixar depended to innovate?

Pixar was innovating on not just one but two fronts: storytelling and computer animation. The culture on which this work depended was very delicate. The storytelling part of that culture seemed especially fickle. In contrast, with engineering projects, you could set a goal and you were likely to see some result, a prototype, a beta, an early version that you could look at and iterate. That didn't make engineering easy, but at least a good engineering manager could find the road map. Storytelling was different. There was no road map. I was learning how it involved much more groping in the dark. The culture had to allow for that exploration. As we laid out a plan for Pixar to grow, we couldn't include in it a line that said, "Make three great stories a year." We had to preserve whatever it was about Pixar that enabled great stories to happen.

Corporations are a lot like living creatures. They have personalities, emotions, and habits. The person at the top might seem to be calling all the shots but is often imprisoned in a culture he or she can do little to change. As corporations succeed, they generally become more conservative. The flames of creativity on which a company is built can easily cool as pressures to perform mount. Success brings something to defend, something to lose. Fear can easily trump courage.

In my days as a lawyer representing start-ups doing deals with large corporations, I had observed how the giant East Coast technology companies like IBM and Digital Equipment Corporation that once ruled the high-tech world had evolved into hierarchical, formal cultures. Orders came from the top. Lines of communication were rigid. Coloring outside the lines was shunned. Their organizations became politicized. The most progressive, innovative contributors did not necessarily rise to the top. Excessive hierarchy and bureaucracy were like a death blow to innovation. I knew that at Pixar, we had to avoid this.

Now I was being exposed for the first time to Hollywood culture. In our efforts to understand the entertainment industry, I had visited executives at Disney, Universal Studios, and other film companies; talked to Hollywood agents, lawyers, and accountants; and read as much as I could on the field. What I found surprised me. I had expected to see the creative, trend-setting, glamorous veneer that defined the image of Hollywood. Instead, I found that Hollywood could be even more defensive and fearful over changing the status quo than the huge tech companies with which I was familiar. Fear and power politics seemed to have a strong grip on Hollywood. The studios wanted to own things: artists, movies, TV, music, whatever it may be. Their instinct was to tie them up, to control them. I had seen this firsthand as I came to understand the terms of Pixar's 1991 deal with Disney.

What this indicated, surprisingly to me, was that the hotbed of creativity that was the supposed hallmark of Hollywood was not all it was cracked up to be. It was much harder than I thought for the studios to take big risks and to innovate. They seemed to trade more on certainty and copycatting than risk. This meant that if Pixar were to raise its flag as an entertainment company, it would have to avoid the Hollywood habits that stifled innovation. If Pixar traded its familial and informal culture for one based on control and celebrity, it could lose the freshness and spirit on which it depended. Maybe my grumbling about Pixar's lonely outpost in Point Richmond, California, was misplaced. Perhaps it was a good thing, making it easier for Pixar to forge its own way.

I could see many challenges to preserving Pixar's culture. But there was one challenge that was rearing its head above all the others. It struck at the heart of Silicon Valley's innovation culture, and it was a festering wound at Pixar that was in danger of becoming life-threatening. As I pulled into Pixar's parking lot after that long commute through the Bay Area and Berkeley, this problem was rarely far from my mind. It involved a little device that had become the glue that held Silicon Valley together: the stock option.

Start-ups were bound together by the opportunity for their founders and employees to share the spoils of success. This was one of the main incentives for joining a high-risk venture versus a more established company. The vehicle for participating in a start-up's success was the stock option, a paper promise that had become the currency of Silicon Valley. Stock options turned Silicon Valley into the modern-day equivalent of the gold rush.

A stock option gives an employee the option to purchase stock in the company in the future. Its value derives from the fact that even though the employee doesn't have to pay for the stock until later, the price the employee pays at that time is set at the value of the stock when the employee receives the option, usually when he or she joins the company. If the company is wildly successful after the employee joins, the value of that stock could grow astronomically, but the employee only pays the price set when he or she received the option. All the rest is profit. For example, if a company's stock is worth $1 per share when a new employee joins, and if that employee receives an option to buy a thousand shares of stock, five years later if the stock is worth $100 per share, the employee still pays only $1. He or she makes $99 profit on each of those thousand shares, or $99,000 of profit. This is how Silicon Valley gives birth to new generations of millionaires and billionaires.

If Pixar had failed in any one area, it was that its employees did not have stock options. Steve had long promised that he would fix this, but it had not happened. This shortcoming was the single biggest source of resentment and bitterness with employees at Pixar. In my early weeks at Pixar, barely a conversation started with me that didn't quickly lead to the question "What about the stock options?" This wasn't a gentle inquiry as much as the bubbling over of a seething cauldron of anger and frustration.

Pixar's employees, especially those who had been there the longest, felt trapped. They felt let down and misled by Steve for not giving them a right to share in Pixar's success. But they had little choice other than to wait and see what happened because they had invested so much time in the company. It would make little sense to leave now, especially when *Toy Story*'s release was imminent.

Making matters worse, Steve had made promises to a handful of Pixar's senior team, giving them a share of Pixar's film profits that might be converted into stock options. I was the most recent of those, having received a promise of stock options when I joined the company. Besides the top executives, everyone else was excluded. This was a disaster in the making. All it would take was one domino to fall, and an exodus of Pixar's talent could happen overnight; if not now, later. That would spell the end of Pixar's capacity to innovate.

On this issue I was caught squarely in the middle. On the one side, Pixar's longtime employees were angry and bitter. There were constant gripes as I made my rounds at Pixar:

"Will Steve take care of us?"

"We've waited a long time for this."

"I hope you make it right."

"I'll believe it when I see it."

On the other side was Steve, who had all the power to decide how many stock options to give Pixar's employees. A stock option plan requires a company to set aside a percentage of its stock for the benefit of its employees. In start-ups that percentage varies, from as low as perhaps 15 percent to as high as 40 percent. Because Steve owned 100 percent of Pixar, every option that went into the stock option plan would reduce his personal stake in the company as those options were exercised by Pixar's employees.

Steve wanted to reduce his share as little as possible. He had in mind the kind of percentage that a new start-up might use, as low as 15 or 20 percent. That might work for a company just starting out, one that might expect to hire 50 or so employees in its first couple of years. But Pixar was far bigger than this. It already had approaching 150 employees, and many of those were seasoned veterans who, by Silicon Valley standards, were entitled to significant stock option amounts.

The problem was exacerbated by the possibility that we might try to take Pixar public soon; Steve was aiming for the end of the year. The price of a stock option is set at the value of the stock at the time the option is granted. Early in a company's history that price will likely be very low because the company doesn't have much value. It might be well under $1 per share. But as the company grows, its value goes up, and so does the option price, maybe to a few dollars per share. Obviously, it is much better for an employee to pay a lower price for stock in a company. As a company approaches its initial public offering, or IPO, its value is presumably growing and growing—which is the momentum that makes the IPO possible—with a corresponding increase in the option price.

Because Pixar was ostensibly close to its IPO, the option price would have to be set much higher than if Pixar was a brand-new start-up. This meant that Pixar's employees who had been there since the early days would be paying a much higher price for their stock options now than they would have had they received them years earlier, when theoretically they should have received those options. There was nothing we could do about that now, but this was going to be a very bitter pill to swallow. It put even more pressure on granting options generously.

Steve did not want to take these factors into account. His position was that "the option price doesn't matter because we'll make the value of the stock so high."

He was also adamant about taking no risk that he would lose control of the company in the future, as Pixar's stock options were exercised by employees, and as Pixar sold stock to other investors. I didn't need to ask him why. He wanted to avoid any risk of being in a position like he had been in at Apple where the board had effectively ousted him from the company against his will.

I understood that Steve wanted to retain control of Pixar, but I felt there was more to it than that. He could have authorized more options in the pool and still retained control. He just didn't want to give up his own shares. When it came down to his own pocket or the pockets of Pixar's employees, Steve wanted the stock in his pocket. On the one side, I couldn't blame him. He was the owner of the company. He had taken all the financial risk.

But on the other side, I grew frustrated with Steve over this. I felt we had a chance to fix an injustice in a way that would allow everyone to win. Giving up a little more stock would make little difference in the wealth Steve would enjoy if Pixar succeeded. In any other start-up, Pixar's key employees would have had stock options years earlier, at very low exercise prices. It was virtually unheard of to put in place a stock option plan so close to a potential public offering. This did not have to be such a battle.

The more I waded into this issue, the more I felt like a punching bag for everyone: Pixar's employees thought I was protecting Steve. Steve thought I was asking for too much for Pixar's employees. It didn't matter that, inwardly, I sided with Pixar's employees. My job was not to take sides but to broker a solution that would work for Steve and the rest of the company. It was the first time I felt myself pitted against Steve, though. He began to get irritated when I brought up the subject of stock options.

"We've already discussed it," he would add curtly. "Just show me the proposed plan."

But I couldn't make a plan without enough stock to put in it.

"When Steve digs in his heels, it's very hard to move him," I complained to Hillary one night. "Most of the time we're on the same page, but we're not on this one and there's little I can do."

"Look, if you've tried everything," Hillary said, "what else can you do? It's his company. It's not your fault."

But I felt I needed to fix it. I could feel the tension building on this issue. Everyone was itching for a stock option plan, but when they saw how much stock was in it, the bitterness would just grow. I had to wrestle more stock from Steve than he wanted to give.

And so, on my long drives between the Berkeley Hills and the San Francisco Bay, I worried. I worried about how seriously we would be taken as an entertainment company. I worried about Disney claiming the space that Pixar was creating. I worried about the pressures a new strategic agenda would put on Pixar's culture. And I worried about Hal Vogel's observation that taking a film company public was a "long, torturous, and expensive obstacle course."

But it was the stock options that bothered me the most. Many of Pixar's employees had staked their entire careers on Pixar, had given it the best years of their professional lives. What kept them there? What kept them from jumping ship for more lucrative opportunities? I reasoned that it could only be because they were passionate about Pixar. Despite all the years of commercial failure, they believed in the potential of their own work, and they wanted to see it through. We could not rely on that for much longer, though. They now needed to be rewarded for it.

Somewhere on those drives, in the quiet of my own car, I realized that no amount of deliberation was going to resolve my worries. Sometimes there comes a point when you jump not because you feel ready or are sure that you'll make it across the chasm, but because the conditions are forcing you off the edge. That's when you find out if you can fly. I felt this was the time to jump. We had to start moving, and resolving the options problem was the place to begin.

As mundane an issue as it might seem, I believed that Pixar's fate hung partially in the balance over how much stock we put in the stock option pool. Too little, and Pixar's key employees might be forever disgruntled, ruining the culture on which Pixar was built. I wasn't sure I had anything further I could squeeze out of Steve, but I needed to take one more final swing at it, even if it meant incurring Steve's legendary wrath. I picked up the phone one night and called him.

"We have to add more stock options," I said flatly. "We can't make it on the amount we have allocated right now. It's not enough. A few percent more, and we can give it a shot and still have a good chance you'll maintain control of the company even after we go public."

"I said I didn't want to revisit this," Steve griped. He was on the verge of dismissing it. I suggested a number. It was as far as I thought he might go.

"Will this be it?" Steve asked, totally exasperated. "Will this be enough options to last for a long while?"

I didn't think it would be. It would barely get us by now.

"Yes," I declared with unfounded confidence. "We'll make it work."

"Then I don't want to hear about it again." And with that, Steve ended the conversation.

I breathed a deep sigh of relief. It could have gone much worse. I would still get a lot of grief over not having enough options to go around, but I had gained enough to now make a case that if Pixar became a big enough success, that would make up for it.

I at last had my first real toehold. The option plan was pivotal to moving Pixar forward. But now the stakes were higher than ever. Those stock options needed to be worth a lot one day. A small win wouldn't cut it for anyone. Pixar was aiming for the big time.

PART II

8

FOUR PILLARS

BY THE END OF THE SUMMER OF 1995, THE TIDE AT PIXAR had turned from the drive to finish *Toy Story* to the countdown toward its release. You could feel the pressure valve letting off steam within the company as the seemingly endless number of production tasks were whittled down. The film crew was visibly more at ease, and by 6:00 p.m. on any given day, the parking lot was emptier than it had been in a while. We had made some strides on the business side also, by winding down the RenderMan sales team and exiting the business of animated commercials.

It was not nearly time to celebrate, though. *Toy Story*'s release date was November 22, 1995, the day before Thanksgiving, about three and a half months away. Between now and then it had to go through the phase of filmmaking called post-production, a slew of tasks that would transform *Toy Story* into a finished product. These included making final edits and last-minute dialogue changes; incorporating final color correction; adding film credits; finalizing the musical score and songs; adding the sound effects for balls bouncing, doors closing, and myriad other noises; duplicating the film for delivery to movie theaters; and more.

Because Pixar did not have its own post-production facility, much of this work occurred at George Lucas's Skywalker Ranch in Marin County, less than an hour's drive away, where Lucas had built a world-class audio post-production facility. During this time period, we at Pixar had no real sense of how the film was coming together. It felt like waiting for the lunar module to emerge from orbiting the dark side of the moon. Pixar was mission control while John and a small crew were on radio silence as they navigated this part of *Toy Story*'s journey. It would be a couple of months before we would see the final product. We were collectively holding our breath.

Besides finishing the film, there were other things about its release to worry about.

"I've seen the latest *Toy Story* trailer," Steve said one Saturday. "It plays too young."

By now, my leg had healed enough for Steve and me to reestablish our weekend walks. This time we stopped at Steve's house afterward and were sitting in the courtyard, admiring his abundant fruit and berry trees.

"We have to keep the pressure on Disney about the trailers," I suggested.

Since the spring, Disney had been showing what were called "teaser trailers," short snippets that hinted at what was to come. The first teaser trailer had been attached to Disney's animated feature film *A Goofy Movie*. I had taken my entire family to the film just to see the one-minute teaser trailer for *Toy Story*. Imagine our disappointment when it didn't play! My first big moment in film dashed in an instant. We later discovered it was in 80 percent of the film theaters where *A Goofy Movie* played, but the Century Cinema 16 theater in Mountain View had not been one of them. My family had to make do with the snippet of *Toy Story* I had at home that they'd already seen a hundred times.

Now Disney was preparing to ramp up the full marketing campaign for *Toy Story*'s release.

"The way the studios market movies is so old-fashioned," Steve griped. "Loud trailers and cheesy billboards. I think we could do better."

The marketing of *Toy Story* was pivotal. Pixar took the idea of family entertainment seriously; *Toy Story* was for all members of the family, not just young children. If Disney aimed the film's marketing campaign only at families with young children, it could drastically limit who might come and see the film. We had learned how crucial the opening weekend box office was; it would set the tone for the film's entire run. Therefore, it mattered how many different trailers there were; whether they appealed to children, teenagers, or adults; what films they were attached to; and the extent of the advertising campaign.

Adding to our concern was our disappointment with how Disney had handled the making of toys and other merchandise for *Toy Story*. Due to a late start, many of their usual merchandise makers had passed on it. We wanted to make sure the marketing went off without a hitch. Steve decided to personally handle the marketing talks with Disney. He had called them about this latest trailer.

"I'm not sure they're listening," he complained to me. "They agree that we need to appeal to different audiences, but I'm not sure what they're doing about it."

In truth, there was not much more we could do besides complain to Disney. The film's marketing was their responsibility, and ultimately we had to trust them. But I was sure it didn't hurt to have Steve breathing down their necks.

Meanwhile, my focus was on putting the finishing touches on Pixar's business plan. By now, Sarah Staff and I had crunched the numbers every which way. But no matter how we looked at it, the fundamental challenge remained the same. The level of success Pixar needed to make a viable business was, by every measure, truly absurd.

Domestic box office performance is the yardstick by which Hollywood measures the success of a film. It refers to the amount of ticket sales in movie theaters in North America. Our profit projections were based on various levels of box office success. For example, if we assumed $100 million in domestic box office revenues for each of Pixar's films, the projections did not work at all. The costs of production and the infrequency of film releases made it nearly impossible to sustain the business. At $150 million in domestic box office revenues, the business began to work. But it didn't really take off until box office revenues exceeded $180 million per film.

But here was the reality: releasing films that consistently performed at the level of $150 million or more had never been done, by anyone. Of all the animated films released by Disney since *Snow White and the Seven Dwarfs* in 1937, only two had a domestic box office that exceeded $150 million: *Aladdin* in 1992, which had earned $217 million, and *The Lion King* in 1994, which had shattered all records with a domestic box office of $313 million. If you excluded *The Lion King* and *Aladdin,* the average domestic box office for Disney animated feature films was far less than $100 million.

And that was Disney films, a brand trusted in every corner of the globe. If you included the animation efforts of other studios, the average was drastically lower. In fact, no studio besides Disney had ever released an animated film that had a domestic box office much above $50 million in its initial release.

How was Pixar, in the new and untested medium of computer animation, possibly going to perform at the levels it needed to succeed? Any way you looked at it, building an independent animation studio required a level of box office success that was not only unprecedented; it was almost unimaginable.

We still needed a business plan, however, a road map to give Pixar a shot at success no matter how improbable. After examining a seemingly endless number of permutations, the plan we finally developed had four pillars.

First, we had to increase Pixar's share of the profits from our films. There was no scenario in which Pixar could become a viable business under the profit-sharing arrangement in the existing agreement with Disney. We tested many possibilities and concluded that the minimum profit share that Pixar would need to achieve its goals was 50 percent. Therefore, the first pillar of our plan called for increasing Pixar's share of the profits to at least 50 percent, which was a four- or fivefold increase over what we had now.

Next, to have any real shot at increasing our share of film profits, Pixar had to be willing to pay all, or a large part, of the production costs of its films. We had learned how Hollywood ran on essentially two currencies: money and star power. Either one was a ticket to bigger opportunities, bigger profit shares, and more clout. Those who didn't have either remained at the whim of those who did. If we were ever to renegotiate our agreement with Disney, or work with any other film distributor when that agreement was over, to begin any conversation about a bigger share of the profits we had to be prepared to pay the production costs of our films. I discussed this with Steve one Friday when he was at Pixar. We were in his office, just down the hall from mine.

"How much do you think we will need to raise?" Steve asked.

"At least seventy-five million dollars," I said. "Competition for talent, carrying costs, and increasing technical challenges are driving production costs up. It won't be long before our budgets hit seventy to a hundred million per film."

"Will seventy-five million be enough?" Steve wondered.

"It would let us finance half the production costs on two films," I said. "That should be enough to get us started. That's no small sum, though. It'll scare away banks and private investors. We can only raise that much by taking Pixar public."

"Maybe we need more. It would be better to have a cushion of a hundred and fifty or two hundred million. Once we're raising money, we might as well have a big war chest."

I certainly had no objection to raising more capital for Pixar. But our chances of raising money went down the larger the amount we sought. For an unproven company like Pixar, investors would prefer to see us put smaller amounts of money to good use before they ponied up more. This wasn't the time to debate that, though. Steve and I agreed on the second pillar of Pixar's plan: take Pixar public to raise money in order to build the studio and to fund our own films.

Increasing our share of film profits and raising money wouldn't be enough, though. We also had to increase the frequency with which Pixar released films. We were presently making one film at a time, which meant a film release every four to five years. There was no way to make the business work at this rate. Again, we tested different scenarios. The ideal rate of film releases, at least according to the numbers, was a new film every year. That seemed far out of reach from where we stood now, but any meaningful increase in how many films we produced would require a drastic increase in the size of Pixar so we could work on productions in parallel. Therefore, scaling Pixar to make films more often was the third pillar of the plan.

Finally, if Pixar was to become a serious entertainment company, we needed people to know about us. Under the terms of the Disney agreement, Disney would have most of the billing, and we feared that few people would understand that Pixar was the creative force behind its films. As it was, the movie posters for *Toy Story* would say, "Walt Disney Pictures presents *Toy Story*," or worse, "Disney's *Toy Story*," with Pixar's name in small print. This would make it hard for the world to fully associate Pixar with filmmaking.

"We have to change how the world perceives Pixar," Steve said one evening when we were discussing Pixar's brand. "Even if Disney gets the billing, people need to know that *we* made these films. We can't build a company without a brand."

That was the fourth pillar of our plan: turn Pixar into a brand.

So that was all we needed to do. Besides making films that would enjoy unprecedented box office success the world over, we simply had to

- QUADRUPLE OUR SHARE OF THE PROFITS
- RAISE AT LEAST $75 MILLION TO PAY FOR OUR PRODUCTION COSTS
- MAKE FILMS FAR MORE OFTEN THAN WE KNEW HOW
- BUILD PIXAR INTO A WORLDWIDE BRAND

Piece of cake.

9

IPO DREAMING

THE LINCHPIN OF OUR PLAN INVOLVED RAISING MONEY, A lot of it. That was the only way we could pay for our own films and gain the clout to earn a bigger share of their profits. The only viable path for a little company like Pixar to raise the kind of money we needed was to take it public. It was simply too much money, and too much risk given Pixar's track record, for traditional banks or other financing sources to consider.

If there is a holy grail in Silicon Valley, it is the initial public offering, or IPO, of a company's stock. This is Silicon Valley's payday, the moment of arrival, when paper money becomes real. Every start-up in Silicon Valley harbored dreams of going public. Only a tiny percentage made it. Of those that didn't make it, some would be acquired by larger companies, even fewer would manage on their own; the rest would shut down. This was because it could take years for start-ups to sustain themselves with their own profitability. Without a steady influx of investment, they just ran out of money.

For the employees of those start-ups that do go public, the promise of riches and the imprimatur of success can become a reality. This is why Silicon Valley was, in large measure, built around the promise of the IPO. Out of a hundred start-ups spawned by the plush venture capital firms that lined Silicon Valley's famed Sand Hill Road, only a very few would be fit enough to make the rare but game-changing leap from being a private to a public corporation.

Corporations are owned through pieces of paper called stock certificates. Stock is simply a share of a corporation. The ownership of a corporation can be divided into as many shares as the corporation wants. If it is divided into a hundred shares, each share represents a hundredth, or 1 percent, of the corporation. If it is divided into a thousand shares of stock, each represents a thousandth of the corporation, or 0.1 percent. The Walt Disney Company has well over a billion shares, each one representing a very, very tiny piece of the company. Anyone can own the stock in a corporation. Steve owned most of Pixar's stock, all except the part set aside to transfer to employees as they exercised their stock options. Even then, Steve would still own the vast majority.

Ownership of the stock in a corporation is either private or public. Most corporations are private, meaning there is no public access to their stock, no marketplace in which to buy or sell it. This was Pixar's present status. There was no way to buy Pixar's stock without knocking on Steve's door and asking him directly to sell some of his. There was also no marketplace in which he could sell his stock, even if he wanted to.

A public corporation, in contrast, is one whose stock is available for purchase and sale by anyone. There is a market for it, like the New York Stock Exchange or NASDAQ. If a corporation is public, any person is free to buy or sell its stock. The more buyers, the higher the stock price. The more sellers, the lower the stock price.

The first time the stock of a corporation is sold to the public is called an initial public offering of its stock, or IPO. From that moment on, the corporation is public because its shares can be bought or sold by anyone.

For any company, an IPO is like adding a rocket booster, full of fuel, to its trajectory. In Pixar's case, an IPO had taken on even more significance. By this time, we had implemented a stock option plan and awarded stock options to Pixar's employees. As I had predicted, many felt they did not receive their fair share. The solution was to make the shares they did have as valuable as possible. This depended on a very successful IPO.

Adding even more pressure was how much Pixar's IPO meant for

Steve. It carried with it the full weight of his return from the wilderness into which Apple had banished him ten years earlier. If there was one event that would unquestionably signify Steve's redemption, it would be Pixar's IPO. This would seal his comeback like nothing else could. It was no wonder, then, that whenever we talked about it, his tone took on a weight and importance of almost biblical proportion.

"I've been thinking about Pixar's public offering," Steve started on the phone one night in early August 1995. "There's never been anything like it. It could be one of the hottest IPOs in the history of Silicon Valley. We're gonna make history, not just in tech but in entertainment."

"It's not going to be easy for investors to get their heads around Pixar's business," I suggested. "We have a lot of explaining to do."

"Why not?" Steve said, a little miffed. "Investors are savvy. They have experience with unconventional business models."

They did, I thought to myself, but not in a good way. One of the lessons I learned from the IPO of my previous company, Electronics for Imaging, was that if there is anything investors prefer it is predictability and stability. They become most nervous when things appear erratic and changeable. And the truth was, nothing about our projections for Pixar had predictability or stability. It was impossible to predict the box office performance for a film, and our film release schedule was erratic to say the least. After *Toy Story*, it would be three years before our next film was released. Predicting Pixar's business performance felt like little more than a guess. Investors might accept an unconventional business model, but I didn't think it was a plus.

In fact, in all my experience in law and business, there was no other transaction that was more fraught with difficulty and risk than launching an IPO. It called for an almost impossible coming together of strategic, financial, legal, and market conditions. IPOs had a long history that proved just how hard they were to pull off. Their origins went back almost four hundred years to, of all things, nutmeg.

If innovation was the harbinger of corporate power in the twentieth century, in the seventeenth century it was spices: nutmeg, mace, cloves, cinnamon, pepper, ginger. These exotic substances were immensely popular in Europe, used to flavor and preserve foods, make medicines and aphrodisiacs, gifts for royalty, and even currency for trading. A huge spice trade existed to source these rare substances from exotic, faraway places like the Banda Islands, ten tiny volcanic islands in the Banda Sea, at that time the only place in the world where nutmeg trees grew. It could take two years for a shipping expedition to journey there and back. To assure the success of these expeditions, governments granted legal monopolies to trading companies that would permit those companies to become the sole source of spice trading.

One of these companies, founded in 1602, was the Dutch East India Company. It grew to become the most powerful and richest company on the planet—in large measure due to the unbridled brutality it unleashed to gain control over the Spice Islands—the first major multinational corporation. It was a dominant force in commerce for almost two hundred years. In 1604, the Dutch East India Company sold stock to investors in a transaction that would be the forerunner of the modern IPO. It used the capital it raised to finance its voyages, and it even created the first modern stock market for the purpose of trading its stock, the Amsterdam Stock Exchange. On that exchange you could purchase an interest in the Dutch East India Company and then, literally, wait to see if your ship came in.

It turned out that giving ownership of a company to individuals who had no personal involvement with that company could be a double-edged sword. On the one side, it ushered in the ability to amass capital in amounts that had never before been attainable. It indeed made it possible, in theory, to raise $100 million to make animated feature films. On the other side, the ability to raise capital from an unsuspecting public also brought with it dangers of fraud that would eventually bring the world to its knees.

For example, how would the potential buyer of stock in the Dutch East India Company know if the fleet of ships returning in several months would have a cargo laden with exotic spices or whether its trove had been plundered by pirates? Worse, what if someone in the Dutch East India Company did know that the fleet's cargo had been stolen by pirates and kept that information quiet in order to sell stock in the company at a high price to buyers who did not have that information? This problem, today infamously known as insider trading, is as old as the spice trade.

In the few hundred years after the Dutch East India Company went public, the many scandals and frauds in trading stock had a minimal impact on the economy as a whole. Investment was limited to the tiny sliver of the population with money to invest. But all that changed in the 1920s.

In the prosperity that followed World War I, the growing American middle class invested in the stock markets on a scale never before seen. This meant that when the stock market crashed in 1929, the economic turmoil that followed was so widespread and so intense that it washed away the financial stability of millions in one fell swoop, bringing the country into the depths of a depression that would last for years. To guarantee that nothing on this scale could happen again, Congress passed a body of laws that, to this day, governs any company seeking to raise capital from the public, laws that are enforced by a government agency called the Securities and Exchange Commission (SEC). These laws would govern any attempt by Pixar to become a public company.

The idea behind modern securities laws is that investors should be left to make their own investment decisions, so long as they are given equal and accurate information with which to make those decisions. The world in which some were in the know and others were not was to come to an end. Taking Pixar public meant Pixar would have to describe and disclose every detail of its business. Life for a public company was life in a fishbowl. Once a public company, there would be nowhere to hide. Nowhere. We would endure a never-ending onslaught of questions about every detail of our business. It would force Pixar into a level of public scrutiny that it had never experienced. We had to be ready for it.

The risks in Pixar's business plan, combined with the perils of taking a company public, conspired to make me cautious. Steve would have none of it, though. I was quite certain he dreamed about Pixar's IPO and saw visions of Pixar's stock price emblazoned across the stock exchanges, a stock price that would announce to the world just exactly what Steve's personal investment in Pixar was now worth. It worried me that he saw Pixar's IPO through glasses that were too rose-colored.

"The markets seem healthy and receptive right now," Steve declared while we were on the phone one morning. "People I know say it's a good time. Other companies are getting ready to go public. Netscape is going to be as big an offering as we've seen in a while. I think Pixar is bigger, and better."

The upcoming Netscape offering had everyone excited. Netscape was credited with inventing the first widely used Web browser, called Navigator. Its public offering was one of the first public offerings in the new Internet space, and it had enjoyed huge attention in the media. Netscape's IPO was scheduled for August 1995, just a couple of weeks away.

"Netscape represents an entire new industry," I replied. "Interest is huge. Investors all over are talking about the Internet. They're not thinking about animation. We'll have to convince them about Pixar."

"They'll get it once they see what we're doing," Steve asserted. "We should plan a Pixar public offering as soon as possible."

"We also have to consider when the market will be most receptive to Pixar," I replied, "before we release *Toy Story* or after. If we do it before, and *Toy Story* sinks, we'll have a disaster on our hands."

"Why's that?" Steve retorted. "We don't have to promise a blockbuster to take Pixar public. We're building a company, not a film. Investors will be buying into the idea of a new kind of entertainment company. If *Toy Story* disappoints, we might never be able to raise the capital we need. Maybe we should do it sooner."

I wasn't sure I agreed. If Pixar raised capital on the promise of *Toy Story*, and *Toy Story* flopped, Pixar's stock price would plummet and it might never recover. Investors might never forgive Pixar if they lost money immediately, and it would be three years before we could prove ourselves to them again with a new film. In a heartbeat, Pixar could go from an exciting, hot company to a has-been known only for its disappointments. In some circles, Pixar already had this reputation. Investors would be even more unforgiving. If we took Pixar public, the timing had to be absolutely perfect. I did not think we could, or should, do it before *Toy Story*'s release.

"Working with Steve can be exasperating," I complained to Hillary one night. "Some of his ideas are brilliant but others are off the mark. It's hard to rein him in sometimes."

"You know how to work with that," Hillary replied. "You did it with Efi. It's similar with Steve."

Like Efi, for as trying as Steve could be, he was in equal measure brilliant and invigorating. But on the issue of Pixar's IPO, I needed a sanity check. If there was one person I could turn to for that, it was my old boss and mentor, Larry Sonsini.

10

ON BOARD

LARRY SONSINI WAS THE MANAGING PARTNER AT MY OLD law firm, Wilson, Sonsini, Goodrich & Rosati. He was a legend in Silicon Valley, and with good reason. Larry was Silicon Valley's resident guru on start-ups and IPOs; he had built the firm advising many if not most of Silicon Valley's most famous start-ups, guiding them and advising them through their initial public offerings and beyond. He was chief legal adviser to Silicon Valley's most prominent CEOs and boards of directors. If Silicon Valley had a consigliere, it was Larry.

Within the law firm, Larry inspired a combination of admiration and awe. He was a brilliant lawyer—efficient, effective, and intensely focused on client service. I also found him to be decent and generous, and I was proud to consider him a mentor. Larry had offered me a job at his firm, given me the opportunity to build a new kind of law practice there, made me a partner, and even supported my decision to leave. I especially admired the pride he took in the firm and its role in Silicon Valley. On one occasion in his office, when we had a few minutes to talk, he compared running the firm to building a start-up: "Our mission is simple," he said. "We serve Silicon Valley companies with as fine a legal counsel as they could get anywhere in the world. They don't need to go anywhere else."

With that goal, Larry had steadily increased the quality of legal services of the firm until it did, indeed, compete with, and in some cases exceed, the very best in the world. As Silicon Valley grew, the firm grew. If Pixar was to go public, it could not be in better hands than Larry's.

I made an appointment to see Larry in his office in Palo Alto, not too far from where I lived. Every time I entered that building, I couldn't help but feel a little nostalgic about my days practicing law. As was his habit, Larry was impeccably dressed, in a well-cut Italian suit and shoes. He was of medium build, trim, fit, with receding hair and was almost twenty years my senior. We quickly got to the point.

"Larry, Steve is pushing hard to take Pixar public," I started, "and there are good reasons for it, but the risks are enormous."

"What's the case for doing it now?" Larry asked.

"We need to finance our own films," I explained. "That's the only way we can increase our share of film profits. That'll take seventy-five million dollars at least. We don't have to do it now, but the release of *Toy Story* will give us some wind at our back, and Steve is itching to make the IPO happen. A lot is at stake for him."

I well knew that Larry understood this. He was also a personal friend and adviser of Steve's.

"How do you see it? What are the risks?" he asked.

"Pixar's financial profile is very challenging," I replied. "We have no earnings track record, revenues are unpredictable, and lumpy, and we have no idea when we might share in more of the film profits. Worse still, after we release *Toy Story*, it's three years before our next film."

"This will all make it a tough sell," Larry said. "It won't be easy for the financial markets to know how to think about Pixar."

"I'm worried about what will happen as investors discover the risks," I added. "Pixar may be an exciting bet to create the next Disney Animation but the risks are huge. We can't hide them. But I'm afraid it will scare investors off before we even get started."

"I agree your best bet is to be as up-front as possible with investors," Larry said. "Pixar has an exciting story, and with Steve involved you'll get attention. Investors will figure out the risks anyway. But it's better if it comes from you up-front. We'll help you craft that side of the story."

I was happy with this meeting. Larry would have been the first person to tell me we were crazy to think about taking Pixar public. It didn't matter that he thought it might be a long shot. I already knew that. But it would matter a lot if he thought we had no shot. With Larry supporting the need to disclose the risks ahead of time, it would be easier to convince Steve, who wouldn't be ecstatic about sharing the precariousness of Pixar's business prospects.

I brought the topic up with Steve on the phone that night.

"We'll have to disclose what we know about Pixar's business risks up-front," I said. "Larry says investors will figure it out anyway. It's better coming from us."

"If that's what you both think we have to do, we'll do it," Steve said, dismissively.

I could tell he wasn't against the idea; he just didn't think it mattered. He was convinced investors would see beyond it, that they would be so enamored with Pixar's vision that the business risks would be minimized in their eyes. That was fine with me. I got what I wanted: tacit permission to disclose the risks.

I had something else on my mind that night, too.

Steve was the only director on Pixar's board. We had to expand the board if we were even to think about going public. Any investors would want to know that Pixar had a professional and sophisticated board of directors watching over the company. But I didn't expect this would be an easy discussion with Steve.

Ten years earlier, Apple's board of directors had blind-sided Steve by abruptly removing him from his responsibilities at Apple due to his extreme and erratic behavior running the Macintosh division. We never openly talked about it, but the way Steve had insisted on control of Pixar when it came time to issuing stock options made me think he hadn't entirely recovered from the Apple debacle even now. Even though Steve would own a majority of Pixar, once Pixar was a public company, its board of directors would be accountable to all of Pixar's shareholders, the minority holders included. This meant that the board would be able to act on its own if it needed to do so. I was quite sure this meant that when it came to selecting Pixar's board members, Steve was going to be more than a little picky.

"It is also time to expand Pixar's board of directors," I suggested. "We need a good board in place long before we go public. We should do it now."

"I want it to be small," Steve said. "I don't like big boards. What's the smallest you think it could be?"

"I would think five or six would be enough," I said. "I'll check with Larry. Let's assume it can be small."

"Six is too many," Steve retorted. "We don't need six. I also want it to be with people I can work with, people who care about Pixar and aren't just doing it for the prestige. I don't want a board with figureheads who know nothing about the company."

"The board has to give us credibility," I said. "Investors will look to the board to validate Pixar's strategy. We can't just fill it with tech people."

"I don't want token Hollywood executives or celebrities," Steve replied. "We need board members who understand Pixar. Who care about Pixar. People we trust."

That narrowed the field a lot. It had to be a small board that would give us credibility in Hollywood, made up of people whom Steve knew well and trusted, and who cared about Pixar's best interests. Enough credibility to satisfy Wall Street; enough intimacy to satisfy Steve. This was going to be a narrow needle to thread.

During the past few months, we had met a number of people who, on paper, would make terrific board members. Edgar Bronfman and Sandy Climan, CEO and COO of Universal Studios, were perfect examples. Most companies would have been thrilled at the possibility that any one of these might join their board of directors. But Steve saw flaws in all of them.

"I like Edgar," he said, "but do we really want to put the CEO of Disney's biggest competitor on our board? Sandy Climan would have the same problem."

The Hollywood executives we knew the best were all from Disney: Michael Eisner, Disney's CEO, and Peter Schneider, head of Disney Animation. Putting a Disney executive on Pixar's board now was full of potential conflicts of interest as Pixar navigated its relationship with Disney and even considered relationships with other studios. It wouldn't work.

There was one more possibility. Sam Fischer, our Hollywood lawyer, had introduced us to one of the senior partners at his firm, Skip Brittenham. Skip was one of a handful of elite Hollywood super-lawyers, counsel to the stars. Sam had insisted we meet him when I'd called to say we wanted to learn more about Hollywood.

Skip was a larger-than-life, charismatic lawyer who seemed to have his hand in much that was going on in Hollywood. He was slightly built, handsome, and mostly bald with long side hair. He dressed in casual suits and had a warm, ingratiating demeanor that made him immediately likable. Skip loved to talk about Hollywood, and there was little he hadn't seen over the course of his legal career. He was already on Pixar's side, because his firm represented us.

On the day I met Skip, as I walked into his office, my eye caught an embroidered pillow sitting on a small armchair. On the pillow were carefully stitched words: "No good deed goes unpunished." Skip saw me notice it and said, "If you understand that, you understand Hollywood." I was struck by this. The words on the pillow were so cynical. I asked him about it.

"You have to understand," Skip said, "there's a reality in Hollywood that will hurt you if you fight it. If you give too much, too soon, you'll end up giving a lot more. It sounds counterintuitive, but keep it in mind."

It did not take long to see why Skip Brittenham was a Hollywood super-lawyer, and it wasn't just because he had a fly-fishing ranch and his own plane to fly there. Skip combined a deep knowledge about the entertainment business and law with an endearing charm that gave him a rare camaraderie with the executives and celebrities he represented. He was able to navigate the seriousness of getting business done with the artistic needs and distinctions of his clients. It was quickly apparent that Pixar, and I, could learn an enormous amount from him.

When we first met Skip, I asked him, "What makes stars rise to the top in Hollywood?"

"People think there's a lot of luck involved," he said. "But I don't think so. You'd be amazed how savvy the top stars are, not just in their art, but in business. It's no accident that they got where they did. They are very, very sharp."

Steve and I agreed that Skip would make a terrific board member. Steve asked me to put out a feeler to see if he might be interested. The message came back that he wasn't. Skip rarely, if ever, sat on boards. I asked if I could speak to him about it. His office arranged a phone call and I talked to Skip from my office at Pixar. Begged would be more accurate.

"Skip," I started, "I know you don't do many boards, and I get why. They take up time. You have to travel to board meetings. Plus it's not the mainstay of your law practice. But this is different. We're not your typical Hollywood company. We're born out of Silicon Valley. We're trying to create this hybrid Silicon Valley–Hollywood company, combining story and technology to do what hasn't been done in generations. You can really help us."

"I understand that," Skip said. "But over the past years I've sat on fewer and fewer boards. I can still advise Pixar, as your lawyer. It's too much hassle for me to be on the board. Besides, you're up in Northern California, far from here."

Skip was our last possibility for a Pixar board member from Hollywood. We really needed this one. I could tell that it wasn't Pixar's inherent risks that were scaring Skip off. It was just the inconvenience. I had to keep trying.

"Skip," I pleaded, "being our lawyer would be fantastic, but we need more. As a board member you'd be invaluable to Pixar's future, and to Steve's. We're trying to be the first company in two generations to change the world of animated feature films. Steve really wants to work with you. We need your help. If we make it, it'll be fantastic to have you be part of it. If not, you can quit the board and you wouldn't have lost much. I'll do everything in my power to make it less hassle for you."

"Let me think about it," Skip said.

Two days later Skip called Steve to say he'd love to join Pixar's board.

I wasn't sure what changed his mind. Perhaps it was my desperation. Perhaps he saw in Pixar an opportunity he wanted to be part of. Perhaps he was intrigued by the idea of working with Steve Jobs. They had certainly hit it off. Either way, he signed up.

One down.

That was as far as I could push Steve in terms of board members whom he did not already know really well. Steve floated the idea that we ask Joe Graziano, Apple's CFO during Steve's time there, to join. He wanted me to meet him. Joe came over to Pixar, where I gave him a tour and we chatted about Pixar's business. I liked Joe right away. He was warm, friendly, very smart, and had a penchant for racing cars that was fun to discuss. It didn't take him long to catch on to what Pixar was up against. Fortunately, Joe was at a stage in his career when he liked taking risks with start-ups. He didn't need Pixar to be a sure thing. He seemed like he would be a loyal and steady hand to help us.

Counting Steve, we now had three board members. We needed one or two more. For me there was one person whom I really wanted to see on Pixar's board: Larry Sonsini.

Larry had not just been a close friend and adviser to Steve over the years; he was known to be a brilliant board member. I couldn't imagine anyone better to help guide us through the thicket of going public and beyond. He met all of Steve's criteria. Steve made the call to ask him. Larry agreed.

Now we had four: Steve Jobs, Skip Brittenham, Joe Graziano, and Larry Sonsini. These would all be fantastic. They were all heavy hitters in their fields, and they would give Pixar much-needed credibility. This was a very small board, though. I was worried we needed more members, but Steve didn't want to add more. I asked Larry if four was enough.

"Yes," he said. "You can add more later, when you're ready."

We had our board. Now we could explore an IPO in earnest.

All roads to taking a company public led through the rarefied world of investment banking. The real IPO game would begin when Pixar began its search for an investment banker. If I thought Steve was picky when it came to selecting Pixar's board of directors, that was nothing compared to how he felt about investment bankers.

11

THE GATEKEEPERS

WHETHER THE GOAL IS TO RAISE MONEY TO PROCURE SPICES in the Banda Islands, or to make animated movies in Point Richmond, California, a business must have a way to find that money. If money is to be raised from the public, that task is the job of a highly specialized and often misunderstood corner of the banking world: investment banking.

Investment banks bring together those who have money—investors—with those who need it—businesses. When companies want to go public, there is no way to do it without an investment banker serving as the intermediary. They are the gatekeepers guarding the pathways that lead to money. If there is a singular function that defines the role of investment banks, it is to certify the quality of the businesses into which investors put their money. An investment bank would have to provide an indelible seal of approval to Pixar's value and credibility as an investment. Only then would we be able to talk to investors directly.

To purchase stock in a company, an investor must assess how to value that stock. Stock is nothing other than a tiny piece—a share—of a company. If a company has ten thousand shares of stock and they sell for $50 each, the company is worth $500,000. If the same shares of stock sell for $100 each, the company is worth $1 million. In order to know how much to pay for stock in a company, an investor has to know the company's value.

Assessing a company's value is one of the chief tasks of investment banks. Their job is to look at every aspect of a company's business—

its history, assets, debts, products, profits, markets, distribution chan-
nels, management team, competition, and anything else relevant to
its success—and make an assessment of its value and the risk of the
investment. They are the ultimate tire kickers. Once their assessment
is complete, the investment bankers find investors and facilitate the
sale of the company's stock. An investment bank's entire reputation
rests on credibly helping investors understand the value and risks of
an investment. This extends not just to IPOs but to all kinds of transactions where valuing a company is at stake.

In exchange for this service, investment bankers earn a little percentage of the amounts invested in each transaction. Although calculated in different ways, this is like charging a small tax on the world's
investments. A percentage of much of the world's financing transactions adds up very, very quickly, which is why the successful modern-
day investment bankers have achieved wealth, power, and prestige at
levels that are fit for royalty. Gatekeeping the world's capital markets
is a very lucrative business.

Investment banks come in all shapes and sizes, some small and local, some operating in every corner of the world. They often special-
ize in different industries and have relationships with different types
of investors. In Steve's mind, however, there were only two worth
considering. These were the undisputed kings of the investment
banking world: Goldman Sachs and Morgan Stanley.

Both Goldman Sachs and Morgan Stanley had stellar reputations
in Silicon Valley, having had a hand in many of Silicon Valley's most
celebrated IPOs, including Apple's in 1980 and, most recently, the famous Internet start-up Netscape, both of which were led by Morgan
Stanley.

There was enormous cachet associated with retaining Goldman
Sachs or Morgan Stanley to lead an IPO. Any hot start-up seeking to
go public would invariably place its first call to one or both of them.
It was common for several investment banks to be involved in each
transaction, with one taking the lead role. That bank would drive all
aspects of the transaction, including the process for valuing the com-

pany, overseeing the SEC filings, introducing the company to investors, and ultimately initiating trading of the company's stock in the public stock markets. Goldman Sachs and Morgan Stanley usually took only the lead position, which meant that they were not often involved in the same transaction. Pixar could use only one of them, a topic that Steve loved to consider.

"Who do you think would be better?" he asked one day as we drove up to Pixar. "Goldman or Morgan?"

"I'm not sure," I said. "For me it depends on how excited they are about Pixar, and especially how excited their analysts are about following Pixar."

Analysts were vital components of investment banks. They were individuals who wrote long reports describing each company and making predictions about its future performance. Long after Pixar's public offering, the analysts at the investment banks would continue to write these reports, assessing Pixar's business on an ongoing basis for the benefit of the investing world. It was vital that we have analysts who were excited to write about Pixar. Without them, it would be easy for Wall Street to forget about us.

"They both have offices in LA," I continued, "and we'll need to speak to their people there to access their entertainment industry expertise."

"Do you think there is any chance that both Morgan Stanley and Goldman Sachs might take Pixar public?" Steve asked.

"That would be extremely rare," I said.

"They might do it," Steve went on. "There's a lot in it for both of them. A chance for each of them to be part of one of the hottest IPOs of the year."

I could see that Steve was not so much interested in which of the two I preferred. He had something else in mind. He wanted both.

"Well, we can ask," I said. "No harm in trying."

If Steve wanted both Goldman Sachs and Morgan Stanley to be involved in Pixar's IPO, I certainly wouldn't be against it. Actually, I'd be ecstatic. I'd be thrilled to work with even just one of them.

Maybe Steve had the clout to tell them they had to work together in order to have Pixar's business. I didn't think we were in a position to be too presumptuous, though, and I worried about blowing it with Goldman Sachs or Morgan Stanley by telling them they'd have to work together.

"Let's meet them first," I suggested. "Then we'll gauge their interest."

The heads of the Silicon Valley branches of Morgan Stanley and Goldman Sachs could not have been more different. Frank Quattrone, of Morgan Stanley, was probably the best-known investment banker in Silicon Valley. He had a legendary, larger-than-life reputation for being bold, gregarious, difficult to impress, and a great fighter once he was on your side. He was tall, with a stocky build, a thick mustache, and an infectious smile. His personality would fill a room. He had been involved in taking many hot tech companies public, and everyone vied for his attention. He was also the lead banker for Netscape's IPO, the hottest IPO of the year so far.

Eff Martin of Goldman Sachs was quieter and more understated. He had a warm smile and conveyed a polished and polite demeanor. If Frank Quattrone came across as Wild West, Martin was more Establishment East. About ten years older than me, Martin had a pleasant, easygoing way about him. He always seemed calm and relaxed.

Steve placed the first call to each of them to invite them to learn about Pixar. They were both enthusiastic. The game was on.

Steve and I prepared a dog-and-pony show, an informal presentation that depicted Pixar's vision, business plan, and the risks associated with realizing that plan. The story, essentially, was that we were going to do in the 1990s what Disney had done in the 1930s, usher in a new era of animated entertainment that would take advantage of a new medium for storytelling, and in so doing create iconic films and characters that would be beloved the world over.

We made a plan that our meetings with Morgan Stanley and Goldman Sachs would begin with Steve presenting Pixar's vision, then I would take the lead on describing our business strategy—the four pillars. That would take us to a discussion of Pixar's business in which the risks and challenges would naturally be a part. Following my earlier discussion with Larry Sonsini, we were well prepared to discuss the risks.

The meetings went off without a hitch. Steve did a fantastic job mesmerizing Quattrone and Martin over Pixar's potential. They could hardly have been more enthusiastic about the vision and strategy. They understood Pixar was not the typical Silicon Valley tech company, and both said they wanted to involve their entertainment specialists in LA. Even the discussion over Pixar's risks had gone well.

"How long do you think it might take for Pixar to share in more of the profits from your films?" Martin asked.

"There's nothing forcing Disney to renegotiate," I said. "They could hold us to the terms of our existing arrangement, in which case it would take until our first three films have been released, maybe seven or eight years from now. If *Toy Story* is a hit, they might be willing to renegotiate early, especially if we're prepared to finance our own films."

"Have you indicated you might want to renegotiate?" Martin asked.

"Our feeling is that it's too early," I explained. "It would be better after releasing our first film, and after we have the funds we need."

"Yes, yes, of course," Martin said. "That makes a lot of sense."

I could tell Steve was antsy in this part of the discussion. He was itching to move on, to turn the talk back to *Toy Story* and the dream, the part where Pixar changed the world. But I knew that although Quattrone and Martin did not know the entertainment industry deeply themselves, they had experts in Hollywood who did. These would be individuals who had spent their careers analyzing the entertainment business. It wouldn't take them more than five minutes to figure out the financial challenges of making computer-animated feature films. I wanted them to think we knew what we were doing rather than look like entertainment neophytes who didn't understand the business.

All in all, these meetings had gone very well, and I would have been thrilled to work with Quattrone or Martin.

"Both of them loved the story," Steve said excitedly. "Next we bring them to Pixar. I think that'll make them even more excited."

I had no doubt that it would. They would be on our home turf at that point. Many companies never got that far with Goldman Sachs or Morgan Stanley. Having them both visit Pixar was a big deal.

After so much skepticism over whether we would be able to take Pixar public at all, I started to feel that perhaps we had more going for us than I had thought. With the world's two most prestigious investment banks gearing up for a visit, it was possible we had a shot. It was even conceivable that maybe, just maybe, we would work with both of them. That would even outdo Netscape.

12

SPEECHLESS

BOTH GOLDMAN SACHS AND MORGAN STANLEY WERE EX-cited to visit Pixar's offices in Point Richmond. These would be show-and-tell meetings. No discussion of risks; just a tour of Pixar—their first chance to peek under the covers. We scheduled the meetings soon after the initial gatherings with Quattrone and Martin.

It was almost impossible for anyone to visit Pixar without coming away completely mesmerized. The rundown and humble nature of our offices, across the street from the oil refinery, belied the artistic wizardry within, turning any visit into a feast of surprises. We made certain to put our best foot forward with the two investment banks. First to visit was Quattrone from Morgan Stanley. He brought along a couple of the junior bankers from his office.

We began with a short talk in the conference room near Ed's and my offices, a small, windowless space with a conference table in the middle and a whiteboard at one end, near the door. Steve, Ed, and I were present for this meeting. Steve began with a quick overview of Pixar's history, an update on *Toy Story*'s production, and our vision for the company.

"Now we'd love to give you a tour," Steve wrapped up.

"Great," Quattrone responded. "Just what we've been looking forward to."

We began in a nearby office where there were two engineers work-ing on 3-D exoskeleton models for Pixar's next film, *A Bug's Life*. The office was unremarkable, like any you might see in Silicon Valley, although you wouldn't often find engineers working on digital models of bug shells.

Then we meandered past a hallway where Quattrone and his team got their first glimpse of something film related. It was a small room with a large, high table in the middle and a shelf around the sides. On the table and shelf were clay models of *Toy Story*'s characters. These models, usually about a foot high, were used to develop film characters, and eventually to help digitize them into 3-D computer models.

"Wow!" Quattrone marveled. "These are exquisite. So this is how you first develop the look of a character?"

"Yes," Ed explained. "It is the first time we see them in 3-D. These are the models we use to build the computerized versions you'll see soon."

"They're extraordinary," Quattrone said. "They belong in a museum!"

We were off to a good start, and we were just warming up.

Then we visited the group who created the artistic renderings of the film's scenes and backgrounds—explorations of color, lighting, mood, and style. There, we showed off the renderings of different scenes in *Toy Story*: Andy's room, the final chase sequence, the aliens in the vending machine.

"This is incredible," Quattrone said. "I had no idea this level of artistry was happening here."

Next up was the storyboard room where we wandered through the thousands of white cards that depicted every detail of the film. Quattrone could hardly believe that we'd have to draw around twenty-five thousand of them before a film's story was finalized.

Then we walked over to the animators' area that had so impressed me when I first visited. We had arranged a visit with one of the animators who demonstrated the painstaking process of bringing the characters to life on their large computer monitors, one tiny movement at a time, all perfectly timed to the film's dialogue track.

For the grand finale, we took Quattrone and his team to the screening room where they laughed at the goofiness of the old couches and then sat down for a screening. We showed them Pixar's short films and a segment from the beginning of *Toy Story*, just as I had seen when I first came to Pixar.

"What do you think?" Steve asked Quattrone when it was over.

"I'm speechless," Quattrone said. "Really. I had no idea what was going on here. This is truly amazing. You have to see it to really get it. We'd have to make sure investors can somehow see this too."

A very good sign.

A few days later, Eff Martin from Goldman Sachs visited. We took him through the same experience.

"This is fantastic!" Martin beamed at the end of the screening. "I love that this is happening right here, away from Hollywood. It is so exciting. Thank you for showing us. I want to get my Hollywood counterparts involved."

Those were the magic words we wanted to hear. The next step with both Goldman Sachs and Morgan Stanley was to speak to their industry experts in Hollywood. That's where we would get down to the nitty-gritty of Pixar's business.

These visits had gone so well I was beginning to think maybe Steve was right. Perhaps both Goldman Sachs and Morgan Stanley would be so enthusiastic about wanting to be part of Pixar's IPO that they would do it together. That would be an incredible coup, almost unprecedented in the start-up world. If we had to choose between them, though, I wasn't sure which way we would go.

"What do you think?" I asked Steve. "Any preference?"

"I'm torn," said Steve. "I like Frank Quattrone, and he's done a lot of important deals. Eff is also great."

"My thoughts too," I said. "I also want to meet their entertainment industry experts. That might sway us."

I looked forward to that opportunity.

We heard from Martin of Goldman Sachs first. A few days after the visit to Pixar he called Steve and asked to meet us at Steve's offices at NeXT. I stopped by there on my way up to Pixar, and we met in a conference room.

"I talked to my Hollywood counterparts," Martin said. "We love Pixar. It's a fantastic story, really fantastic, and we want to be part of it."

This is exactly what we wanted to hear.

"Our concern is the timing," Martin went on. "The length of the Disney contract injects a lot of uncertainty about when you'll be able to earn more of the profits from your films. We're thinking it would be better to wait until there is more visibility into increasing your profits, and then take it public. That would give you a much better chance. How does that sound to you?"

It sounded terrible. Goldman Sachs didn't want to take the risk that it might take years until Disney would renegotiate or until we could talk to other studios. But we needed to raise capital in anticipation of that renegotiation. This was a thinly veiled "no." Steve was shocked.

"I don't think you get it at all," he protested. "We can't wait that long."

"I hear your frustration," Martin tried to empathize, "but right now there's just too much risk. We think it's better to wait."

After Martin left, Steve seemed dumbfounded.

"They just didn't get it," was all he had to say.

But it was okay. We needed only one lead investment bank. Morgan Stanley had taken Apple public and perhaps it was fitting that they do another Steve Jobs IPO. Quattrone had promised to get back to Steve quickly, and it was just a couple more days before he did. But he didn't ask for a meeting, as Martin had done. He just picked up the phone and called. Steve contacted me right away with the news.

"I spoke to Frank Quattrone," he started.

"Great!" I said. "What are the next steps?"

"None," Steve replied. "They're not interested."

A rare silence on the phone.

This was a huge blow. I wasn't sure what to say. Steve didn't sound like he was in the mood to talk.

"Did he say why?" I asked.

"Something about the risks of blockbuster films and their unpredictability."

That is all I got from Steve.

In one instant, Steve's dreams of an iconic IPO had been dashed. There would be no Goldman Sachs. No Morgan Stanley. Just like that, the gatekeepers had closed the gate.

13

WEST COAST SWAGGER

AS I PUT DOWN THE PHONE AFTER STEVE TOLD ME ABOUT Morgan Stanley's rejection, all of my fears about Pixar came rushing back. Perhaps I had allowed Steve's exuberance and the bankers' early enthusiasm to cloud my view of Pixar's business risks. Before we had engaged Goldman Sachs and Morgan Stanley in discussions, I would have said that working with either one of them was a long shot. I wouldn't have been at all surprised if they had turned us down. But somewhere in the process I had let myself believe they would want to go forward. That made the rejection sting all the more.

Over the next couple of days, the magnitude of what had occurred sunk in. I didn't hear much more from Steve about it. He just went quiet. I also didn't want to make a big deal of it at Pixar. There was too much excitement over *Toy Story*, which was opening in just over three months. Moreover, no one was thinking much about Pixar's investment bankers. They were thinking about the IPO, though. Everyone knew this was the only way to bring value to their stock options. The buzz around the company was that we were racing toward the release of *Toy Story* while also having an IPO in our sights. The last thing I wanted to do was deflate the *Toy Story* balloon with bad news on the IPO front.

As usual, I found plenty of time to think on my long commute.

In the first place, I didn't like how things had played out with Goldman Sachs and Morgan Stanley. I understood that it was common for companies to be passed over somewhere in the process of interviewing with investment banks, but I felt we never even had our day in court. I was confident Quattrone and Martin had talked to their banks' Hollywood experts, but then we were dismissed out of hand, without ever having the chance to make our case to them. That left a bitter taste in my mouth. Now I had another reason for making Pixar's IPO a big success: to prove to the world's two largest investment banks that they were wrong. They might be the kings of the investment banking hill, but they were far from almighty. We'd show them.

More significant was whether their rejection signaled a bigger issue with taking Pixar public. Were they reflecting what any investment bank would say? It was certainly possible because Pixar's financial profile was so risky and so unconventional. Moreover, if we wanted to do an IPO this year, the window was rapidly closing on us. It took time to bring investment banks up to speed, and it wouldn't help that another investment bank might wonder why Morgan Stanley and Goldman Sachs turned us down. If we missed this crucial window, with our next film at least three years away, who knows how long it might be before we could raise the capital we needed? That put the entirety of our business plan at risk. We needed someone fast.

One possibility came to mind, an investment bank that I had done business with before: Robertson Stephens.

Robertson Stephens had been the lead banker on the IPO for my previous company, Electronics for Imaging. I had a great relationship with them, and I was pretty sure they liked and trusted me. They were one of a handful of boutique investment banks that specialized in high-tech public offerings. In Silicon Valley they had a stellar reputation, but they didn't have the size or clout of Morgan Stanley or Goldman Sachs, and they had no expertise in the entertainment industry. That would normally count them out of representing an entertainment company.

But we were running out of options. If Robertson Stephens came on board, we would certainly need another investment bank that did bring clout in the entertainment world. I also liked Robertson Stephens. They prided themselves on being as effective as the big players, only nimbler and more efficient. If they saw Pixar as a hybrid technology/entertainment company, there was a chance they might just take a swing at it.

My first step was to give Larry Sonsini a call. He knew Robertson Stephens well. If he thought this was a bad idea, I wouldn't take it any further.

"I like it," Larry said. "The firm has a great relationship with Robertson Stephens; so do you. I agree we can bring someone else in on the entertainment side. It's worth a shot."

Once again, Larry's backing gave me momentum. Now I had a plan that depended on convincing one local technology industry investment bank to do an entertainment IPO, and then finding another investment bank that would give us credibility in the entertainment world. In a sense, we needed to be struck by lightning—twice.

Steve also had to be on board, and I imagined he would not be thrilled about Robertson Stephens, an investment bank he probably knew little if anything about. Even if Steve saw this as the backup plan, if he had any hope of fulfilling his IPO dream this year, we needed some new investment bankers, and we needed them yesterday. My next conversation was with him.

"We need a banker on board right now if we're to have any shot at doing an IPO this year," I said. "How do you feel about me giving Robertson Stephens a call?"

"Robertson Stephens?" Steve said skeptically. "I've never dealt with them."

"I know them well," I said. "They're good, really good. They've been one of the most active investment banks in the tech industry. They can do as good a job as Goldman or Morgan. But they're local. No entertainment experience. Just tech."

"I thought we need clout in entertainment," Steve said.

"We do. If they're interested, we'll need to find an investment bank to join them that does know entertainment. It's a long shot, but I think it's worth a call."

"Give it a try," said Steve, a little less than enthusiastic.

The founder and chairman of Robertson Stephens was Sandy Robertson. He and my former boss, Efi Arazi, were good friends, and I had met Sandy a number of times. He was the ultimate gentleman banker, very polished, with a West Coast daring and swagger. He was also an influential and important figure in San Francisco. I knew he wouldn't be involved in any of the day-to-day discussions with Pixar, but one word from him and his team would take us seriously.

He was delighted to hear from me.

"How's Efi?" was the first thing he asked.

"He's great," I said. "He's off on some new ventures now. I know he'd love to see you."

"And what are you doing now? I hear you're at Pixar, working with Steve Jobs."

"That's right," I said. "As a matter of fact, that's what I'm calling about."

I recounted to Sandy a summary of the Pixar story.

"Of course we'll take a look," he said. "This sounds thrilling. We'll be right back to you."

Within a few hours I received a call from two investment bankers at Robertson Stephens, Brian Bean and Todd Carter. They wanted to learn as much about Pixar as quickly as they could. I arranged a time to visit them right away in their swank offices in San Francisco's financial district.

Brian was the senior of the two, a delightful character who wore colorful suspenders and who loved art, culture, and new challenges. Todd was more junior and would be the person on the ground, the one who would pull together all the details. Todd looked like the all-American boy, tall, blond, handsome, the kind who had probably been voted "most likely to succeed" in high school. He was respectful and articulate. I liked both of them right away, although I couldn't imagine what Steve was going to make of them—endearingly quirky Brian, and Todd who looked like he was barely out of college.

I invited Brian and Todd to Pixar, where we gave them our dog-and-pony show and took them on the tour, just as we had done with Goldman Sachs and Morgan Stanley.

"This is fantastic," Todd Carter gushed, "just fantastic."

"Agreed," said Brian. "I love what you're doing here. It's so authentic, so creative. It's different from what we usually do. But we like different."

There it was, the West Coast swagger I hoped to find. I could swear these two bankers had caught the Pixar bug, and they might just be crazy enough to run with it despite the risks. But I recalled we had gone this far with Goldman Sachs and Morgan Stanley. It was the *next* step that we needed, the step where they really started to piece together what Pixar was all about.

Unfortunately, Steve was skeptical.

"I'm not sure about those guys," Steve said. "I liked them okay, but could they really pull this off? Do they have the clout we need with investors?"

"If they say they can pull it off, they will," I said. "Larry has done a lot of deals with them. You could check with him. They know what they're doing. But first we have to get them on board. We're not there yet."

Steve remained worried about whether they'd be good enough. I was worried about whether we could get any investment bank interested at all.

The next day Todd Carter gave me a call.

"We love Pixar's story," he said. "We want to get into the details. I also want to bring along one of our financial analysts to help with that. Our only issue is we don't have an analyst who's an expert in the entertainment industry. But one of our digital media analysts, Keith Benjamin, is really interested in this. He'd love to learn more. How would that be with you?"

How would that be with me! I just about cried. Todd was apologizing for not having an entertainment specialist, only a media specialist who wanted to learn more about Pixar. I had never expected they would have an entertainment analyst. He was handing me a lifeline and apologizing because it wasn't in my favorite color.

"No problem," I said. "No problem at all. The entertainment business has been new for me too. We'll bring Keith up to speed."

They all came over to Pixar. Brian Bean, Todd Carter, and Keith Benjamin from Robertson Stephens; Steve, Ed, Sarah Staff, and me from Pixar. We sat in a conference room and finally had the meeting I had been waiting for.

We walked the Robertson Stephens team through the details of Pixar's vision, business plan, and risks. We told them we were aiming to change entertainment history in a way few companies had ever had a chance to do, and we described the four pillars it would take to make it work: raise the money to finance our films, expand the studio to handle more productions, make Pixar a worldwide brand, and increase our share of film profits. But there were risks. Big ones. Wall Street would have to understand that.

"Thank you," Brian said sincerely. "This has been immensely helpful. Give us a couple of days. We'll be back to you."

Later that day I received a call from Todd Carter. He thanked me for the meeting and wanted to explain the process by which they would make their decision.

"The decision is made by our Commitment Committee," he said. "That comprises all our top people and they make the final decision on every deal."

"Any idea how it looks for Pixar?" I asked him.

"I wish I could say," Todd replied. "You're very aware of the challenges in Pixar's business model. We're excited about Pixar, we love the vision, but we have to be certain our investors can tolerate the risks. My personal recommendation is that we go for it, but it isn't my decision. I think it'll be close."

There wasn't much there to make me feel comfortable. I could only sit and wait. It was hard to be patient, though. I hadn't expressed it to Todd, but by this point I was flat out of options. If Robertson Stephens's committee voted thumbs down, our chances of an IPO anytime in the near future would truly evaporate.

Two days later Brian Bean called.

"Our Commitment Committee made its decision," he started.

I held my breath.

"We're in," Brian told me. "We think our investors will go for this. We know we have to get them on board for the long term, but there's enough that's exciting here that we think they will. We'd be honored to be the lead banker for Pixar's IPO."

I put down the phone with a lump in my throat. Lightning had struck. This was huge. My first call was to Steve.

"Robertson Stephens is on board," I said.

"That's great news," Steve said. He sounded excited but also cautious. I think he was still getting used to the idea of working with an investment bank he really didn't know.

"I need to give them a signal that we want to make them the lead on the deal," I went on. "We'll need others involved, but we have to give them the lead now if we want to go through with this."

"I want to talk to their CEO first," Steve said.

The CEO of Robertson Stephens was Mike McCaffrey. I didn't know him, but he had a reputation as a great banker and a terrific guy. I arranged a meeting for a few days later. Todd Carter and Mike McCaffrey came over to Pixar to meet Steve, Ed, and me. We all liked Mike immediately. He was tall, athletic, and articulate. He came across as sharp, grounded, and very respectful toward Pixar and Steve. After the meeting, Steve pulled me aside.

"I have one request," he said, "and it's nonnegotiable."

"What's that?" I asked.

"I want Mike McCaffrey at every stop on our road show."

My heart sank a little. This was crazy. The road show was when the bankers would arrange a two-week or longer whirlwind tour for Pixar to meet potential investors in every corner of the country, and even in some corners of Europe. It was a grueling slog to share our story with as many investors as possible, and it was unheard of for the

CEO of an investment bank to go on a road show. Ushering us from city to city to meet investors was considered the grunt work for the junior bankers. Mike McCaffrey probably hadn't done that kind of work in more than twenty years. He was running the entire operation of Robertson Stephens.

I wanted to say to Steve, "Are you kidding?!" but I stopped myself. As irrational as this demand was, this wasn't the fight to pick. Steve needed to feel confident in our bankers, and if this was the only way to get him there, I would give it a shot.

"I'll ask," I told him quietly.

Somewhat sheepishly I explained the predicament to Brian Bean and Todd Carter.

"I realize this is unconventional," I said. "But Steve has a lot at stake here. It is crucial that Steve is excited and on board. He liked and trusted Mike. It will give him the confidence that this will go well. Would you mind asking him?"

They did. And Mike said yes, in what for me was one of the greatest acts of business sportsmanship I had seen. Even Brian Bean and Todd Carter seemed surprised. Mike McCaffrey, the CEO of one of the tech industry's preeminent investment banks, was going to jump into planes, trains, and cars and join Pixar on what would undoubtedly be a high-pressured and exhausting road show. I never asked him why he did it, but I was pretty convinced it was a gesture of pure deference toward Steve. Steve may have been down and out for a while, but he still commanded respect in Silicon Valley circles. This must have been Mike McCaffrey's way to honor that.

"Mike's in," I told Steve excitedly. "He said he'd join us on the road show."

"Fantastic," Steve replied. "Then we have an investment bank to lead the deal."

For the first time in a long while, I felt it was actually possible that the wind had begun to shift.

14

HOLLYWOOD CRED

IT DID NOT TAKE LONG FOR MY EXCITEMENT AT SECURING Robertson Stephens as the lead investment bank to wane a little. We still had no one who would certify Pixar's credibility as an entertainment company, and we needed that if we were to convince the investment community we had what it took to make it.

Morgan Stanley and Goldman Sachs would have been perfect because they had stellar reputations in Hollywood. But Robertson Stephens was unheard of in those circles. I liked Keith Benjamin, the Robertson Stephens analyst who would write the reports on Pixar that Wall Street would read. He was thoroughly engaged in Pixar, inquisitive, smart, and enthusiastic. But few in the entertainment industry would know him. We needed somebody whose word would give Pixar immediate credibility in Hollywood.

I was sitting in my office one day when I was struck with an idea. I had read and reread Hal Vogel's book *Entertainment Industry Economics*. I remembered that his experience in entertainment came from being an industry analyst. I checked the book, which said he had been the senior entertainment industry analyst at Merrill Lynch since 1977. He had also been ranked as a top entertainment industry analyst by *Institutional Investor* magazine for several years in a row. This would make him one of the best, if not the top, entertainment industry analysts on Wall Street.

I didn't expect that Hal Vogel would have much interest in Pixar, especially because it was his book that described the perils of financing film companies through the stock markets. Still, he'd know the field well, and maybe he'd have some ideas. I thought it might be worth talking to him.

I gave Todd Carter at Robertson Stephens a call. Todd knew I was on the lookout for some entertainment clout in our deal and he was eager to help. It didn't take long for Todd to discover that after seventeen years at Merrill Lynch, Hal Vogel had left just a short while earlier, at the end of 1994. He was now managing director and senior analyst of entertainment, media, and gaming at Cowen and Company, a boutique investment bank based in New York that I had never heard of.

"Would you like me to reach out to him?" Todd asked.

"That would be great," I responded. It was not uncommon for the lead investment bank to solicit interest from other banks. That would spare me the embarrassment of taking any rejection directly.

"Do you know anything about Cowen and Company?" I asked Todd.

"Not a lot," Todd answered. "They're a very small player in the IPO business but they've gotten more active in recent years. They're unknown out here."

Todd placed the initial call to Hal Vogel, who indicated he was happy to have a conversation. I didn't know if that was good or bad, but at least I hadn't been dismissed out of hand. We arranged a time to talk over the phone. I began the conversation cautiously.

"Thanks so much for talking," I said. "I learned a lot from your book. I know you're not high on film companies raising capital in the stock markets, but I think it's Pixar's only shot. If you have a few minutes, I would love your advice on how to go about getting entertainment coverage for Pixar."

This was Hal's chance to remind me how terrible an idea this was. But instead he replied, "I'd love to learn more. I've had my eye on Pixar from afar."

Much less painful than I was expecting. I recounted Pixar's story to Hal over the phone.

"I love it," Hal said. "Just love it. You're doing everything that the entertainment industry needs."

"What?" I thought to myself. I had my armor on but no barbs were coming my way. In fact, Hal could not have been more positive, jovial, and friendly.

"What do you mean?" I asked him.

"Technology is a huge driver in entertainment," Hal explained. "Companies that combine great story, technology breakthroughs, and seasoned management will lead the way into the future. Pixar has all the ingredients. Believe me, it's rare. I'd love to be part of this. Maybe Cowen can be part of your IPO."

If Hal had seen me at that moment, I'm quite sure he would have been shocked to find my jaw on the floor. He saw in Pixar something we barely saw in ourselves, and certainly something Goldman Sachs and Morgan Stanley had not seen. If Hal Vogel thought what we were doing at Pixar was important, well, maybe it was!

This was a far, far cry from our dismissive rejection by Goldman Sachs and Morgan Stanley. Here was one of the top analysts in the field saying we had all the ingredients for success. Moreover, he wanted in on the deal. If Cowen and Company was involved in Pixar's IPO, Hal Vogel would play a pivotal role in educating investors about why Pixar mattered in entertainment.

First, though, I had to convince Steve. If I had been worried that Steve didn't know much about Robertson Stephens, I could be certain that he had never heard of Cowen and Company, nor probably had anyone he knew. I'd already stuck my neck out with Robertson Stephens. Now I was asking Steve to trust Cowen and Company on the strength of one entertainment industry analyst.

I thought the best place to start was to have a meeting. I described to Steve Hal Vogel's reputation and suggested it might be great for him and the banking team at Cowen and Company to come for a visit. We set up a time to meet them at Pixar.

Adele Morrissette was head of digital media investment banking at Cowen and Company. She visited Pixar with Hal Vogel and we hit it off straightaway. Adele was bright, engaging, easy to talk to, and straightforward. She saw Pixar as a great story and as a great opportunity for Cowen and Company. She thought that with Hal behind it, investors would feel better about the risks and would be more likely to give Pixar a chance. Hal remained just as enthusiastic about Pixar as in our first conversation.

"What do you think?" I asked Steve after the meeting.

"I like Hal," Steve said. "He knows his stuff, and he gets Pixar."

After the fiasco with Goldman Sachs and Morgan Stanley, I think Steve really appreciated that.

"But," Steve continued, "they're a complete unknown for IPOs. Do we need them on board to get Hal to cover Pixar?"

It was a good question. Analysts at investment banks could cover any companies they wanted, not just their clients. It was possible that Hal would write about Pixar even if Cowen and Company was not involved in the IPO, but for a new public company, coverage by a top analyst was notoriously difficult to gain.

"You're right," I said. "Hal could write about Pixar even if Cowen isn't involved. It's a big risk, though. We have to start the ball rolling with entertainment coverage in order for Pixar to be taken seriously. I wouldn't take a chance on it. I'd rather see Cowen in on the deal and know that Hal will cover Pixar."

"Will they take third position on the deal?" Steve asked.

"I'm pretty sure they will," I replied.

It was fairly typical to have three investment banks involved in an IPO. There was no magic number. Some IPOs used two investment banks; some used four or more. It depended on the size of the offering, access to investors, and the need for specialized industry expertise. The Pixar shares sold in the IPO would be allocated among its investment banks. Giving Cowen third position meant that they would have the smallest allocation, which made sense because they would likely have a smaller roster of clients who invested in IPOs.

"If they'll take third, it's okay with me," Steve said. "We'll still need someone else in second position."

I was more than pleased. I was sure Cowen and Company would go for it. It meant that Hal Vogel would be Pixar's analyst.

Lightning had struck again.

Cowen and Company was happy to be involved, and they assigned a delightful young banker named Jill Dallas to help with the deal. With that, we now had two investment banks, one of which had an analyst whose credentials in the entertainment industry were impeccable.

By now I felt I had extended myself quite a bit with Steve. I understood full well that it was not his dream to take Pixar public with a boutique tech bank and a small New York bank that no one in Silicon Valley knew. To him, this was the backup plan. To me, this was our shot at actually pulling it off. I felt confident for the first time in a while, and I wanted Steve to see it.

"This is going really well, Steve," I said shortly after we heard Cowen and Company was on board. "Between Robertson Stephens and Cowen, we can get this done."

"I hope so," said Steve, "but we still need a third banker. What do you think of Hambrecht and Quist?"

Like Robertson Stephens, Hambrecht and Quist was a well-known boutique investment bank in Silicon Valley. They had been involved with Apple's IPO in 1980, playing second position behind the lead, Morgan Stanley. Steve knew their CEO, Dan Case, who had started talking to Steve about Pixar. Steve had not considered Hambrecht and Quist to lead our deal, but he thought it might be a good idea to have them involved.

"They'd be great," I said. "They're another tech bank so they won't help much on the entertainment front. But we've got that covered well enough. Let's go for it."

It didn't take long to get them on board. With that, we had our investment banking team: Robertson Stephens as the lead, Hambrecht and Quist second, Cowen and Company in third position. Now the real work would begin.

"We have a chance to make this happen," I said to Hillary one night toward the end of August. "I'll be out of commission working on this for the next couple of months. But this is our shot."

"Steve's ready for it too?" Hillary asked.

"Yes, he's on board. Ready to go. Even excited I would say."

"Good luck," Hillary said. "This is the chance you've been hoping for."

We'd need that luck. Actually pulling off an IPO was going to be a lot harder than finding investment banks. We would now begin endless meetings with the bankers as they pored over every single detail of Pixar's history, financial information, and business plan. There would be teams of lawyers and accountants checking, double-checking, and triple-checking compliance with every nuance and requirement of the securities laws. There would be continuous discussions and debates over how to value Pixar, how to price its stock, and the exact timing for taking it public.

Most of all there would be the crafting of the document around which the entire transaction would pivot: Pixar's prospectus. This mind-numbingly detailed legal document would be filed with the SEC and then delivered to every potential investor. The prospectus would disclose in painstaking detail every facet of Pixar's business, qualitatively and quantitatively, and would contain page after page of discussion of the risks that every investor should know about. It would describe Pixar's history, vision, business plan, technology, animation and production processes, competition, risks, executives, board members, stock ownership, stock option plan, and countless other details relevant to understanding the company. It would be as long as a book and take many weeks and many nights in a room full of investment bankers and lawyers to craft its every word. After that, it would be subject to the comments of the SEC to which we would have to respond in detail. If anyone along the way — investment bankers, lawyers, accountants, or the SEC—was not happy with that prospectus, there would be no public offering.

But this was exactly the shot I had hoped we would have. It was now approaching a full year since Steve had first called me. Pixar's IPO had been foremost on his mind from day one, and here we were, after a roller coaster of twelve months, ready to roll up our sleeves and see if we could actually get this done.

15

TWO NUMBERS

STEVE ONCE TOLD ME THAT THE GESTATION OF GREAT PROD-
ucts takes much longer than it appears. What seems to emerge from
nowhere belies a long process of development, trials, and missteps.
If anything proved that case, it was Pixar. The gestation of *Toy Story*
could be traced back sixteen years to when Pixar had been the computer graphics division at Lucasfilm. It had been a long and arduous
path since then, with no end of challenges. This made it especially
ironic that in one week in November of 1995, Pixar's entire future
would depend on just two numbers: the opening weekend box office for *Toy Story*, and the price at which Pixar's shares sold in its IPO.

The first number, the opening weekend box office for *Toy Story*,
would tell us how well *Toy Story* would perform overall. It was scheduled for release on November 22, the Wednesday before Thanksgiving, and Disney told us it could make a good prediction of the opening weekend box office, and indeed the film's overall performance,
solely on the basis of that week's Friday night box office performance.

This meant that after all those years of evolving the technology
and then four more years of actually making *Toy Story*, Pixar would
learn on a single Friday night in November what the world thought
of its work. It reminded me of the hundred-meter sprint in the Olym-
pic Games. A lifetime of training to become the fastest runner in the
world came down to a single ten-second performance. If the world
fell in love with *Toy Story*, Pixar would have a chance to usher in a new
era of animated entertainment. If it didn't, Pixar might be written off
as another company that tried but never quite hit the mark.

"What opening weekend box office would make you feel really good?" Steve asked me as we were taking a walk in Palo Alto one Saturday afternoon.

"Anything above ten million," I said. "Even if we hit eight million we're on the board."

"My number's fifteen," Steve said. "If we hit fifteen to twenty, they'll project a total domestic box office of over a hundred million. Then no one will question Pixar's arrival."

This was the umpteenth time we'd had this discussion. We loved to speculate about *Toy Story*'s box office potential and what it meant. A domestic box office run — meaning the total North American ticket sales — of $100 million would be sweet indeed. It was a magic number in the film business, and very difficult to achieve, even more so in animation. In all of film history, only four animated feature films had a domestic box office greater than that, and all of those had been made by Disney: *Beauty and the Beast, Aladdin, The Lion King,* and *Pocahontas.*[4]

After Disney, the dropoff was precipitous. Only three non-Disney animated feature films had achieved a domestic box office at or around $50 million: Universal's *An American Tail* in 1986 and *The Land Before Time* in 1988, and Tim Burton's *The Nightmare Before Christmas* in 1993. In fact, in the past five years, if you excluded the four Disney blockbusters, of the seventeen other animated feature films released by major studios or well-known independents, the average domestic box office was a little under $14 million. That's *total* domestic box office, not the opening weekend. In animation, for all practical purposes, Disney had been the only game in town for over fifty years. In an environment this harsh, what would it take for Pixar to claim victory?

— —

4. Box Office Mojo, http://www.boxofficemojo.com/genres/chart/?id=animation .htm. *The Little Mermaid* went over $100 million in a second release that occurred after 1995. This number also excludes *Who Framed Roger Rabbit?*, a live action–animation combination.

It was almost ludicrous to bet Pixar's success on its first film doing something no other studio had done besides Disney. We needed another standard. Tim Burton's *The Nightmare Before Christmas* seemed a good one. It had quite a few parallels with *Toy Story*. Released in 1993, the film had enjoyed rave reviews, was made using a nontraditional technology called stop-motion animation, and was distributed by Buena Vista Distribution, Disney's film distribution company. Originally slated to be released under the Disney banner, it had been shifted to Disney's Touchstone Pictures banner for fear that some of the content was a little dark. It had scored $50 million in the domestic box office (which went up to $75 million after its rerelease years later). At least if *Toy Story* did $50 million, we could claim the same respectability as *The Nightmare Before Christmas*.

"What about *The Nightmare Before Christmas*?" I reminded Steve. "We would hardly be in poor company if we performed as well."

"I love Tim Burton's work," Steve replied. "It's no shame to do fifty million. Crossing a hundred would put us in a different league, though."

For a total domestic box office of over $100 million, *Toy Story* would need an opening weekend in the $15 to $20 million range. Excluding the four Disney blockbusters, the average opening weekend for animated feature films during the past five years was under $3 million. No matter how we measured it, we were reaching for the sky.

The second number that would define Pixar's future was the price at which Pixar's stock would start trading as a public company. The moment Pixar went public, its stock would begin to trade on the NASDAQ stock exchange—a computerized trading system on which most Silicon Valley IPOs were launched. Of all the issues in Pixar's public offering, there were none that occupied Steve's thinking more than what Pixar's stock would sell for when it first went public.

The first stock price was the price at which Pixar sold stock to investors. We were planning on selling roughly six million shares of stock. If the stock price was $10, we would raise $60 million. If it were $20, we would raise $120 million, and so on. After that moment, those six million shares would be in the hands of investors, and they would be free to buy and sell shares among each other just like any other publicly traded stock. It was that first sale that determined how much Pixar itself received.

The price of Pixar's stock as it traded in the market *after* that first sale would also be important. It would determine the total value of the company at any given moment in time—and the total value of Steve's holdings as well as the stock options held by Pixar's employees. Given the total number of shares of Pixar stock that existed, if Pixar's stock traded at $10 per share, Pixar would be worth about $370 million, and Steve's 80 percent share around $300 million. If it traded at $20 per share, Pixar would be worth $740 million and Steve's portion around $600 million. In other words, Pixar's stock price at the end of its first day of trading would not just signify Steve's comeback, it would quantify it.

The way the first stock price—the price at which Pixar's stock was initially sold to investors—would be determined was as much art as science. When Pixar filed its prospectus with the SEC, it would include a *proposed* price for Pixar's first sale of stock. That proposed price would be our investment bankers' indication of a fair value for investing in Pixar. All the tire-kicking work that the investment bankers went through was to establish that one number. Until Pixar's stock actually started to trade, that proposed price would be the so-called definitive number on Pixar's value.

However, it was just a *proposed* price, the number that the investment bankers thought investors should be willing to pay for Pixar stock. The actual number would not be determined until the first day of stock trading, which wouldn't happen until weeks after our SEC filing. During that time we would be hitting the road to meet investors, and their level of interest would indicate whether the actual first sale of Pixar stock should be at, above, or below the proposed price. In Netscape's recent IPO, for example, the proposed price had been around $14 per share, and after its road show the opening price had been double that, $28 per share. In the first few hours of trading, the stock price had doubled again.

On the IPO road show we would spend a little over two weeks in San Francisco, Los Angeles, New York, Boston, London, and a few other cities, going from office to office telling our story to potential investors. Sometime after each visit, the investors would let our investment banks know their level of interest in Pixar. Once the investment bankers saw the actual level of interest from investors, they would adjust the opening price accordingly. If investors were wildly excited, the opening price would go up from the proposed price. If interest waned, it would go down. If it really plummeted, they could even cancel the IPO.

Setting the proposed price for an IPO was a very delicate balancing act. The lower the stock price at the opening of Pixar's IPO, the less funds Pixar would raise from selling its stock, but the higher investor demand would be. On the other hand, the higher the stock price at the opening, the more funds Pixar would raise, but the risk was that investor demand might be lower, thereby putting downward pressure on the price. These were numbers that Steve and I discussed incessantly.

"We're worth more than Netscape," Steve asserted one evening when we were talking over the phone. "They've only been around about a year and are losing money. If Pixar's films are hits, we'll make more than them. We should be worth more."

Netscape had been valued at a little over $1 billion when its stock began to trade on August 9. By the end of that day, it was worth over $2 billion. We were not privy to how that valuation had been calculated, but we did know there had been an investor and media frenzy over investing in Netscape's stock due to the enormous interest in the Internet.

"We'll have the same level of interest," Steve went on, "if not more. We can value Pixar at two billion dollars."

But in my mind, no amount of number crunching could get Pixar to a value of $2 billion. I would have been surprised if our investment bankers were thinking about a quarter of that number.

"It's a huge risk," I tried to push back. "If we model our IPO on Netscape, the biggest IPO frenzy in years, we might blow the whole thing. We're better off getting out of the gate, keeping investors happy, and letting the stock build momentum."

"As more investors learn about Pixar they'll want in," Steve went on. "Parents will want to buy shares of Pixar stock just so their children can have some. It'll be like owning a few shares of Disney, something to treasure."

It was certainly possible that parents might want Pixar stock for their children. Steve and I had recently signed the version of Pixar's stock certificate that would be issued to stockholders. Emblazoned on the bottom were five characters from Pixar's short films and *Toy Story*. It might even be a collector's item one day, but I could not imagine that the volume of shares purchased for this reason would have any impact on Pixar's stock price.

"I don't think that will be enough to make a difference in the stock price," I said. "The price will be driven by big investment firms buying and selling larger blocks of stock, not families buying stock for their children. Ultimately, it's not even up to us. It's up to Robertson Stephens and our other banks."

"But they may not get it either," Steve retorted. "We have to make sure they understand Pixar's value."

I was quite sure that Robertson Stephens did get it, and I worried that Steve was overreaching. Even if he was correct about the value, it was much better to reach it by allowing market momentum to lift Pixar there rather than demand it at the outset. The last thing we needed was the press to report that we asked for too much and disappointed investors. It might mean we would raise slightly less money for Pixar, but it would be better for everyone in the long term if there were confidence in Pixar's stock.

Eventually our investment bankers came up with their own verdict. They thought Pixar's stock might quickly level out in the high teens, giving Pixar a value of around $700 million. They wanted the proposed price to be $12 to $14 per share. That would provide some cushion so that the price would have room to go up after the initial sale. That meant the proposed price would value Pixar at around $500 million, an enormously respectable number.

But Steve needed to be on board.

"If we start at twelve to fourteen dollars when we file with the SEC," I told him, "and if the road show goes well, we could double it, just like Netscape did. If we double it, Pixar will be valued at a billion dollars. We'll have a shot, but we take much less risk starting conservatively and letting the market be the judge. All the bankers are on board. Me too."

At least I could project a path where Pixar was worth a billion dollars. This would translate into a huge payday for Steve, who would own the vast majority of it, and create opportunities for Pixar to raise more money later on if we needed it.

"I still think we're worth more than Netscape," Steve replied, "and I don't want to leave money on the table. If Pixar is worth more, investors should pay us for it so Pixar has the money."

"The downside is too great," I pushed back. "If we price it too high and end up disappointing investors, our stock will languish and no one will benefit. A half-billion-dollar value is more than respectable, and we have a chance of doubling or tripling it. I think we should trust our bankers on this one."

"Let me think about it," Steve said.

A couple of hours later he called me.

"We'll go with it," he said. "I think we'll have so much interest after our road show that we'll double the opening price."

I breathed a huge sigh of relief. We had our starting place.

On October 12, 1995, we filed Pixar's prospectus with the SEC, showing a price range of $12 to $14 per share of stock. We had worked immensely hard, not just on the technical details but on the quality of the language. The SEC told us informally it was one of the most finely crafted prospectuses they had seen, a compliment that had the old lawyer in me beaming with pride. After a few weeks of back-and-forth, the SEC approved our filings, and Steve, Ed, and I were ready to hit the road to introduce Pixar to investors.

We would need a slide show to tell Pixar's story, one that wove together Pixar's history, aspirations, business plan, and risks, together with a video showcase of our work. Together Steve and I mapped out what the slides needed to say, and then Steve went to work on them himself, requesting images, data, and numbers, and when he needed them. Then he'd ask me to take a look, and we'd make revisions.

Steve paid attention to every nuance of the slides, even details that, as far as I could tell, were invisible to the naked eye, like font kerning — which is adjusting the space between letters — and font smoothing to make sure the curves on each font were perfect. He hired a presentation professional, Wayne Goodrich, to help finalize these details and to make sure that at every single stop on the road show, all the pieces were in place to show the presentation and video perfectly.

So there it was. As we headed into November, Pixar was racing toward a sequence of events that on the strength of just two numbers — *Toy Story*'s opening weekend box office and the opening price for Pixar's IPO — would say yay or nay to sixteen years of effort, almost $50 million of investment, and the tireless work of some of the world's most talented storytellers and programmers. The month would look like this:

In the second week of November, we would begin the IPO road show that would last two weeks.

Then, on Sunday, November 19, Disney would hold the premiere for *Toy Story* at the El Capitan Theatre in Hollywood.

On Wednesday, November 22, *Toy Story* would be released into movie theaters all over North America.

On Saturday, November 25, we would have our verdict on *Toy Story*'s opening.

Finally, if all that went well, sometime the following week Pixar's stock would begin trading and we would become a public company.

Beyond that, there wasn't much happening.

16

EL CAPITAN

MY DAUGHTER SARAH WAS STANDING BY THE FRONT DOOR of our house. Now seven years old, she was always the first one ready, especially if we were doing something fun.

"Come on," she said. "The car is here. We have to go!"

I could trust Sarah to keep us on track. She was wearing a pretty black-and-white outfit, a skirt and top, with a white ribbon in her hair. It was Sunday, November 19, and we were heading to the San Jose airport where Hillary, Jason, Sarah, and I would fly to LA. There, a car would take us to the newly renovated El Capitan Theatre where Disney was holding the invitation-only premiere of *Toy Story*. Even better, next door to the El Capitan, Disney had created the "*Toy Story* Funhouse," a building that would be full of games, food, and shows based on *Toy Story*. Sarah was going to take no chances that we might be late.

A few days earlier, we had concluded the IPO road show. Steve, Ed, and I had told the Pixar story over and over again. We had described Pixar's business plan and all of its risks and answered every question the best way we could. Our investment bankers had been with us the entire way, and Mike McCaffrey had indeed joined us at every stop.

But it was hard to read the investors' response. They rarely, if ever, jumped up and down with excitement. Investors didn't want to cause a frenzy that would drive the stock price up before they bought it. Robertson Stephens appeared happy with how we did, but it would be a little while before we knew how that would translate into demand for Pixar stock. The best thing we could do while we waited was to press forward and enjoy *Toy Story*'s premiere.

We landed in LA early that afternoon and were picked up at the airport to go to the premiere. As we approached the El Capitan Theatre, evidence of Disney's marketing campaign for *Toy Story* was everywhere.

"Look!" Sarah shrieked. "A *Toy Story* poster."

If we had harbored earlier reservations about Disney's marketing effort for the film, they had more than made up for it of late.

"This holiday season the adventure takes off when toys come to life," began the trailer that had been playing in the movie theaters for weeks.

"Two heroes, ready for anything, except each other," it went on. And then, at the end: "Walt Disney Pictures presents the first ever computer-animated motion picture."

Disney was hitting all the right chords, and they continued to do so in a massive poster and billboard campaign that filled highway billboards, bus stops, and the sides of buses throughout the country. Everyone at Pixar had shared a nervous excitement these last couple of weeks that all but bubbled over once we started to see the first billboards go up on local highways. *THE TOYS ARE BACK IN TOWN*, one said in huge, bold, black letters with the *Toy Story* characters in full color. Other posters emphasized individual characters. Rex the dinosaur had one that said, *I'M A NERVOUS REX!* Woody's said, *DON'T YANK MY STRING!* The bottom of each poster said, *COMING TO LIFE NOVEMBER 22.* It was becoming hard to miss the growing drumbeat for the film.

Now we had reached the dropoff point at the El Capitan.

"We all just get out of the car like we know what we're doing," announced Jason, now ten, smiling.

Jason saw the humor in just about anything we did. We had all been excitedly bantering about walking down the carpet to enter the theater. We would not, strictly speaking, be walking down the red carpet that led to the TV cameras. That was for the stars. Ours was right next to it, though, and it would be as close as we had ever been to the red carpet feeling. We'd still be walking right by the reporters and fans who were lining the street.

"As far as anyone knows," Hillary chimed in, "Jason might be a voice in the film. Why don't we walk behind him like his entourage?"

Jason liked that. Sarah giggled. The car arrived.

"This is it!" Jason reminded us. "No one trip."

With that caution, we were ushered out of our car and relished every moment of walking down the carpet. Before we knew it we were sitting in our seats, watching as the theater began to fill up.

"Look, there's Tom Hanks," Hillary announced excitedly.

Indeed, there Hanks was, in the flesh, walking into the theater. His star could not have been brighter at that moment, fresh off the summer's hit film *Apollo 13*. We saw many of the "voices" in the film as they came in: Tim Allen, Wally Shawn, John Ratzenberger. Even Michael Eisner, Disney's CEO, was present, which we took as a special compliment to Pixar given the number of Disney premieres to which he must be invited. And of course we saw John Lasseter, Ed Catmull, and the other key contributors at Pixar, all accompanied by their families, as Disney had made this into a truly family event.

The only one missing was Steve. He was not a big fan of the El Capitan Funhouse idea, feeling it was money spent on reaching too few individuals, and he had wanted a Silicon Valley premiere to highlight where *Toy Story* had been made. He had arranged a special screening of the film in San Francisco for the next night.

Soon the theater filled up, and as the lights went down, a quiet hush filled the room. With great anticipation, we all settled in to watch the world's first computer-animated feature come to life. And come to life it did!

It didn't take long to realize we were watching not just a movie but the making of film history. I had seen much of the film in storyboards, rough animation, and unlit sequences, but seeing the final form, with the songs, the soundtrack, the depth of color, was just stunning. I had never seen final animation of the creepy mutant toys in Sid's house, and I found myself choking up when Woody and Buzz realized that these ghoulish creatures just wanted to help them. I loved it even more when they helped Woody and Buzz escape from Sid's house. I cheered inside when I saw the outdoor scenes where Woody and Buzz flew on a rocket ship, seeing not just an amazing movie moment but a technical accomplishment that had seemed impossible just a few months earlier.

As the film ended, the clapping and cheering in the theater lasted all the way through the closing credits. When the lights went up, the room filled with excited chatter.

"That was great!" Jason declared. "The end is amazing."

"The 3-D look of the film is fantastic," Hillary said. "It was beautiful to watch."

"I've seen so many clips of the film," I said, "but seeing the whole thing was mesmerizing. I was thinking, 'How did they do it?' even when I've *seen* how they do it."

"Sarah, what's your favorite part?" Jason asked.

"I like when Woody tells Etch to draw," Sarah said, "and when Buzz flies around the room."

"But you know my very favorite part?" Hillary added.

"What's that?" Jason replied.

"Seeing Jenna's name as one of the *Toy Story* babies in the credits!"

Of course. Hillary was not soon going to forget that.

After the film, we were ushered directly into the Funhouse, a three-story spectacle of *Toy Story* delights for children. There we spent the next two hours exploring the Green Army Men Room and its obstacle course of fake lakes and bridges, the live Western band in Woody's Roundup, the laser-shooting gallery in Buzz's Galaxy, and the assortment of junk foods in Pizza Planet Café, including the slushy alien slime, as if there were not enough sugary treats.

We got stuck, however, in Mr. Potato Head's Playroom. This was an arts and crafts extravaganza in which, once Sarah started playing with the drawings and Lite-Brite games, all she wanted to do was stay. It was only the sound of clapping and ushers gently encouraging us to leave that made us finally move. All the operators at the Funhouse had lined the hallways to the exit and were clapping as we moved through them, giving Sarah a feeling of being whisked away. We found our way back to our awaiting car and made the journey home, where we arrived totally tired but thrilled. We had been part of a Hollywood moment. I don't think Jason and Sarah could understand why I had ever doubted joining Pixar.

With the thrill of *Toy Story*'s premiere behind us, we were at last heading into the two weeks that would count the most.

17

PIXR

"CAN I STOP BY ON MY WAY HOME?" I ASKED STEVE ON THE phone as I left Pixar two days after the premiere. It was Tuesday, November 21, the day before *Toy Story*'s official release.

This was one conversation I wanted to have in person.

"Sure, come on by."

As I walked through the gate on the side of Steve's house, I felt a chill down my spine. Goosebumps.

Steve was in his home office. He sat at his desk, working on his computer.

"Robertson Stephens called me this afternoon," I started.

Steve had been anxiously awaiting the results of our road show.

"We did it, Steve," I said, quietly. "We did it," my voice grew louder. "Investors want in. Our stock offering will be oversubscribed. Robertson Stephens is ready to go. They want to launch Pixar's public offering at the end of next week."

"Any idea what the price will be?" Steve asked.

"Not precisely. But Robertson Stephens think there's a good chance the IPO will go over the proposed twelve- to fourteen-dollar price, well over. Interest is very high."

"Wow," Steve said, a smile creeping across his face. "This is fantastic."

"It's amazing," I said. "Investors loved our story. They understand we've got a lot of work ahead of us, that this is a long-term investment. But they believe in Pixar. They believe we can do it. They want in."

"Great," Steve said, taking it all in. "This is really great."

The final price for the IPO would not be set until a day or two before the offering. In the meantime, there was that other number we had our eye on: *Toy Story*'s opening weekend box office.

On the morning of Saturday, November 25, all I could do was pace. We had arranged a chain of phone calls through which we would know how well *Toy Story* had performed Friday night. I would receive a phone call from Sarah Staff, who was plugged into Pixar's source of box office information. We needed to know the precise number, and we needed to know how to interpret it. We had learned that Thanksgiving film releases were a little unusual compared to a normal weekend. In the first place, the film was officially released on Wednesday, the day before Thanksgiving. Friday itself was the huge post-Thanksgiving shopping day, so that had to be factored in also. Disney had promised to help us make sense of the numbers.

"When will you hear?" Hillary asked.

"They said by around 10:00 a.m.," I replied.

It was now approaching 10:30. It would be only moments before we knew the first magic number, that of *Toy Story*'s opening weekend box office. I'd take $10 million, I reminded myself, but something north of $15 million would be very sweet indeed.

"I'm nervous," Hillary said.

Twenty minutes later, the phone rang. I rushed to answer it.

"Yes, yes. I see. I get it. Thank you. Yes, I'd love the details. You have my fax number. Thank you."

I hung up the phone, trying to absorb what I had just been told.

"So?" Hillary couldn't wait.

"It's *massive*," I said. "Massive. They didn't believe it was possible. Disney predicts a weekend box office close to thirty million! Friday night's box office alone was close to eleven and a half million."

Hillary and I high-fived.

"Wow!" Hillary exclaimed. "It's way better than any of us even imagined."

"Thirty million!" I continued. "Even more, audience polling is off the charts. Disney thinks the film will have a huge run. It will sail past a hundred million, and probably past a hundred and fifty million."

Five minutes later the phone rang again. It was Steve.

"It's amazing," Steve started excitedly. "I've talked to Disney marketing, I've talked to John. I've talked to Eisner. This is huge. They're thinking this could be the biggest film of the year."

The biggest film of the year so far had been *Batman Forever*, with a total domestic box office of $184 million. Second was *Apollo 13*, with $172 million. It had never really occurred to any of us that we might reach into that territory.

"Are you serious?" I said. "That means it'll get close to two hundred million."

"It's possible," Steve said. "We did it, Lawrence. We totally did it."

I felt chills down my spine again as I got off the phone and shared what Steve had said. *The biggest film of the year. Pixar. Toy Story.* It was hard to compute. We were dumbfounded. Audiences were falling in love with Woody and Buzz. "My goodness," I thought, "these are going to become cultural icons, like Mickey Mouse and Bambi." That first number, the opening weekend box office, had totally exceeded our wildest expectations.

The mood at Pixar on Monday morning was jubilant. More than jubilant. Ecstatic. I don't think a scrap of work got done as everyone recounted their weekend experiences taking friends and families to see the film. The air was filled with a mixture of humble pride and total disbelief at the size of the box office numbers.

My team and I had little time to take it all in, though. Robertson Stephens had confirmed they were ready to go. Wednesday was the target day for Pixar's IPO.

Later that day, I called Steve.

"Robertson Stephens thinks they can price it over twenty dollars per share," I told him. "Far above the twelve- to fourteen-dollar range."

That $12 to $14 had been the proposed price before we met investors. Now we were talking about something way beyond that.

"They're thinking twenty-two dollars," I went on. "Their investors want in on this, although if the price is much higher than that, they're worried some might balk. That values Pixar at eight hundred million dollars, and means we'll raise over one hundred forty million in cash."

"Are you sure that's as high as they're willing to go?" Steve asked.

"I am," I said. "I'll arrange a call for you to talk to Mike McCaffrey so you can discuss it with him directly. It's an incredible price. And there are still worries about the risks in Pixar's business model."

Steve talked to Robertson Stephens's CEO, Mike McCaffrey, and we had a separate call with Pixar's board members. They all approved.

"Congratulations," Steve said to all of us. "We've got ourselves a deal. Let's make it happen."

We had agreement on the opening price.

Two days later, on Wednesday, November 29, Steve, Ed, and I huddled around a computer in the San Francisco offices of Robertson Stephens. The NASDAQ stock market had opened at 6:30 a.m., about thirty minutes earlier. Robertson Stephens was ready to launch Pixar's stock, which would trade under the symbol PIXR. With us from Robertson Stephens were Todd Carter, Mike McCaffrey, Brian Bean, and Ken Fitzimmons, who was in charge of actually placing the stock in the hands of investors. It was his task to make sure trading began smoothly. The NASDAQ stock exchange is not a physical place like the New York Stock Exchange. There is no bell to ring, just stock symbols on a computer screen.

A little after 7:00 a.m., six million shares of Pixar stock were placed with investors at $22 per share. They were immediately tradable by any person who wanted to purchase Pixar's stock.

"There it is!" Todd Carter exclaimed. "Pixar's first trade."

We could see our symbol PIXR for the first time. We were live. Pixar was a public company.

But the trading did not begin at $22. That was the price the first investors paid to Pixar to acquire the stock. It immediately jumped up into the high thirties. Demand was off the charts.

We all stared at it, partly beaming, partly in disbelief.

Todd Carter broke the silence. He turned to Steve.

"Congratulations, Steve," he said. "You're a billionaire."

At the end of the first day's trading, Pixar's stock was at $39. That gave Pixar a market value of close to $1.5 billion and did indeed make Steve a billionaire. I later heard that while I was glued to the computer screen watching Pixar's trades, Steve had stepped into a nearby office and made a phone call to his friend Larry Ellison, the founder and CEO of Oracle Corporation. All he apparently said was "Larry, I made it."

The next day's headline in the *Wall Street Journal*'s report on the IPO read:

STEVE JOBS IS BACK IN THE SADDLE AGAIN, BECOMING A BILLIONAIRE IN PIXAR IPO

The article said:

> *There are plenty of analysts who think the market's valuation of Pixar, at a total of $1.46 billion, is a sign of investors gone mad. Disney will get 80% to 90% of the revenue from "Toy Story," and has locked Pixar into a three-picture deal through at least 1999 that promises to be a lot more rewarding for Disney than Pixar.*[5]

Responding to similar skepticism over Pixar's valuation, the *LA Times* quoted Steve saying, "It's not for me to decide what the value is — that's why we have a market. But we are only the second studio in 60 years to produce a blockbuster animated feature film —

— —

5. G. Christian Hill, "Steve Jobs Is Back in the Saddle Again, Becoming a Billionaire in Pixar IPO," *Wall Street Journal*, November 30, 1995, http://blogs.wsj.com/wsj125/2014/11/29/nov-30-1995-pixars-ipo/.

and we're doing it in a new medium of 3-D computer graphics."[6]

That turned out to be no mere understatement. *Toy Story* went on to become the biggest film of 1995, clocking in a total domestic box office of just under $192 million by the end of its run. At the time, it was the third-biggest animated feature film ever released, behind only Disney's *Aladdin* and *The Lion King*.

At the end of the day that Pixar went public, if anyone had seen me as I walked out into Pixar's parking lot to drive home, I'm sure they would have noticed an extra bounce in my step. I felt something between disbelief and jubilation. For most of the past year, I had been utterly wrapped up in what was right in front of me, simply trying to move everything ahead, sometimes little more than an inch or two. Now, in the space of one whirlwind week, Pixar had taken off. We had gone from a sleepy company that the world had all but forgotten to having one of animation's hottest film releases ever and one of the most successful IPOs of the year. The stock price—which had been the source of so much angst just a few months earlier when we were issuing stock options—was higher than anyone at Pixar expected. It was immensely gratifying to think about how much Pixar's team of humble, patient, groundbreaking geniuses deserved it.

Years later, I learned more about my own role in Pixar's IPO. I met up with Todd Carter, who told me how close a call Robertson Stephens's decision to take Pixar public had been. Their Commitment Committee that made the decision had met not once, not twice, but three times to discuss whether investors would tolerate the built-in risks. They were right on the fence about whether to proceed and had especially worried about Steve's insistence on too high a valuation, and whether investors would be comfortable with Steve dividing his responsibilities between both Pixar and NeXT.

Todd also explained how important my influence had been in tip-

— —

6. Amy Harmon, "Like 'Toy Story,' Pixar Stock Is a Hit Its First Day on the Street," *Los Angeles Times*, November 30, 1995, http://articles.latimes.com/1995-11-30/business/fi-8751_1_toy-story.

ping the balance. The committee trusted that my view of the risks aligned with their own, and they believed I would be a grounding influence when it came to valuing Pixar. They also felt I would compensate for Steve's commitment at NeXT. As flattering as that was, it was me who remained grateful for how Robertson Stephens came through for Pixar, staking its reputation on a crazy bet for Pixar to make it big in Hollywood and doing it before we had even released our first film.

If that Commitment Committee had come down the other way, everything would have been different. We would have been flat out of time for an IPO in 1995, and who knows how hard that would have made it to raise the capital we needed to build Pixar, when we needed it? Any way you looked at it, Pixar's fate had hung on the slenderest of threads.

As jubilant as I was about the IPO, I also understood that my responsibilities were just beginning. I now had all the pressures of being the CFO of a public company. The coming months would call for an enormous amount of finesse as the Wall Street analysts initiated their reports on Pixar, and the investment community began to scrutinize our ability to execute our business plan. After all, the IPO was just one of the four pillars we had described. We still had to drastically increase Pixar's output, earn a much bigger share of our films' profits, and build Pixar's brand. Pixar was far from reaching a stable orbit. This moment, however, was one to take in and to truly remember. We had navigated the long, torturous, and expensive obstacle course that Hal Vogel had so presciently described in his book, and we had come out of it on top.

But this wasn't the end of Hal Vogel's part of the story. Some years later, he made a small editorial change in his book. Just below the paragraph in which he described stock offerings for film companies as "investment nightmares," he added a new paragraph:

A rare exception, however, was the late 1995 IPO of Pixar, in which 6.9 million shares were sold at $22 per share, raising a total of around

$150 million. The Pixar offering was a great success because the com-
pany not only introduced new computer-generated technology in the
making of Toy Story *(released the week of the IPO), but also was*
backed by a multifilm major studio distribution agreement with
Disney and led by a team of management and creative executives
with impressive and well-established credentials.[7]

I am probably the only person in the world to notice this amend-
ment to Hal's book. But it still makes me smile every time I think
about it.

---

7. Vogel, *Entertainment Industry Economics*, p. 117.

PART III

18

FROM THE HEART

AS MUCH AS RAISING $140 MILLION MIGHT SEEM LIKE A big win, it still had to be transformed into actual business success. Like raising money to procure spices from the Banda Islands, all the risks of the voyage were still ahead of us.

To investors, even *Toy Story*'s success would quickly become yesterday's news — last year's spice journey. Sustained performance is the hallmark of business success, and Pixar was still a far cry from it. This depended on the other pillars of our plan: making films more often than every four years, enjoying more of the profits from those films, and turning Pixar into a brand. Before we could tackle those challenges, however, we had to face the biggest challenge of all: how to make *great* films. Without that, no matter what else we did, Pixar might easily join the long history of one-hit wonders that littered the entertainment highway.

Coming up with a second act after a big hit is a thorny challenge. The problem with success, even a little success, is that it changes you. You are no longer walking along the same precipice that drove you to do great work in the first place. Now you have something to defend: a reputation, money in the bank, a brand, real customer expectations. Success can take the edge away.

To keep the Pixar engine going, we had to produce another hit, and then another, and then more after that. How could we make sure that Pixar kept its creative edge? We couldn't call a meeting, trot out a whiteboard, and write across the top: *MAKE A BLOCK-BUSTER*. It was like trying to clone Mozart.

Two issues, in particular, were central to the challenge: how often to make films, and who would have the final say over creative choices.

By the end of 1995, Pixar was well into development on its second act, a film called *A Bug's Life*. John was directing it, but with his commitments to market *Toy Story*, he had given Andrew Stanton a big role in making the film, one he hoped would groom Andrew to direct his own films in the future. Work on the story had begun over a year earlier, in 1994, and Disney had approved the film during the past summer.

Once again, the story team was skirting the edge of what was possible technologically: the exoskeletons of bugs were far more complicated than the plastic surfaces of toys; the film was set almost entirely outdoors; the miniaturized world of insects called for a luminous glow created by the sun shining through leaves and trees; and, perhaps hardest of all, the film was centered around an ant colony. A handful of ants was not going to cut it; we needed legions of them. This challenge fell to Bill Reeves, who was leading a team to invent technology to animate ant crowds automatically.

A Bug's Life was not slated for release until the end of 1998 at the earliest, almost three years after *Toy Story*. We had to decide when to put future films into production. This called for tackling one of our four pillars: make films more often. The question was—how often?

"It's a tradeoff," I said to Steve one evening over the phone. "The more often we release films, the more risk we take with creative quality. The less often, the more risk we take with Pixar's financial viability."

"What release rate would reduce the business risk?" Steve asked.

"The numbers show releasing a film a year at a minimum," I said. "Even two films a year, but I can't see us getting to that."

The next time we were at Pixar, we took the issue up with Ed.

"It's too big of a leap," Ed said. "The story team isn't ready for a film a year."

The story team, often described as Pixar's brain trust, consisted of John Lasseter, Andrew Stanton, Pete Docter, and Joe Ranft. Lee

Unkrich, *Toy Story*'s editor, also played a key role. They had all been pivotal in the making of *Toy Story*, and they were slated for big things in the future. The genius of John included not just the ability to make great films but to recognize and to groom others to do the same. Sometimes Steve, Ed, and I referred to the story team as the "John Lasseter School of Animation Direction."

It was still early days in developing new directors, though. With only one film under Pixar's belt, we were not certain how long it would take. Moreover, because each film required a host of artistic, technical, and production capabilities, we also didn't know how much time it would take to hire enough people to scale up. Pixar had around 150 employees while it was making *Toy Story*, an almost comically small number for all it was doing. This number would need to grow a lot.

"As much as I'd like to see it," I said, "everyone is balking at the idea of a film a year. But a film every two years makes the numbers all but impossible to work. If we miss on a film, that means we'd have a dry spell of four years. We'd lose too much lift."

Another option was to release a film every eighteen months. We could still hit the two big release windows, a summer release one year, a winter release the next, although the financial numbers did not work as well as they would if we released a film every year. We would need bigger hits, and any disappointment would hurt more. But we could make a case that a film every eighteen months might work, and this is where we compromised.

When we mapped out what it would take to accomplish a film every eighteen months, it became clear that we would need to expand the size of Pixar by three or four times at least. From that point on, the challenge became where to find the talent to make that happen. The level of artistic, animation, and technical talent within Pixar was rare, almost impossible to duplicate. Multiplying it would be like building two or three World Series baseball championship teams from scratch. We would need a full system of scouts capable of finding and signing the right people.

I hired Rachel Hannah to head up the hiring process. With an infectious enthusiasm, Rachel skillfully put in place the systems that would find the talent we needed from the world's best animation, technical, and artistic sources. We also had to train the new hires so that they could be effective as quickly as possible. Ed had the vision and took on the task of creating Pixar University, hiring Randy Nelson to head it up. Together, they built an entire school within Pixar for training new and existing Pixar employees. Their vision for Pixar University went beyond merely professional development and training to encompass a full range of fine arts education that would evolve and perpetuate Pixar's creative depth and talent.

We also hired Sarah McArthur, an executive from Disney, to head up Pixar's production staff. Sarah had a stellar reputation in the industry, having had key roles in *Beauty and the Beast* and *The Lion King,* and served as senior vice president of production at Walt Disney Feature Animation. She was a huge catch for Pixar, something we could never have dreamed about before *Toy Story*'s success.

When it came to scaling creative quality, however, it was the second challenge that would have more significance for Pixar's future than any other: Who would have approval over Pixar's creative choices? Coming into Pixar I had no awareness of the importance of this decision. Now it scared me more than any other. I was simply astounded at how many ways it was possible for a film to go awry creatively.

Each film began with a "pitch" or a "treatment." This was a simple vision of what the film was about. In the case of *A Bug's Life,* it was something like "a film about a group of misfits who save an ant colony from an evil gang of grasshoppers." The pitch would then outline the basic elements of the story and its main characters. On the strength of that pitch, production funds would be committed to develop the story and push the project further along.

The pitch was just the beginning of a long sequence of creative checkpoints in the making of a film. Someone needed to approve the storyboards, script, character designs, and artwork; the computer models of every character; the actors who would voice the characters;

the number of sequences in the film and how those sequences were animated; the musical score and any songs; the film's title; and even the length of the film.

Moreover, these approvals were repeatedly required in the process. Creative vision does not spring forth fully formed. It evolves, meanders, and all but stumbles its way to fruition. The four thousand storyboard drawings for a film were typically redrawn five or six times each in the process of making a film. Who was going to be responsible for these approvals? We were looking at investing upward of $100 million of investors' money in filmmaking. We had to watch over it all very responsibly.

Disney had a well-honed system for making creative decisions. The executives there — Jeffrey Katzenberg, until he left, Peter Schneider, and Tom Schumacher — had a hand in every step of the creative process. The directors of Disney's animated films very clearly answered to the top executives, and very little went forward without executive approval.

It was easy to see why Disney worked this way. Creative mistakes can be very expensive to fix. If there is a significant change to the story or to one of the main characters deep into the production process, the change ripples through every aspect of the film. It doesn't take much to rack up millions or even tens of millions of dollars in unplanned costs. Most executives are not built to take this kind of risk, so they like to keep a close watch on the creative process. In fact, I was now beginning to understand why so many entertainment companies really didn't like to take much creative risk at all. Executives often kept creative development on a short leash, preferring safer bets over riskier experiments.

As the stakes grew for Pixar, we felt even more pressure to have some sort of executive oversight to make sure Pixar's creative processes did not go astray. We had a small band of story artists who had released one film and were now facing production budgets that would soon begin approaching $100 million per film. We worried about how much freedom the creative team should have. Ed, Steve, and I met with John to discuss the matter one Friday when Steve was at Pixar.

"I understand the concern here. I really do," John said. "But we don't want to make safe films. We want to keep breaking barriers in story and animation. Our story team is like no other. It has incredible vision and depth. We have to rely on it."

"What about Disney?" Steve asked. "They've made some great films but their executives like Jeffrey Katzenberg provided creative oversight."

Katzenberg had overseen Disney's resurgence in animation, presiding over the development of *The Little Mermaid, Aladdin, The Lion King,* and other films. Now he was off building his own animation studio at DreamWorks. Bringing up Jeffrey Katzenberg to John, however, was a bit like showing a red cape to a charging bull. Katzenberg's first animated feature at DreamWorks was about ants, just like Pixar's next film. Pixar felt Katzenberg had developed the idea after hearing about Pixar's film.

"We're not making films like Katzenberg," John retorted quickly. "We have ideas for incredible, original stories. It's so rare to do original work. That's what we can do. It's what we *have* to do."

"How do you see the creative decision process moving forward?" I asked.

"Our films must come from the heart," John explained. "It's not just about entertainment. It's about telling stories that audiences connect with emotionally. The way to do this is to make our films personal, to make certain they mean something to our directors."

John had such passion in his voice, such sincere conviction, that it was almost impossible not to be moved by it. He literally touched over his heart as he spoke.

"We have to trust our story team," he went on. "They have to believe we trust them."

"So what you're saying," Steve said, "is that we should bet on our creative talent, no matter the risk."

"Yes," John replied. "I know that's asking a lot, but it is what I think we should do."

What John was asking us to do was unprecedented. He wanted us to put all creative approvals in the hands of Pixar's story team. It just wasn't done. Disney had never done it. And those few directors in Hollywood who did have complete approval over their films had long track records of making iconic films. The truth remained that Pixar had released one film, and most of its future directors would be directing a feature film for the very first time. If we gave them unfettered control over creative decisions, we could end up with production overages that would not just sink us financially, but they'd make us look like the Hollywood novices we were.

After John left the meeting, Steve asked Ed what he thought.

"From Pixar's shorts to *Toy Story*, we've done it the way John described," Ed said. "Only now the stakes are higher as we try to make more films and our production budgets go up. But we have to take John's thoughts seriously. So often studios sacrifice story by playing it safe."

We walked through our options. The first was to insert ourselves more into the filmmaking process. No one would think it unreasonable for Pixar's Office of the President to have a say in the films we made. As obvious as this seemed, especially by Hollywood standards, we well understood that we had no experience or qualifications to judge creative choices. Yes, we had our personal taste and opinions just like any other person, but evaluating story had a depth, an art, a physics to it. Moving from our personal views of a film to a professional critique was a gigantic leap. As alluring as it might be to try, we just did not have the confidence that we could guide the stories ourselves.

The second option was more enticing.

"We could hire someone to oversee Pixar's creative choices," Steve suggested. "With *Toy Story*'s success, I'm sure we could lure someone here to help with this side of the business."

"You could talk to Joe Roth at Disney," I suggested. "I'm sure he'll have some ideas."

Over the next few days, we looked into hiring a creative executive and reviewed a few names that came our way. Nothing really lit our fire, though. In animation, no names came up at all. The top names in animation already worked for Disney or DreamWorks. At best, we would have to settle for a creative executive from live-action film.

I could also sense something else at work. Our search for a creative leader was lackluster, and it wasn't just because we couldn't find anyone. John's pleas had struck a chord.

Steve and I had a chance to talk it over one weekend.

"Isn't that the way we should be making great films?" Steve said. "From the heart of the filmmakers? Why would we want anyone else to interfere with that? The focus should be on creative vision, not deadlines and budgets."

"Disney's made some great films with executive oversight," I pointed out. "We all love *Aladdin* and *The Lion King*."

"But did they have a John Lasseter?" Steve mused.

This was a great question. Disney certainly had animation directors with stellar reputations, but John and his young team seemed to be cut from different cloth. They were virtually inventing how to tell stories in the entirely new medium of computer animation.

"And we're aiming for something different," Steve added. "Truly original films. Stories that have never been seen or heard of before."

At this point, my job as chief financial officer should have been to remind Steve about the huge risks of cost overruns, to cite cases of films notorious for budget excesses and box office disappointments, and to recount the dangers of creative teams running amok. By this time I was aware of examples of all of them. I didn't bring them up, though. That wasn't why I came to Pixar. I came because I had believed in Ed, John, and Pixar's team. Now, I found myself surprised to find Hollywood so risk averse. I loved the idea that filmmaking could use a dose of Silicon Valley bravado.

Moreover, John was not saying, "Bet on me." He was saying, "Bet on our team; bet on our process." He would be the first to say how much that process relied on the relentless critique of each other's work and the willingness to put aside ego just enough to hear that critique. When I added it all up, every start-up impulse within me said this was the time to bet on our team. That would be the Silicon Valley way of filmmaking. No hedging. Bet on innovation. Bet on greatness. Take the shot to change the world.

"We don't have to do this the Hollywood way," I said. "I'm completely on board with that."

Ceding creative control to John and the story team wasn't the rational decision, though. A more traditional approach would be to say, "Don't break the mold; don't be so naive that you think you can do things better than they're done in Hollywood." I also wondered what Wall Street would think when we told them the three members of Pixar's Office of the President would have no say over creative decisions.

The next week, when Steve was at Pixar, he grabbed Ed and me to discuss it all one last time. From my conversations with Ed, I knew he was behind this approach already.

"So we trust John and the team," Steve said. "We bet on them."

"Yes," said Ed.

"It's the right call," I added.

This decision meant that from that point on, all creative decisions for Pixar's films would be made by John, Andrew, Pete, Joe, and their growing team. Steve, Ed, and I would have no input into the content of Pixar's films, no approvals over the creative process. If John and his team wanted to make a silent film about a robot falling in love, we would not interfere. If they wanted to change the main character of a film halfway into production, we would support it. We would sit on the sidelines and watch Pixar's creative team work, helping them, supporting them, nurturing them in whatever ways we could, but not intervening with their creative choices.

Although I was fully behind the decision, as chief financial officer I still took a big gulp. It was a very risky move because it meant we could lose control over our production budgets and deadlines. In effect, we were valuing the upside of creative freedom over the downside of budgets and deadlines running off the rails due to creative mistakes.

Now, some might say it was easy to cede creative control when you have someone like John Lasseter on your team. But in my experience it is never easy. And it was certainly never easy for Pixar. Every one of Pixar's films went through a series of hair-raising creative crises that repeatedly tested our decision. Creative excellence is a dance on the precipice of failure, a battle against the allure of safety. There are no shortcuts, no formulas, no well-worn paths to victory. It tests you constantly.

But I felt really proud of our decision. We had chosen to truly empower talent, to send a signal to Pixar's creative leaders that we trusted them. I cannot say this approach would be right for every company. But I can say that whether you're making bottled water, mobile games, or computer chips, the decision of who has control over the creative elements is among the most important any team will make. Fear and ego conspire to rein in creativity, and it is easy to allow creative inspiration to take a back seat to safety. It is one thing to cite the adage "Story is king." It is another thing entirely to live by it.

19

ANATOMY OF A DEAL

AS THE CALENDAR TURNED TO 1996, PIXAR HAD ORGA-nized itself for not one but two productions. *A Bug's Life* was in full production, and work had begun on *Toy Story 2*, a sequel to *Toy Story* that was slated to bypass theatrical release and go directly to the home video market. Disney had enjoyed great success in recent years with direct-to-home-video releases like *The Return of Jafar,* a sequel to *Aladdin*. Because these sequels would not have the benefit of widespread theatrical distribution, they had to be made at far less cost than the original film in order to make financial sense.

I was on record as being skeptical about Pixar's ability to reduce its film production costs enough to justify a direct-to-video release. We were running into similar challenges trying our hand at producing a *Toy Story* video game. The game was great, but the production costs were prohibitively high. Disney had honed ways to make less expensive sequels in traditional animation, but Pixar did not have a method to make lower-cost computer animation.

Another problem with *Toy Story 2* was that it would extend the Disney contract because it would not count as one of the three original films we had to deliver under that contract. Here I had been looking for every angle to get out of that agreement, and this was going to make it last longer. There was a lot of momentum to make a sequel, however. Pixar's creative and production teams thought they could find ways to make it quicker and at less cost than a theatrical release, and it would at least have the benefit of helping with the carrying cost issue — paying for production employees who would otherwise have no film to work on. On the theory that it would take much less time than a theatrical film, we decided to go for it.

At the same time, Steve and I were turning our sights toward another of our plan's four pillars: increasing our share of film profits. This hinged on the terms of our film distribution agreement, presently with Disney but in the future potentially with any of the major studios: Disney, Universal, Fox, Paramount, Warner Brothers, or Columbia.

For two generations, these studios controlled the business of film distribution. Through their extensive networks, only they could deliver films into movie theaters in every corner of the world. In the United States alone a big movie would open in 2,500 to 3,000 theaters. For this kind of reach, Pixar would have to strike an agreement with one of the major studios, and that agreement would spell out Pixar's share of the profits. It would also describe the terms for one of our other pillars: branding. If our films were to be distributed under the Pixar brand, whatever studio was distributing our films would have to agree.

Our choices were: either we rode out our existing contract with Disney and then entered a new contract with Disney or any of the other major studios, or we renegotiated our contract with Disney now. If we rode out the existing contract, we would have maximum flexibility at its conclusion, but that could take up to eight years. In short, it all came down to evaluating which option was better for Pixar: renegotiating now with Disney, if that was even an option, or entering a new agreement later with Disney or another studio. Much like the IPO, this topic began to occupy a lot of my time with Steve.

"If we're going to make a move to renegotiate with Disney," I suggested one night in early January 1996, "we should start thinking seriously about it right away, while *Toy Story*'s success is still fresh."

"Or maybe we're better off waiting," Steve said, "until we're free to negotiate with other studios and have more flexibility to pick our best distribution partner."

Neither of us was sure whether or when to approach Disney to try to change our deal. We understood that if we did it now, we might get better terms even for our next two films, but if we waited, we might get even better terms later, when we were free of that agreement. We went back and forth, often switching sides in the discussion. Making the move now made sense only if we thought we could negotiate a deal that would be strong enough to justify giving up our options in the future. But how would we know?

There is no formula for easily making this type of assessment. In business relationships, or virtually in any relationships for that matter, there are two factors that determine one's capacity to effect change: leverage and negotiation.

Leverage means bargaining power. It is the muscle you have to bring about change in your favor. The more leverage, the better your chances to get what you want. In poker, leverage would be the equivalent of the actual strength of your hand. *Negotiation,* in contrast, describes the tactics you employ to extract the best terms you can, given your leverage. It is about how you play the hand. Courage, fear, tenacity, trustworthiness, creativity, calm, the willingness to walk away, to behave irrationally—these all play into negotiation. Leverage is an assessment of bargaining strength; negotiation is how you put that bargaining strength to work for you. A good negotiator can make more out of the same leverage than a not-so-good one.

In Pixar's first agreement with Disney, Pixar had fared poorly in terms of both leverage and negotiation. Pixar had not had much leverage because it had just closed down its hardware business, was struggling to remain afloat, and had never made a feature film. In terms of negotiation, I felt Steve had been caught in a rare weak moment. This was more than four years ago, though. Steve liked to cite the adage "Fool me once, shame on you; fool me twice, shame on me." What had occurred four years earlier was not going to happen again.

We needed to understand how much leverage we had in order to negotiate a good deal with Disney now. If we approached Disney and didn't have the muscle to back us up, we would be politely, or maybe not so politely, dismissed out of hand.

One Friday in late January 1996, when Steve was at Pixar, we stepped into the small, windowless conference room near my office to discuss where we thought Pixar stood in relation to Disney. As we often did, we wrote down the main points of discussion on a whiteboard. There was one in the front of the room, with a wooden casing around it. We had discussed all of these points before, but it was helpful to see them in one place. Steve took a whiteboard pen and made two columns: Disney and Pixar. Under the Disney column, he would write the points that gave Disney leverage. Under the Pixar column, he would write the points that favored Pixar.

Point one for Disney: **NO OBLIGATION TO CHANGE CONTRACT**

"We know there's nothing that can force Disney to negotiate with us," Steve said. "They have a three-picture deal and they can stick to that contract simply because they want to."

"They have us tied up for two more films," I added. "They keep most of the profits, and we can't talk to any other studios until we're done. It's a great deal for them. Why would they change it?"

Steve added a second point in the Disney column: **CAN INVEST IN COMPUTER ANIMATION THEMSELVES**

The impact of *Toy Story* had made Disney examine its own potential in computer animation. They might easily assume that they could hire the best talent they could find and build up their own capability.

"If Disney makes a substantial investment in computer animation," Steve said, "they may have no interest in extending their agreement with us."

"Disney has plenty of resources to do it," I added. "Plus they also have time on their side. Their deal with us could buoy them for a few years while they build up their own capacity in computer animation. We're basically giving them the lead time they need."

This was a potentially perfect strategy for Disney. They could use

Pixar to tide them over until they no longer needed us, reaping most of the profits along the way. Then they'd have their own computer animation capability ready to go and could easily jettison Pixar.

"Another point for the Disney column," I added, "is that Disney will undoubtedly think it offers Pixar more than any other studio can offer, given its expertise in animated films."

Steve wrote in the Disney column: OTHER PIXAR OPTIONS INFERIOR

Disney was clearly better at distributing animated feature films than anyone else. It had extraordinary merchandising capability for churning out toys, clothes, and other branded items; it had the very best theme parks for showcasing the films and their characters; and the imprint of the Disney brand on an animated film gave it a cachet that no other studio could provide. Where else could Pixar find that kind of distribution clout? Disney might well conclude that Pixar needed Disney far more than Disney needed Pixar, and they might be right. It would certainly diminish our leverage with them.

Next Steve added to the Disney column: PIXAR ONLY ONE HIT

"We've had only one hit," Steve said. "Before we prove we can repeat it, Disney might be reluctant to change our deal."

This was the one-hit-wonder problem. One hit did not make for a track record.

"Anything else in Disney's favor?" Steve asked.

"We've talked about this," I said, "but maybe Eisner's interest in animation is waning. He just bet big by buying ABC, which includes ESPN. Animation could be on its way to becoming a sideshow for him."

Michael Eisner was Disney's CEO. He had a reputation for being mercurial and hard to read. The notion that he might not care all that much about animation seemed a bit far-fetched, but it was possible he was more interested in television and other media outlets than animation. He had just spent $19 billion to buy ABC. Maybe it spelled a new direction for Disney.

Steve wrote in the Disney column: **ANIMATION MIGHT BE LOSING PRIORITY**

The Disney column now read:

DISNEY

- **NO OBLIGATION TO CHANGE CONTRACT**
- **CAN INVEST IN COMPUTER ANIMATION THEMSELVES**
- **OTHER PIXAR OPTIONS INFERIOR**
- **PIXAR ONLY ONE HIT**
- **ANIMATION MIGHT BE LOSING PRIORITY**

Any one of these factors wouldn't bode all that well for Pixar. Collectively, they added up to a bleak outlook for Pixar's leverage. Some might say Disney had all the bargaining power, that Pixar was just a fly on the side of the elephant. Disney could let us hang around for as long as we were useful, then swat us away in an instant.

There was another column, though.

The first thing Steve wrote in the Pixar column was: **IPO $ TO PAY FOR PRODUCTIONS**

"We can now pay for our own productions," Steve said. "Disney doesn't have to pay for all the costs."

This was why we had done the IPO. If money talked, we now had quite a bit of it. We anticipated that production costs for Pixar's next film might approach $50 million, and production costs for future films more still. If we offered to put up half of it, this would surely get Disney's attention.

Then I added a second point: *TOY STORY* **SUCCESS**

Steve wrote it in the Pixar column.

"No one expected *Toy Story* to be so successful," I said. "Least of all Disney."

Toy Story was still playing in theaters and had surpassed $170 million in the domestic box office, vastly exceeding Disney's expectations. Much to their surprise, the quaint experiment in computer animation had gone mainstream. The world might not know that Pixar made the entire film, but Disney knew, and it would make it harder for them to brush off Pixar and computer animation as a sideshow.

"By itself it doesn't compel Disney to renegotiate," I added, "but it would make them more inclined to keep Pixar happy."

Skip Brittenham, the Hollywood super-lawyer now on Pixar's board of directors, had told us how success talks in Hollywood. If that was true, Pixar's star was shining a lot brighter these days. That would surely give us some leverage.

"There's also the DreamWorks factor," I added.

DreamWorks was founded in 1994 after Jeffrey Katzenberg's well-publicized resignation from the Walt Disney Company over CEO Michael Eisner's decision not to promote him to president of the company. As chairman of the Walt Disney Studios division, Katzenberg had overseen the revival of its animation business. Together with its two other founders, Steven Spielberg and David Geffen, DreamWorks's vision was to produce live-action films and a brand-new animation studio that would compete directly with Disney.

The implications of DreamWorks for Pixar were twofold. First, DreamWorks Animation was a potential competitor to Pixar. Second, and more important to this discussion, DreamWorks's competitive threat to Disney might make Disney less willing to alienate Pixar. Better for Disney to keep Pixar in its camp than risk not one but two serious competitors in animation when, for the preceding sixty years, it had none.

"Katzenberg would like nothing more than to trump Disney in animation," Steve said. "He's a thorn in Disney's side. If Eisner loses Pixar to another studio, and DreamWorks succeeds in animation, Eisner could go down as the Disney CEO who lost animation."

Steve wrote in the Pixar column: **DREAMWORKS THREAT TO DISNEY**

Then Steve made another entry in the Pixar column: **BETTER DEAL IF WAIT**

"If we don't do a deal with Disney now," Steve said, "we'll get a better deal later when this contract is over. We'll then have multiple studios bidding for Pixar's business. We might even be able to keep eighty or even ninety percent of the profits, much more than we're likely to get from Disney now."

"We can't count on that," I countered. "If our next films underperform, maybe we get worse terms later. This point can cut for or against us. Also, if we renegotiate with Disney now, we might get better terms right now, even for *A Bug's Life*."

"But I think there's a premium we have to pay for a partnership with Disney," Steve added, "because of their experience in animation compared to the other major studios. If we go with another studio later, we can get even better terms."

I agreed that Pixar would pay a premium to be in business with Disney, probably in the form of Disney keeping more of the profits than we might have to relinquish to another studio. I also felt that any deal with another studio would depend on our track record then. There was no need to press the point now, though.

The chart now looked like this:

DISNEY	*PIXAR*
NO OBLIGATION TO CHANGE CONTRACT	IPO $ TO PAY FOR PRODUCTIONS
CAN INVEST IN COMPUTER ANIMATION THEMSELVES	*TOY STORY* SUCCESS
OTHER PIXAR OPTIONS INFERIOR	DREAMWORKS THREAT TO DISNEY
PIXAR ONLY ONE HIT	BETTER DEAL IF WAIT
ANIMATION MIGHT BE LOSING PRIORITY	

It was difficult to assess how this would shake out. Both of us had leverage. But did Pixar have enough to force a negotiation now, and on favorable terms? I felt we had enough to find out. Just one of our points might be sufficient to bring Disney to the negotiation table. And we were not afraid to wait if it didn't materialize now.

"I think we should go for it," I said to Steve.

"It would be better if Disney approached us," Steve replied. "We just had this huge hit. Wouldn't Eisner want to keep us happy?"

Steve was right. It would be much better if Disney made the first move. We didn't want to appear weak, or needy. I was nervous about Pixar making the first move too.

"It would be better," I agreed. "But everything we've learned suggests that's not how Eisner works. He keeps things close to the vest. Even if Disney did want to sweeten the deal for Pixar, there's nothing compelling them to do it now. Maybe we make the move while the glow of *Toy Story* still shines brightly."

"But if they say no," Steve added, "it might poison the relationship, making the next two films harder to make."

"I hope it wouldn't affect the film productions," I said. "We have to keep the business and creative relationships separate."

"Let's look at what we want if we do approach them," Steve continued.

This was another topic Steve and I discussed a lot. If we approached Disney to renegotiate our deal, we had to be crystal-clear about what we wanted. This was about our negotiating strategy.

The natural tendency in negotiations is to engage in positional bargaining. This means taking a position knowing that it is not a final position, and holding in reserve a backup position. The danger of positional bargaining is that it forces you to think about backup positions, which weakens your conviction in your original position. It's like negotiating against yourself. Plan A may be your optimal outcome, but inwardly you have already convinced yourself to settle on Plan B.

Both Steve and I had a strong distaste for approaching negotiation this way. We preferred to develop our positions without thinking through a backup. Once Steve decided what he wanted in a negotiation, he developed something akin to a religious conviction about it. In his mind, if he didn't get what he wanted, nothing else would take its place, so he'd walk away. This made Steve an incredibly strong negotiator. He would dig into his positions with a fierce, almost unbreakable grip. The risk, however, was in so overreaching that we would end up with nothing. If we were not going to have a backup plan, we had to be very careful about knowing what we wanted.

Steve changed the whiteboard pen for a new color, and in a different part of the board he wrote: **NEW DEAL**

Below that he wrote: 1. **CREATIVE CONTROL**

"We need control over our creative destiny," Steve asserted. "We've proven we can make a great film. We can't go on indefinitely beholden to Disney to approve our creative choices."

Unless you were Steven Spielberg, Ron Howard, or another celebrity director, it was almost unheard of for an independent production company whose films were being funded by someone else to have creative control. That usually belonged to whoever was putting up the money. We had already decided that John and his team would have creative control *within* Pixar. Now we wanted to diminish any outside influence over them.

"It will help that we are willing to fund our films," I added, "but Disney will be nervous about this so long as they're putting up even some of the money."

Nevertheless, we both agreed that creative control was essential to Pixar's future.

"Another must-have is favorable release windows," I said.

It mattered a lot when films were released, especially big-budget family films. There were two optimal dates: early summer and Thanksgiving, which runs into Christmas. No other time periods came close in terms of box office opportunity. Any contract we entered, with Disney or anyone else, would have to guarantee that Pixar films enjoyed optimal film release windows. Steve wrote on the whiteboard: 2. **FAVORABLE RELEASE WINDOWS**

"Disney has to treat Pixar film releases like its own," Steve added to emphasize that point.

Then he wrote: 3. **TRUE 50/50 PROFIT SHARE**

This was a big one. All of our financial projections told us that we had to keep at least 50 percent of the profits from our films.

"A true fifty-fifty," Steve said. "Calculated fairly."

"Not using ancient Hollywood accounting terms that favor the studios," I added.

"That leaves the branding issue," I went on. "Pixar's films under Pixar's name."

We had discussed this endlessly. Steve wrote: **4. PIXAR BRAND**

"We made the films," Steve said. "The world needs to know that."

That was the fourth pillar of Pixar's business plan.

"Anything else?" Steve asked.

"Of the big issues, no," I said. "These are the ones we stick to, no matter what."

Now the whiteboard had a column that said:

NEW DEAL

1. **CREATIVE CONTROL**

2. **FAVORABLE RELEASE WINDOWS**

3. **TRUE 50/50 PROFIT SHARE**

4. **PIXAR BRAND**

We understood there would be many other issues in any renegotiation, but on these four matters our plan was to hold firm. If we gave up on any of these, Pixar's future would be jeopardized too much. These were our deal breakers.

"I think we're ready," I said.

"I'll call Eisner," Steve replied. "I'll tell him what we have in mind."

I felt sure this was the right move. It was a little scary, though. If Eisner shut the door on us because he thought we were overreaching, our chances of improving our financial situation in the near or even the medium term would evaporate. But we had thought this through every which way. It was time to set in motion a renegotiation with Disney. We could not predict what would happen next, but one thing was clear: when Steve picked up the phone to call Eisner, there was a lot at stake for Pixar.

20

POKER TIME

STEVE CALLED EISNER IN EARLY FEBRUARY 1996 TO OPEN
talks for a possible renegotiation with Disney. He explained that we
were willing to use our newly raised funds to pay for all or part of the
production costs of our films, and he summarized the four provisions
that meant the most to us. Eisner responded by saying he was interested in the discussion. He said he was open to those four provisions,
and that he would want to extend our existing agreement by adding
more films to it, which we had expected. The conversation had gone
well. Eisner said he would get back to us soon.

We then organized ourselves for a negotiation with Disney. I was
to oversee all the details and the contract drafting, much as I had
done with Pixar's IPO, while Steve would interface with Eisner to resolve the impasses. We assembled a team to make sure we left nothing to chance. We wanted to draft the contract ourselves, and we retained Gary Moore to do it. Gary had done work for Steve at NeXT
and represented Pixar in our patent licensing deals with Microsoft
and Silicon Graphics. Although, like us, Gary had no experience in
entertainment law, he was a superb lawyer and an expert draftsman.

For coverage on the entertainment side, we had Sam Fischer, our
entertainment lawyer. Sam and I had forged a great relationship, and
I saw him as a trusted partner as we navigated the world of Hollywood. We added a couple of Hollywood experts to help us with
the accounting provisions we would have to draft to give us a true
share of the profits. We also had Skip Brittenham, who was on Pixar's

board of directors. He would help with the big issues and could step in with Michael Eisner if we needed it. This was the A-team of Hollywood contract negotiations. We were not going to falter for lack of legal muscle.

What happened next, however, surprised us. In a word, it was —nothing.

After Steve's initial call with Michael Eisner, we expected some sort of rapid follow-up. Someone from Disney to call Steve, or me, to get the ball rolling. But no one did. It was as if the conversation never happened. A couple of weeks went by, and Steve placed a call to Eisner to follow up on their conversation. Eisner repeated his interest in a deal and said he would get things going. More weeks went by. Still nothing.

This pattern repeated one more time, after which Steve began to feel frustrated. He felt Eisner was toying with him, saying one thing on the phone but doing nothing in actuality. We understood that for Disney, this was one deal among many, maybe not even a very important one, but that didn't explain why Disney's actions belied what Eisner had told Steve on the phone. Eventually, Steve began to take it personally.

"Maybe Eisner just doesn't like me," he said one day in the spring of 1996. "He tells me one thing and never follows through. I don't get it."

Steve's reputation preceded him, and maybe Eisner didn't trust him. They were both accustomed to being in control. Maybe they rubbed each other the wrong way. But I wasn't convinced that was the reason Disney was failing to follow up. I had checked with Sam Fischer, who also reminded me that Eisner had a lot on his plate with integrating ABC into Disney. That merger, which had been completed just a couple of months earlier, had been the second-largest merger in US history, after the $25 billion acquisition of RJR Nabisco Inc. by the private equity firm Kohlberg Kravis Roberts in 1989. Sam thought it was a bit odd that nothing had come out of Eisner's office, but he didn't feel it was due to friction between Eisner and Jobs.

"I'm not sure it's personal," I told Steve. "We're asking a lot of Disney here, terms they've probably never given anyone. I doubt anyone's got a fifty-fifty profit share, especially in animation, and certainly not the branding arrangement we're asking for. There are many reasons why Eisner might be taking his time, not the least of which is the recent ABC acquisition."

I felt patience was the key. Disney hadn't said no. But Steve was not accustomed to being brushed off, and he didn't like it. The more time went by, the more his frustration grew.

Finally, one day in exasperation, he exclaimed to me, "I don't know if I can work like this!"

For a potential deal to fall through because the leaders on either side could not get along would not be unprecedented, but I didn't think this was the time to call off our effort to initiate a negotiation, at least not yet. I had met Eisner briefly myself a few months earlier, before *Toy Story* came out. In one of my trips to Hollywood with Steve, we stopped by to say hello. The meeting had been a friendly visit to touch base on the upcoming release. I had been quite impressed with Eisner. He was tall and slender, in his mid-fifties. He wore a suit that seemed to fit a bit large and entered the room with a casual lope. He came across like a favorite uncle, engaging and charismatic. We had chatted casually about the film business and the marketing for *Toy Story*'s release.

Remembering that meeting, I said to Steve, "Everyone we know has said the same thing about Eisner. He keeps his cards very close to the chest. There's no evidence that this is personal."

Skip Brittenham had offered to intervene a number of times, although we hadn't taken him up because we didn't want to appear desperate. But now, enough time had passed.

"How about taking up Skip's offer?" I said. "He could find out what's going on, with a light touch. Why not give him a call?"

Steve spoke to Skip, who said he would float some feelers and see what he could learn. He wouldn't make a call exclusively for this purpose but would wait until he had some other business at Disney that gave him a natural opening.

Skip came back to us a couple of weeks later, now around May. Steve and I talked to him on a conference call.

"I think they're interested in talking," Skip said. "They do want a partnership with Pixar. They just want to get their head around the terms. We're asking for a lot. We just have to be patient."

Skip was right. A short while after that call we heard the first signal that Disney finally wanted to talk. Eisner called Steve and told him he wanted to move things forward. He wasn't prepared to say he agreed with all the points Steve had asked for, but he remained open to them. Eisner proposed moving the negotiation along to see where they stood on all the details. He had assigned a young executive by the name of Rob Moore to oversee the process. Moore was executive vice president and CFO of Walt Disney Pictures and Television.

But Steve remained skeptical.

"Maybe we shouldn't proceed without final agreement on the main issues," he complained.

I didn't disagree with that. Sometimes it's better to have clarity upfront. But I felt it was important to maintain the momentum.

"Eisner knows where you stand," I suggested. "And we'll be sure to reiterate that with Moore. I think we should let this move forward to see where it goes."

Steve agreed but wanted to be sure we didn't take our eyes off the main issues.

When I first spoke to Rob Moore over the phone, my expectations were not all that high. Disney's contract negotiators had a reputation for being unyielding. They were seen in the industry as deal killers more than deal makers. I assumed Moore would be one of them.

But Moore was nothing like what I expected. He was engaging, up-front, and had a good sense of humor. He had an ease about him that I liked; it almost caught me off guard. It did not take long for us to plunge into the details of the deal. We spelled it all out, first in summaries and then in actual contract drafts. Moore proved to be immensely constructive. In a company that was known for being ruled directly from the top, he was not afraid to think for himself, and he was willing to take chances to get things done.

This deal was immensely complicated, requiring a whole slew of provisions on Hollywood accounting, film release windows, merchandising, production approvals, and many others. There were many places it could go wrong.

And sure enough, in November of 1996, after six months of effort, we hit a wall.

On the issue of branding, we had requested that Pixar have equal billing to Disney. We knew that Disney would never allow Pixar to have 100 percent of the brand credit. And in truth, of all the studios, we didn't mind co-branding with Disney because they brought enormous credibility to animation. But we insisted that it be exactly equal billing.

Eisner was balking because he felt Disney would be doing too much to build Pixar into an entertainment powerhouse and that one day the deal would end and Disney might have created its worst enemy. In his view, it was enough for Pixar to receive credit for producing the film, but no equal billing with Disney and no branding on the toys and merchandise. That was his line in the sand.

I could see Eisner's concern. If computer animation took off, little Pixar might actually become a threat to Disney one day. But we had no backup position for this point. We had to decide whether to walk away from the deal or to accept something less on the branding issue. Disney had agreed in principle to all our other demands, with details that still needed to be worked out. On this one issue, Pixar's fate hung in the balance.

If we walked away now, we would give up all our other gains and suffer under the terms of the existing agreement for years, taking our chances that we could enter a better deal with Disney or another studio later. If we went forward with the deal, our profits would quadruple now, but we wouldn't have the brand credit we wanted. Everyone needed to weigh in: Steve, Ed, John, and me. Whatever we did, we had to do it together. We met one day in our usual conference room at Pixar.

John had been completely immersed in making *A Bug's Life* and supervising *Toy Story 2*. A meeting like this was rare. He well understood that if we wanted him there, something big was afoot.

"I've spoken to each of you," Steve began. "The negotiation with Disney has not been easy. We've made a lot of progress, but we've hit the wall on the branding issue. I'm not happy about it. Pixar needs to be a brand. These are *our* films. We deserve full credit for making them."

Steve had not the slightest air of conciliation. He spoke like this was an affront.

"Why won't they let us do it?" John asked.

"Eisner's afraid of building Pixar into the next great brand in animation," I chimed in.

"The principle just isn't fair," Ed said. "We make the films and they get the credit."

Ed almost never seemed ruffled. But he was miffed over this. The issue of brand credit had become a matter of principle.

"If the next two films succeed, Disney takes the credit," I said. "If they don't, Eisner blames Pixar and cuts us loose."

"Why can't they just do what is right?" John said. "We're creating these stories and characters here, in this building. Not down there. All we want is the credit for doing that. Why would they want to take that from us?"

For John this was fully emotional, and it was easy to see why. He had spent years developing these characters. They were like children. Pixar's children. I was quite sure he didn't feel like seeing another poster that said "Disney's *Toy Story*" with Pixar in small print.

"Let's consider the other side of this," I said. "If we walk away, we give up a fifty-fifty profit share on our next two films. If those films are blockbusters, that could be worth fifty million dollars for each of them."

The new agreement would supersede the old one, giving the next two films the benefit of all the new terms.

"But what's it worth to turn Pixar into a brand?" Steve asked. "That could be worth as much or more later, when we are free of Disney and own all the rights to our films. Look how audiences trust the Disney brand. They go to films and theme parks on the strength of it. If Pixar had a brand like that, we might make a lot more later than we give up now."

"But we'd be stuck with the old agreement in the short term," I said.

"Don't you think that's worth it for the long term?" Steve asked.

"I'm not certain," I said. "We'd be betting on ourselves, that's for sure, but the short-term price is very high."

"They've known about this from the very beginning of the negotiation," Steve added. "If this was such a problem, they should have told us long ago. We make these stories and characters. They're ours. How can we let anyone else take credit?"

Emotions were really running high over this. There was no spirit of compromise in the room.

"Our only move is to end the negotiation," I said. "We'd have to walk away. No going back."

"I don't want to force the decision," Steve said, "but I don't think we'll feel good about ourselves if we yield on this. We'll be miserable when we see Disney taking the brand credit all over again. We'll have our self-respect if we walk away, and I think we'll get better terms later anyway."

"I'm in too," John said. "We'll get through the next two films, and then we'll have all the flexibility we want."

"Me too," Ed said. "We've been through a lot to get here. We'll make it work."

Coming into this meeting, I had been on the fence on this issue. I knew this was one of our walk-away issues, but I needed to feel sure that we weren't allowing our pride to stand in the way. Principles were important, but we couldn't afford to be cavalier. After all, Pixar had exactly one film to its name. We had secured all the economic terms we had wanted from Disney, and we would be walking away merely because Disney, the only company in two generations of animated entertainment to become a household brand, didn't want to share the billing equally. I also wasn't sure Pixar's stockholders would care about the branding if Pixar quadrupled its share of film profits.

But there are moments when principle matters, and this was looking like one of them. There was no way we were going to feel great if we ceded to Disney on the branding issue. And at Pixar it was vital to feel really good about what we were doing. It went to the core of our culture. How could we make great films while seething over someone else taking too much credit? It wouldn't work.

"I'm on board," I said. "We have to live with our choices, not just profit from them."

We were unanimous. We had decided to walk away.

I felt really proud of our decision. Steve was on his soapbox, defending Pixar's rights, willing to stake it all on what he thought was right. John, Ed, and I were right behind him. If Pixar was going to take a fall on this, we were going to do it together.

I called Rob Moore and told him the deal was off. I don't think he was altogether surprised. He and I had discussed the branding provision extensively. He knew how important it was to us. Rob took this kind of outcome in his stride. Some deals made it. Some didn't. I was quite sure he would quickly move on to another Disney matter.

For me, though, there was a bigger letdown. After the call with Rob, I felt deflated. It was really over. As I did sometimes when I needed a break, I took a walk around Point Richmond. There was a quiet park not too far from Pixar's office, with great views of San Francisco Bay. I well understood the risks of trying to craft a deal as complicated as this one. I'd been doing it my entire career. I agreed with Steve that we would still have our chance, after we finished the next two pictures. But this put even more pressure on those pictures being hits. And we were walking away from what would have been a sweet deal for Pixar. Very sweet. We had gotten so close.

Now we had to wrap our heads around a future that looked less and less likely to include Disney. Once again, we were rolling the dice.

21

THE LAST 20 PERCENT

FOLLOWING THE BREAKOFF OF THE DISNEY NEGOTIATION, John and Ed were quickly engulfed in the creative and production challenges posed by *A Bug's Life* and *Toy Story 2* while, back in Palo Alto, Steve spent a quiet Christmas holiday with his family. I returned to the task of building Pixar's infrastructure. My team was responsible for meeting Pixar's growing computer, facility, and human resource needs, as well as all the financial planning aspects of expanding the studio. The computing needs alone were staggering. As the technical sophistication of the films increased, so did the computing power required to generate the images. Fortunately, we had hired Greg Brandeau, a brilliant computer systems expert, to head up that effort.

As we were wrestling with the challenges of growing the studio, it came as more than a little surprise when, a couple of weeks into 1997, while I was sitting in my office, Steve called to share some news.

"Eisner called," Steve said. "He wants to resume talks."

"What?" I exclaimed incredulously. "You're kidding!"

"He has an idea to break the logjam," Steve went on. "I said I was open to talking, but I didn't want to waste time. We aren't going to change our position. He asked for a day or two and he would be back to me."

"We've heard that before," I said a little skeptically. "He did reach out, though. Unusual for him."

We waited patiently, wondering what Eisner had in mind. Two days later, he called Steve again.

"He wants to finish the deal," Steve reported. "As soon as possible. He'll give us equal branding."

"Wow," I said, almost in disbelief. "That's a big, big turnaround. What was his idea to move things forward?"

I was quite sure there would be a price to pay if Eisner was willing to give us the branding.

"He wants rights to buy stock in Pixar," Steve went on. "He feels that if Disney is going to help build Pixar's brand, it ought to have the right to benefit from it. By owning a piece of Pixar, he can justify yielding on the branding."

"This is fantastic!" I said immediately.

It was brilliant. Eisner did care about animation. He did care about Pixar, enough to want to buy a piece of the company. This was huge.

"Did he say anything else about the investment in Pixar?" I asked.

Steve explained that Eisner hadn't spelled out any details. He had said Disney didn't need to own a large percentage of Pixar. He didn't want to compromise our independence, just participate in the company's success. Again, this was perfect. But Steve was cagey.

"We need to think about this," he said. "We don't want to open a back door for Disney to control Pixar through owning our stock or a board seat or something."

"We can structure a deal to protect us from that," I said. "Larry Sonsini will know how to do it. Eisner didn't say he was looking for control or a board seat. I'd take him at face value."

Steve said we could explore it. If our lawyers could guarantee a way for Disney to invest passively, we would consider it. I jumped on it immediately. I called Larry, who said he would make sure all of Steve's concerns were alleviated.

Larry and his team structured the investment to address our concerns, and Eisner remained true to his word. The door was open to accomplish everything we wanted, now, before our next film, years before I thought it would be possible. We mustered all our resources, and in early February I all but moved to LA to work in Disney's offices where Rob Moore and our respective teams would finalize the details of the deal.

In contract negotiations, as in many other endeavors, the last 20 percent can take 80 percent of the effort. It is in the last 20 percent that the precise details are spelled out. One challenge is the inordinate amount of time spent on drafting contingencies that will likely never occur. For example, if an earthquake strikes Point Richmond and delays Pixar's completion of a film, should Pixar be in breach of contract for delivering a film late? To what degree should Pixar be expected to protect against the risk of an earthquake? It's actually not an unreasonable question, especially when making a film on the edge of the infamous San Andreas Fault.

Or, if Disney and Pixar share the costs for buying computers to make films under the agreement, can Pixar use those computers for other, non-Disney projects? If so, should it reimburse Disney for that usage? Because it is possible to conjure up a virtually endless list of risks and contingencies, one of the marks of a good negotiator is knowing where to draw the line so that things can move forward. In negotiation, there is a constant tension between momentum and fear. It comes down to an exercise in risk management.

One illustration of this idea came early in the draft agreement in a clause called "Treatments." This provision said, simply, that for each picture under the new agreement Pixar would submit to Disney one or more film ideas in the form of a treatment. But what would constitute a treatment? Could it be one line on an index card: "A father goes on an adventure to find his son; oh, and they're both fish"? That probably wouldn't make the cut. So the agreement spells out the details: a written treatment less than three pages that can be the basis for a screenplay.

But Pixar often presented its treatments orally, using sketches and short storyboards. What if that was the preferred method? The agreement needed to cover that possibility too. And Disney wanted to make sure that the treatments were for original stories, not sequels or prequels, so all that had to be defined.

Once Pixar delivered a treatment to Disney, what happens next? Can Disney take as much time as it wants to respond? Three months (too long for Pixar); two weeks (too short for Disney)? What if Disney doesn't respond at all? It's off doing better things; it's bored with Pixar films; the treatment slips to the bottom of someone's inbox. That's a hard one. Can Pixar just go ahead and do whatever it wants? After all, Disney had its chance to review the treatments. It's not Pixar's fault if Disney doesn't respond. Then again, if Disney fails to respond and Pixar does proceed without Disney's blessing, is it reasonable to demand that Disney will put its full brand and distribution muscle behind a film it never approved?

Most of these contingencies would, of course, never happen. In the real world, the most likely scenario was that Pixar's story team would have a collaborative working relationship with Disney and they would review and work out the proposed film treatments in a harmonious way, without once resorting to the contract. Most disputes in life don't depend on a contract for resolution. But once you commit things to a written contract, it needs to cover the risks in a reasonable way so that if things do go wrong, you know where you stand.

The clauses covering treatments were just one provision. Multiply this by a hundred and you have the scope of complexity in this negotiation: What were Disney's rights to oversee production at Pixar? How much access would Disney have to Pixar's technology? Would Pixar have a say in the marketing of the films? How would film production budgets be set? What about approvals for budget increases? What were Disney's rights to use characters from Pixar's films in its theme parks? How about its new line of cruise ships? Should Pixar be paid for that?

One clause dealt with a category of products called "derivative works." These are new products based on the original movie, like sequels, prequels, TV shows, video games, ice shows, Broadway musicals, and theme park rides. Would Pixar have a right to produce those itself? If so, how would the costs and profits be shared, and what

were Disney's obligations to distribute them? If Pixar did not produce the derivative works and Disney did, should Pixar be paid? How
much?

As complex as all these provisions were, they paled in comparison
to the provisions that spelled out how film profits would be calculated and shared. Those, literally, required a degree in accounting to
understand.

It fell to Rob Moore and me to wrestle each one of these provisions to the ground, and for our team of lawyers to draft and negotiate the contract language that would spell them out. Moore and I
were like two sparring partners, back and forth, and back and forth
again as we crafted solutions to every detail of Pixar's future relationship with Disney. We quickly fell into a working relationship that often felt like we were on the same team, working to address a seemingly endless list of challenges. We presented solutions to Steve and
Eisner, and if they didn't like them, we went at it some more. Piece by
piece the agreement finally came together. By the time we were finished, the four central issues that had been put on the table way back
with Steve's first call to Eisner were resolved.

On the matter of creative control, the agreement said that in any
picture directed by John Lasseter, Pixar would have final creative control; in any picture directed by someone who had previously directed
or co-directed an animated feature film that did better than $100 mil-
lion in the US box office, Pixar would have final creative control; and
in any other circumstances, Pixar and Disney would have joint final
creative control. This meant that even first-time directors, like Andrew Stanton or Pete Docter, could have creative control if they had
previously directed a successful film with John Lasseter, which is exactly what was happening with Andrew on *A Bug's Life*.

On the matter of release windows, Disney agreed to release Pixar's
films in the optimal summer or holiday period release times and to
give those films enough time to succeed. They agreed, in essence, to
treat Pixar's films like their own.

With respect to dividing the profits on the films, we agreed on a true 50/50 split. After paying Disney a standard fee for use of its film distribution network, and after recovering the marketing costs for the film, profits were to be divided equally between Disney and Pixar. The agreement included detailed provisions for calculating profits; to our knowledge, that was the first time these provisions had ever been written in this way.

Finally, with respect to branding, the agreement included provisions that I was also quite certain had never been done before. It stated that the Pixar brand would be established as a coequal brand in connection with the films, and that the Pixar logo would be used in a manner that was "perceptually equal" to the Disney logo. Even if the style of each logo was different, or one logo was in capital letters and the other used lower case, they still had to *appear* to be the same size. This also meant that from this point on, Pixar's films would be marketed under the banner "Disney • Pixar," not "Walt Disney Pictures presents . . ." In short, Pixar would share the brand on everything associated with our films equally with Disney. Never again would we be seen as inferior to Disney for the work that we did.

"Pixar's gonna be a brand," Steve said to me after we had finalized the terms of this provision. "Everyone will know we made these films."

"That's right," I said. "All the way down to the Buzz Lightyear action figures and T-shirts. We did it."

On February 24, 1997, Rob Moore and I sat in a conference room at Walt Disney's headquarters in Burbank. Before us were final copies of the new Co-Production Agreement between the Walt Disney Company and Pixar Animation Studios. Each of us took a pen, and Moore on behalf of Disney and I on behalf of Pixar signed the agreement. It was done. We had completed the final two pillars of Pixar's business plan—a 50 percent share of profits on our films and Pixar's brand recognized the world over.

Of all the deals I had ever completed, I don't think I ever felt more elated.

The next day the *New York Times* reported:

*The Walt Disney Company announced an unusual 10-year part-
nership yesterday with Pixar Animation Studios to jointly make five
films in a deal that reflects the value Hollywood increasingly places
on the lucrative field of animated movies.*

*Disney and the fledgling studio will equally share the costs, profits
and logo credit on the five films. The studios will essentially be sharing a brand, as the movies will be called Disney-Pixar productions.*[8]

Yes, indeed, the press had picked up on the part of the deal for
which we had been willing to risk it all: the vaunted Disney had
agreed to share top billing with Pixar.

For a long time afterward, whenever Steve and I passed a Disney
store we would run in to examine the Buzz and Woody dolls and
other merchandise from Pixar films. We would look at the tags so we
could see the Disney • Pixar logos equally displayed on the back.

I am quite certain there were no others in the store who were smiling so gleefully at the tiny logos on the back side of the labels.

— —

8. Steve Lohr, "Disney in 10-Year, 5-Film Deal with Pixar," *New York Times*, February 25,
1997, http://www.nytimes.com/1997/02/25/business/disney-in-10-year-5-film-deal-with-
pixar.html.

22

A LITTLE CREDIT

PIXAR'S IPO, THE DISNEY RENEGOTIATION, OUR DECISIONS over creative control, building the studio, and many other mission-critical initiatives had filled our plates during my first two years at Pixar. Not every issue that came along served some major strategic initiative, however. One small matter in particular had caught my attention and ignited my fervor.

It arose in early 1998, as Pixar approached the release of *A Bug's Life,* and it involved the issue of film credits. I waded into this topic naively, and I am not sure I would have pursued it so fiercely had I not already felt some injustice over an earlier incident about sharing credit.

That injustice had its origins in a magazine article about Pixar that appeared in September 1995, the groundwork for which Steve had been laying for some time. Earlier that summer, Steve began to covet the media outlets that might let him tell the Pixar story, cleverly intermingled with his own. In this domain Steve was a master, displaying a level of strategy and patience akin to a leopard stalking its prey. He would settle for no less than a big kill, a feature story in a major magazine. He would even pass on lesser stories in order to hold out for the big one. Steve tested his relationships with reporters at *Time, Newsweek,* and other outlets to see who might be interested. Ultimately, it was Brent Schlender at *Fortune*'s Silicon Valley office who showed the most interest.

Steve invited Schlender to Pixar, where he took the grand tour and spent time with each of the key players. He also spent a good amount of time with Steve. In its September 18, 1995, issue, *Fortune* delivered exactly what Steve had wanted—a huge feature story, the first to usher in Steve's comeback and Pixar's new strategy. The cover of the magazine said "Steve Jobs' Disney Deal." The first two-page spread of the story was, on the left side, a full-page, giant-size close-up of Steve's face, and on the right side a giant headline that read:

STEVE JOBS' AMAZING MOVIE ADVENTURE

The heading on the first page of the story said:

DISNEY IS BETTING ON COMPUTERDOM'S EX-BOY WONDER TO DELIVER THIS YEAR'S ANIMATED CHRISTMAS BLOCKBUSTER. CAN HE DO FOR HOLLYWOOD WHAT HE DID FOR SILICON VALLEY?

The piece set up Steve's comeback and positioned Pixar with pitch-perfect precision. In describing what *Toy Story* meant for Steve, Brent Schlender wrote:

> *The release of* Toy Story *marks the beginning of a new chapter in the storied career of Steve Jobs. If the movie's a hit, he'll rub shoulders with the kingpins of the brave new world of digital entertainment—moguls like Eisner and Steven Spielberg and megastars like Hanks and Allen. Jobs may in fact have found, at last, his natural element—a business in which fantasy and technology actually enhance each other. With Pixar and* Toy Story, *the "reality" Jobs creates just might, for once, exceed his own rhapsodic rhetoric.*[9]

It was a fantastic story for Steve, and for Pixar, well reported by Schlender. Around Pixar, though, the reaction was muted. Certainly it was the most exciting piece written on Pixar in years, the first to

— —

9. Brent Schlender, "Steve Jobs' Amazing Movie Adventure," *Fortune*, September 18, 1995, http://archive.fortune.com/magazines/fortune/fortune_archive/1995/09/18/206099/index.htm.

describe Pixar's new image as an entertainment company and to introduce the world to its filmmaking prowess. But something felt off. I had been around companies when they received great press. The usual measure of high fives and celebration was curiously absent here. The reactions at Pixar were more like polite, politically correct gestures of approval than a joyous celebration over a media coup.

Given Pixar's historic anxiety about Steve, it was easy to see why the article had been received with mixed reactions within the company. The story focused too much on him. It sounded like *he* had architected Pixar's film strategy and direction almost on his own. It is not until the fifth paragraph of the article that Pixar is mentioned, and then it refers to *Toy Story* as "Jobs' new movie." Certainly Steve deserved a lot of credit for sticking with Pixar through all the lean years, but even though the article went on to describe Pixar in some detail, including several great photos taken within Pixar, it still made Steve front and center stage in a story in which he had spent much of the time on the sidelines.

Although I found Steve to be quite a private person, when it came to the public eye, he didn't like to share the spotlight. His ability to weave stories around big ideas was legendary, and he applied them with equal force to his own story. Working for Steve meant working in the shadows; he wasn't terribly generous when it came to publicly sharing credit. I was okay with that. I minded more, however, when I thought the entire company had been overshadowed somewhat. This is perhaps why, when I did have a chance to shine a small spotlight on the work of others, I became more than a little passionate about it.

My opportunity arose over the seemingly innocuous issue of film credits for *A Bug's Life*. These are the names of the production crew that scroll quickly across the screen at the end of a movie, the part where the audience is grabbing their jackets and leaving the theater. Those at Pixar who were assigned to a particular film would automatically be included in the film credits. But what about those individuals at Pixar who were not assigned to a particular film but worked across all Pixar films?

Most of those people worked for me, in finance, human resources, facilities, purchasing, and other administrative and support functions. These dedicated contributors worked night and day on Pixar's films—they certainly were not working on anything else—but because they were not assigned to a particular film, their names would never be included in the closing credits on screen. Everyone else at Pixar, for those few brief moments while the credits scrolled down the screen, would see their names in the spotlight. Even if no one but their own families sat there and watched the credits, at least for them it would be a shining moment, a source of personal and family pride with a lasting glow. I felt my team was entitled to that same experience.

That team included Sarah Staff, my right-hand person who managed Pixar's financial and accounting systems and played a central role in our IPO; Greg Brandeau, the brilliant information technology manager in charge of Pixar's exceedingly complicated computing needs; Tom Carlisle, our tireless facilities manager who took care of our growing workspace needs with boundless enthusiasm and skill; Rachel Hannah, who built from scratch the hiring processes we needed to grow the company; Milan Parikh, manager of Pixar's budgets who had followed me from my last company and worked with tireless poise as we developed Pixar's business plan; Lisa Ellis, who had been at Pixar long before I joined and managed our health benefits; Mary DeCola and Kathi Cozzetta in accounting; Bryn Richardson in investor relations; Katherine Singson, Katherine Sarafian, and Jonas Rivera in marketing and creative resources; Robert Taylor in film accounting; Marty Eshoff in budgeting; DJ Jennings in purchasing, who would do anything to make sure Pixar's vendors delivered on time and on budget; and my amazing assistant, Diane Phillips. All told there were forty-two individuals on the list.[10]

In the celebrity world, these individuals, like me, may have had lit-

---

10. The complete list is available at http://www.imdb.com/title/tt0120623/ fullcredits?ref_=tt_cl_sm#cast.

tle notoriety, but in my world they were stars. They went to incredible lengths to help Pixar succeed. Many worried not just about their own area of responsibility but about the company in general. For them, Pixar was personal. They were Pixar's unsung heroes, the supporting army whose names would never appear in the spotlight but whose efforts were every bit as important as anyone else's.

"They should all get a credit," I said to Steve one day. "It costs us nothing to add the names of all those in Pixar's administration at the end of the film credits. It will mean an extra few seconds of screen time, that's all. How about it?"

"Maybe Darla is the person to talk to about it?" Steve suggested.

That wasn't a yes or a no, but it was an opening. I took it.

Darla Anderson was the co-producer of *A Bug's Life*, along with Kevin Reher. She had run Pixar's commercials group and this was her first feature film. I had pushed hard for her to get the position. She was happy to check with Disney on the credit question.

Darla got back to me a couple of weeks later.

"Sorry," she said. "It's a no-go on the credit idea. Disney is very particular about film credits. They've never done this on their own films. They won't do it on ours."

The request had been blown off in one brief instant by Disney. That didn't seem fair. I had to figure out why they were being so difficult about this.

I learned that film credits had evolved to become somewhat of a resumé for those who had them. They were not handed out lightly. Moreover, Disney had evolved an in-house style where it did not give its administrative employees film credits, so they did not want to break that tradition for Pixar. I remained unmoved, though. These were *our* films. We had just negotiated a contract that made that clear. Pixar had creative control. This should be *our* decision. I went back to Steve about it.

"I don't want to take no for an answer on this one," I said. "It's an opportunity for us to do something really meaningful for Pixar's employees, at no cost to anyone."

"If you can get the support of John and Ed," Steve replied, "we'll press Disney on it."

John and Ed were both members of the Academy of Motion Pictures and understood the politics of film credits very well. I arranged a meeting with them to discuss it.

"The problem," John explained, "is that Hollywood takes film credits very seriously. They don't want to dilute what credits stand for by adding names that are not strictly speaking on the film crew. For them, it's a matter of precedent."

"But animation is different," I asserted. "We don't have film crews that disperse when production ends. Our staff is working day and night, the same as the production crews. We're all in the same building, working alongside each other for the same purpose."

We discussed it some more, but we didn't resolve the issue. Ed suggested we take some more time to think about it.

A couple of days later, Ed and I revisited the topic. I reiterated that this was just about fairness. It was arbitrary to cut out so many people who were all working toward the same goal. We brainstormed ways we could address it without upsetting the status quo.

"How about if we come up with a different kind of credit," Ed mused. "Something at the end that is distinct from the regular credits."

"That would be fantastic." I said. "That's all we're trying to do. I don't mind if it's not the same as the other credits. I just want to see the names up there on the screen."

Finally, a breakthrough.

Following that meeting, Ed, John, and I, working with the producers of *A Bug's Life*, developed the idea of a "thanks to" credit that would be below and distinct from the normal credits. Steve went along with it and took the idea to Disney.

A couple of weeks later the answer came back.

"They're okay with it," Steve said, "with one exception."

"What's that?" I asked.

"No credits for Pixar's executives. They won't break that precedent."

I understood immediately what that meant. Steve and Ed had already received a more than well-deserved executive producer credit on *Toy Story*. As executives, none of us would be included in this new credit for *A Bug's Life*, however. This would leave me as the only member of Pixar's senior executive team who would never see his name on screen. Everyone who worked for me would.

I had to admit this stung a little. It would have been nice to see my name up there, even once, if only for my family. It wasn't to be, though. But no matter. I had accomplished what I wanted. My next move was now crystal-clear.

"That's great," I said to Steve. "We got it done. Thank you for taking this up with Disney."

The new credits were added to *A Bug's Life* for the first time. At the end of all the normal credits, just when it seemed they were all over, emerging from the bottom of the screen came these words:

THANKS TO EVERYONE AT PIXAR WHO
SUPPORTED THIS PRODUCTION

and then the names of all of Pixar's finance, marketing, and administrative personnel appeared. Of all my moments at Pixar, seeing this for the first time stood out as among the most gratifying. It meant even more when it became an ongoing tradition for all of Pixar's films.

To this day my family knows that when we watch a Pixar film, they have to sit all the way to the very end of the credits when I will excitedly watch for the list of supporting personnel to hit the screen. I choke up every time I see it. I don't know many of those individuals personally anymore, but I do know how hard they work, how important they were to the film, and how deserving they are, for one fleeting moment, to see their names in lights.

23

FLICKERS

THE SIGNING OF THE NEW AGREEMENT WITH DISNEY WAS not the only event of import to occur in February 1997. Apple Computer bought NeXT, an enormous coup for Steve. It was hard not to miss the irony of Apple purchasing the company Steve had started in defiant rebellion against Apple. I could not see the whole picture at that moment, but the signing of the Disney deal and the sale of NeXT to Apple triggered a chain of events that would mark a change in my journey with Steve. An ever-so-gentle pull was now beginning to take us in different directions. It would take time to see where that direction would bring me. For Steve, the change came sooner.

Steve was thrilled about selling NeXT to Apple. NeXT had launched its first computer in 1988 but had failed to compete in the burgeoning market for workstation computers. In 1993 it had shut down its hardware business to focus on selling its operating system and development software. In selling the company to Apple, Steve had found a face-saving parking place for NeXT, and a chance to keep its advanced software technologies alive. It was no wonder he was excited about it.

"NeXT's software will be the core of a new-generation operating system for Apple," he told me after the sale. "They really need it."

As Steve's responsibilities at NeXT began to wind down, I wondered if his day-to-day involvement at Pixar might increase from the weekly visits that were now his custom. But nothing changed. Pixar was steadily working on *A Bug's Life* and *Toy Story 2* and putting the expansion plan into place. Steve seemed happy with the way things were working at Pixar and he showed no inclination to change it.

During this time, my own relationship with Steve evolved. It was freer from the pressures of the past two years. We had accomplished in two and a half years what we thought might take ten. With the IPO and the Disney deal behind us, Steve was more relaxed. He would often stroll over to my home on the weekend and we'd go for a walk or sit in the backyard and talk. Our conversations meandered from Pixar to world affairs to our children and personal lives.

One time I was in the midst of a medical emergency. Someone in our immediate family had developed a potentially very serious medical problem. Steve called one evening when we were deciding what to do. Hillary answered, and when Steve asked how she was, she just broke down and cried. After she explained the problem, Steve immediately said, "I'll find you the best doctor in the world and bring them here if you need it."

It turned out that the best doctor was in San Francisco, an hour away by car. We were very fortunate that the issue was ultimately resolved. Hillary never forgot Steve's offer, however, and always appreciated him for it.

In several of our talks around this time, especially after the sale of NeXT, Steve mused about Apple. He felt Apple had long ago lost its way, that it was more adrift than ever, rapidly becoming a shadow of its former self. He blamed a string of CEOs who he thought had no idea how to restore Apple's greatness. Steve felt that buying NeXT would help Apple but wouldn't be nearly enough.

Slowly I began to realize that Steve's musings were in fact the visible flickers of an internal raging fire. Steve's designs on Apple's future were far more than theoretical. I confirmed this one Saturday in early summer 1997 when we met in Palo Alto.

"I'm thinking about going back to Apple," Steve said. "Apple's board is asking if I'm interested."

"Wow!" I said. "That's huge. How do you feel about it? They've been adrift for a long time and need a ton of help. Are you sure you want to take that on?"

"I'm not certain," said Steve, "but I could try. I wouldn't even take a salary. I'd have a chance to share my ideas and to assess what needs to be done."

As soon as Steve said this I realized he had made his decision. Steve wasn't sure Apple could be saved. And the last thing he wanted was to return to Apple and then be held responsible if he failed to rescue the faltering company. Not taking a salary was a way of saying, "You're not paying me so don't blame me if the company sinks." If he did turn it around, there would be ample opportunity for reward later. It was a no-lose scenario.

But he was looking for something else from me.

"Look, if you decide to do it, don't worry about Pixar," I said. "It's under control. Now that the Disney deal is behind us, we know what to do. And it's not like you're going away. We'll be in touch like we always have, even if you can't come up to Point Richmond as much as before."

What I surmised Steve had wanted in this conversation was to make certain we wouldn't think he was abandoning Pixar. In a way, he wanted Pixar's tacit permission and blessing to go back to Apple. I knew he would have the same conversation with Ed and John. I also knew they would support him completely. This was because, among all the changes that had occurred during the past few years, there was one more that gave him a level of confidence that I was certain mattered a lot. After a rocky relationship with Pixar that had lasted the better part of ten years, Steve had gained something that was sorely missing when I joined the company: *respect.*

This became abundantly clear to me one day at Pixar when the executives were invited to a screening of one of the films under development. As was our habit, we all gathered in the screening room where we watched the most current reels of the film. At the end of the screening, John turned to Steve and said, "Steve, what did you think?"

"Looked good to me," said Steve. "Though it doesn't really matter what I think."

"It does matter," John insisted.

"No. You guys decide," Steve said. "I trust you."

"But we *want* to know what you think," John said emphatically.

It was a small moment, one that I doubt registered with anyone. For me it signaled something that I had never seen before at Pixar. The creative team, the team to whom we had long ago ceded all creative responsibility, *cared* about what Steve thought. In the world of Pixar, there was no greater accolade. It implied the highest level of respect. In fact, throughout Pixar there were no lingering traces of animosity toward Steve. He had come through for the company and was now seen not as feared owner but as trusted protector. We never discussed the subject, but subconsciously I feel certain it mattered to him a lot.

In fact, looking back, I believe that this and other experiences Steve had at Pixar brought about changes in him that were vital for what was about to occur.

One such change was that Steve now understood the entertainment industry. He was no longer just a high-tech CEO but also an entertainment industry CEO. Very few executives could lay claim to being comfortable in both worlds, a qualification that would become essential as Steve steered Apple through the complex thickets of music and entertainment.

I also feel the process through which Steve and I deliberated Pixar's business and strategic challenges had an impact on him. His commercial failures at Apple, NeXT, and the early years at Pixar had occurred in large measure because he had ignored business realities. The Lisa, the original Macintosh, the NeXT Computer, and the Pixar Image Computer had all missed the mark because they were overpriced or ignored important market considerations. At Pixar, melding business realities with creative priorities was always integral to our collaboration.

Finally, of course, Steve had now regained the mantle of success. He had joined the ranks of billionaires. Nothing that happened at

Apple would take that away from him. Even if Apple flamed out, his comeback would still be intact.

When you added it up, there were many aspects of Pixar that had a big influence on Steve: becoming a billionaire, experiencing a stellar comeback in the eyes of the public, learning the ins and outs of the entertainment industry, enjoying a transformed relationship with Pixar, and bringing both business and creative imperatives into harmony. Combined with Steve's aesthetic genius and product vision, these influences made for a very potent force as he jumped into the vortex at Apple. Indeed, Pixar may have been an interlude in Steve's journey—one that remains the source of most of his wealth—but without Pixar one could make a case that the revolution ushered in by Steve's second act at Apple might never have occurred.

As Steve and I were wrapping up our discussion about his possible return to Apple, I was moved to share one more thought with him.

"I know you're itching to get back to Apple," I said, "but you're in a different place now than you were a couple of years ago. You have a chance to take care of other aspects of life too. Time for yourself, family, friends, developing in other ways. Don't forget about those."

Steve didn't respond to this. I meant it as a hint about aspects of his life I thought could use attention. When I joined Pixar, I was acutely aware of Steve's reputation for harsh behavior—he was legendary for it—although I had never experienced it in our personal relationship. From the moment we met, our collaboration was always constructive and respectful, even when we didn't see eye to eye. I could not recall an angry word between us. This did not mean I never witnessed Steve being ill mannered or dismissive of others. He could be unforgiving, with little tolerance for mistakes.

At Pixar, however, this type of occurrence was rare. It helped that we aired everything together and that, unlike at Apple and NeXT, Steve was not Pixar's product maker. He didn't make the films. For Pixar to really take off, he had to rely on others to a degree he had perhaps not done before. I now felt that same spirit of trust and collaboration we had enjoyed at Pixar might benefit Steve in other ways.

When Steve rejoined Apple in July of 1997, I couldn't help but feel a little empty. It spelled a change in the journey we had taken together these past few years. We had walked, talked, debated, plotted, laughed, shared, and worried our way to take Pixar where it needed to go. Steve was moving on to a new world now, one into which I was not going. My job was at Pixar: to see through the implementation of the new agreement with Disney, to keep a steady hand on the business direction, to work with Wall Street and our investors, to keep an eye out for Pixar's well-being.

Over the next ten years my relationship with Steve would continue to evolve in ways I could never have predicted. He was diagnosed with cancer in 2003 and underwent a series of treatments over the ensuing years. I spent much time as bedside companion while he fought the challenges of the disease and its treatments. I would visit him at home often, slipping inside to see if he was there. On many of those visits no words were spoken. We'd just watch an episode of one of his favorite TV shows.

On the best days, Steve would eagerly show me the products he was working on at Apple. I first listened on an iPod, talked on an iPhone, and played on an iPad in Steve's office at his home. He invited me to all of Apple's big product announcements where I sat quietly at the Moscone Convention Center in San Francisco as he mesmerized the world year after year. I even saw the stunning designs of a yacht that Steve dreamed about building. Steve's aesthetic genius extended far beyond the domain of technology.

But there were also parts of Steve's life he didn't share. Steve had a way of separating the different aspects of his life, he alone holding the keys to every compartment. If you were in one compartment, you had little access to the others. As Steve's celebrity status skyrocketed and he went on to meet leaders and celebrities from every corner of the world, I felt my own role in his life recede. But so long as his health was good enough, he would often meander over to my house to go for a walk or sit together. And I remained welcome to slip into the kitchen door of his house and walk to his room for a visit until the very end.

In times of illness and hardship, it is hard to know if one is saying the right thing, or is doing the right thing. There is no guidebook, no formula for getting it right. At the end of the day, perhaps, Steve was born more for action, less for being gentled by others, for taking stock, for being worn down by illness. I was often left wondering if there was more that I could do. It was impossible to know. During this time, Steve showed much gratitude for our friendship. I felt happy to know it. And I certainly felt the same way.

It is not for me to take the measure of a person. I feel sure, however, that my work with Steve at Pixar was important for both of us. I was very fortunate to work with Steve—he was a magnificent sparring partner. And I remain more grateful than I can express that back in late 1994, he picked up the phone to call me.

During the time of Steve's illness, while he was still at the helm of Apple, we were to have one more adventure, one more time when we had to navigate a new course. This would be our last time working together, and it would bring our Pixar journey to a fitting finale.

24

JUST KEEP SWIMMING

ON OCTOBER 21, 2005, IN A *USA TODAY* COLUMN CALLED "Managing Your Money," Matt Krantz wrote:

Pixar's stock had been a big star, too. The past five years, shares have gained 171% — that's 22% compound annual average growth. That truly is incredible, if you consider that the broad Standard & Poor's 500 stock index is down the past five years.

But the stock had trouble squeezing into its superhero tights in the second half of 2005.[11]

Pixar's stock had indeed been a star. Over the previous five years, the value of Pixar had crept up from $1.5 billion to $3 billion to almost $6 billion. With Steve still owning the vast majority of it, he had now gone from billionaire to multibillionaire. More importantly, the run-up in Pixar's stock reflected an unprecedented run in Pixar's films. The five original films under the new agreement with Disney had been *A Bug's Life, Monsters, Inc., Finding Nemo, The Incredibles,* and the soon-to-be-released *Cars. Toy Story 2* had ultimately been released as a theatrical animated feature film sequel but did not count toward the five original films required by the agreement. Collectively, these films had an average domestic box office exceeding $250 million. They also won a slew of awards.

— —

11. Matt Krantz, "Pixar Could Be an Incredible Buy," *USA Today*, October 21, 2005, http://usatoday30.usatoday.com/money/perfi/columnist/krantz/2005-10-17-pixar_x.htm.

A Bug's Life won a Grammy for Best Instrumental Composition. *Toy Story 2* won a Golden Globe for Best Picture—Musical or Comedy, and a Grammy for best song written for a motion picture. *Monsters, Inc.* received four Academy Award nominations and won an Academy Award and a Grammy for best original song. *Finding Nemo* won an Academy Award for Best Animated Feature Film. *The Incredibles* was nominated for four Academy Awards and won two of them, for Best Animated Feature Film and Best Sound Editing. Ten years earlier, had I told Wall Street that Pixar's films would perform this way, both in terms of box office performance and in accolades, I am quite sure I would have been laughed out of town.

I had left my day-to-day role as Pixar's CFO in April 1999. I took a sabbatical to pursue a series of personal interests that eventually led me in some new directions. At that time Steve asked me to join Pixar's board of directors. As a director, it was my job to look out for Pixar strategically, similarly to the way I had always done. Consistent with the *USA Today* column, and despite Pixar's unprecedented success, in 2005 I found myself once again worrying.

The laws of physics suggest we cannot go in one direction forever. Sooner or later, something will slow us down. Whether it be stocks, housing prices, economies, or entire civilizations, even the biggest booms stall. We build castles, churches, and monuments believing they will last forever; our perception of solidity often belies an underlying movement that is difficult to perceive. Sometimes we can see the wave of change coming. But more often we are swept along in it. In my mind, Pixar was facing such a wave.

When a company's stock price goes up and up on the strength of its business growth, the first sign that its rate of growth is slowing can create enormous downward pressure on its stock price. Pixar's last two films, *The Incredibles,* released at the end of 2004, and *Finding Nemo,* released in the summer of 2003, had been Pixar's biggest films to date. *Finding Nemo* had taken in almost $1 billion worldwide. These films had enjoyed heights of success so dizzying that I feared the slightest hint of a slowdown would send Pixar's stock tumbling.

As the *USA Today* article had described, this had already happened on the news that DVD sales might be slowing down. The stock had recovered, but the evidence was strong that it was in rarefied air, made even thinner by Pixar's continued dependence on blockbusters. One small slip and the danger of a big fall was high. This would hurt not just Pixar's stockholders but the company as a whole. Shareholder cries for change can create enormous pressure on a corporation. It was better to be on top of it.

The solution was to find a way to diminish the risk that a small disappointment might cause the stock to plummet. There were two ways to do this. One was to use Pixar's highly valued stock to purchase other companies. The effect of purchasing other companies would be to diversify from animation so that if animation experienced a downturn, it would not have as devastating an impact on the company. Diversification had been Walt Disney's strategy all those many years earlier.

The other way to diminish the risk was to seek a buyer for Pixar. If a large corporate conglomerate were to buy Pixar, Pixar's stockholders would exchange their Pixar stock at its present soaring value for the stock of the larger corporation where they would enjoy much greater diversification. Over the years, Steve and I had speculated occasionally on how Pixar might ultimately end up being purchased by Disney, but we had never taken this on as a serious possibility.

But by October 2005, I was convinced that Pixar had to at least explore one of these two directions. The financial pressures to produce blockbuster after blockbuster were enormous, and it would not take much to burst Pixar's balloon. On one of our weekend walks, I broached the issue with Steve.

"I'd like to talk about Pixar's stock price," I said.

"What's on your mind?" Steve asked.

"I think Pixar's at a crossroads," I said. "Its valuation is too high to stay still. If we have any miss, any miss at all, even a small one, Pixar's value could be cut in half overnight, and half of your wealth will go with it." I paused, and then added, "We're flying too close to the sun."

"We've had an incredible run," I went on. "Ten years of block-busters. But I think it's time that either Pixar uses its sky-high valuation to diversify into other businesses, just like Disney did, or . . ."

"Or we sell to Disney," Steve finished my sentence.

"Yes, or we sell to Disney, or anyone else that offers the same opportunity for diversifying and protecting Pixar as Disney does."

We discussed the first of these options, Pixar diversifying into other businesses.

"To diversify would require expanding Pixar's management team," I said. "Pixar's current management team is tuned for animation. It doesn't have the bandwidth or the experience to investigate and acquire other businesses. We would need executives who know how to do that, and as CEO you would have to find them. Between your Apple responsibilities and your health, I'm not sure it's feasible."

Steve clearly did not have the bandwidth for this option. Although there was plenty of reason for hope with his health, he needed to take care of himself. He was still fully immersed at Apple; there was no way he could take on anything else. The combined effect of Steve's health and the animation focus of Pixar's management team led us to option two: finding a buyer for Pixar, the most obvious one being Disney.

"Let me give it some thought," he said. "I hear what you're saying. Maybe we should talk to Larry."

I agreed. Larry Sonsini was still on Pixar's board of directors. He would help evaluate what to do. Steve and I paid a visit to Larry a few days later in his Palo Alto office. He liked the idea a lot. He agreed that Pixar's value as a company had reached stratospheric heights that would be hard to sustain. He suggested a meeting with Disney to test the waters.

One never knows if an event that appears detrimental is in fact part of a larger pattern that we cannot see. A year and a half earlier, in early 2004, as the co-production agreement that I negotiated long ago with Rob Moore was coming to an end, Steve called off talks with Disney to extend the agreement. The *New York Times* reported, "The residue of several years of testy relations, and Mr. Jobs's distaste for the way Mr. Eisner conducted business with Pixar, may have amplified the typical problems of partnerships into irreconcilable differences."[12]

Eisner responded by saying that the terms Pixar demanded were simply more than Disney could bear. Ten years of unprecedented success had, perhaps surprisingly, done very little to bring Steve and Eisner close enough to find a way to continue the relationship between Pixar and Disney.

Even more, Eisner's failure to find a way to extend Disney's agreement with Pixar added dramatically to mounting pressures on him. Roy Disney, nephew of Walt Disney, resigned from Disney's board of directors in 2003 and had been waging a "Save Disney" campaign that criticized Eisner's management style and leadership and called for his resignation. Breaking off the Pixar relationship added much fuel to the fire.

Roy Disney was insistent that without being a leader in animation, Disney would lose its creative soul. Eisner had been unable to withstand the pressure, and on September 9, 2004, he announced he would step down when his contract ended in two years. A few months later, in March 2005, Eisner's successor was announced: Bob Iger, who joined Disney as president of ABC Television after Disney acquired ABC in 1996. At the end of October 2005, Eisner abruptly resigned from Disney, both as CEO and as a board member, leaving Iger for the first time in complete control. This was the exact moment we began to contemplate the possibility of selling Pixar to Disney.

If there was any time to discuss an acquisition, or any other kind of relationship, this was it. The big question was: How important was animation to Iger? Disney had thriving businesses in television,

12. Laura Holson, "Pixar to Find Its Own Way as Disney Partnership Ends," *New York Times*, January 31, 2004, http://www.nytimes.com/2004/01/31/business/pixar-to-find-its-own-way-as-disney-partnership-ends.html?_r=0.

theme parks, and live-action motion pictures. Iger had risen through the ranks at ABC and was more steeped in the world of television than the world of animated feature films. It was not clear if he would see animation as a relic of Disney's past or an essential part of its future.

To find out the answer to this question, we arranged a meeting with Iger and Dick Cook, then chairman of Walt Disney Studios. Steve had already had some dealings with Iger over launching Disney content on Apple's soon-to-be-announced video iPod. Steve, Larry, Ed, and I attended on behalf of Pixar. We gathered in a conference room at Apple's offices in Cupertino, California.

From the moment the meeting began, the tune of Pixar's relationship with Disney changed. Gone were the second-guessing and posturing that had characterized Steve's relationship with Eisner. With Iger there were no games, no politics, no posturing. He was smart, straightforward, and up-front. It was the most positive meeting between the two companies at that level in a decade.

Steve took an immediate liking to Iger, which would blossom into a close collaboration and friendship. Moreover, Iger made it clear that animation was very important to him, and to Disney. He said it was the heart and soul of the company and bringing it back was central to his vision for Disney. Iger did not have to be so forthcoming with us about this. The more he claimed Disney needed animation, the more leverage Pixar might have. But that was his style. With Steve, it worked like magic.

"I like him a lot," Steve said after the meeting. "What do you guys think?"

"Iger gets Pixar," Larry said, "and he wants to use Pixar to redesign Disney. This is fantastic."

I agreed.

At that meeting we floated ideas of how the two companies might work together, ranging from a film distribution agreement as before, to a joint venture, to an outright acquisition by Disney. By the end of the session, all options remained on the table for discussion.

Afterward, it did not take long for the acquisition idea to gain momentum. From Pixar's side, it came down to two issues. First, as would be typical for any acquisition, was the matter of price. Customarily a buyer will pay a premium for acquiring full control of a company, and there was much room for negotiation on what that premium might be. The second issue was a matter that would be considered unusual for an acquisition, and it became the defining concern in this one. We wanted Disney to agree that Pixar's operations and culture would be fully allowed to continue to run the way they always had. We had worked incredibly hard to protect and preserve Pixar's way of doing things, going back all the way to the time when we decided that Pixar's executives would not intervene with its creative processes. This acquisition had to preserve everything we had worked for; there was no way that we would be willing to do it otherwise.

"Disney has to agree *not* to change Pixar," Steve said. "Ed and John have to be on board. They have to believe this is about preserving what we've created."

This, for us, was a deal breaker.

Iger came through immediately. He said that not only did he want to preserve Pixar's way of doing things, he wanted that way of doing things to infect the culture of Disney Animation so that Disney would become more like Pixar. This was a vision we could all get behind.

The next step was for Pixar's board of directors to assess Disney's business and assets to make sure that we could recommend to Pixar's shareholders that exchanging Pixar stock for Disney stock made good business sense. Along with our advisers and investment bankers, I spent some time at Disney learning about its businesses and financial status. What I discovered made me even more positive about the deal.

The strength of two of Disney's businesses, in particular, surprised me. These were Walt Disney World and ESPN. These were rock-solid businesses that looked to me as though they were positioned marvelously for years of solid growth. Financially, this made the transaction look even better, an almost perfect fit. Shareholders of Pixar would be exchanging their investment in a highly risky animation company for a diversified investment that included some of the highest-quality media assets in the world, including Disney World, ABC, and ESPN. Those assets would also include Pixar, of course. I returned with a strong recommendation that, financially, this made great sense.

On January 24, 2006, Disney announced it would acquire Pixar for $7.4 billion. Steve still owned just over 50 percent of Pixar, giving his Pixar stock a value of almost $4 billion. In an instant, he became Disney's largest shareholder. Both Steve and Iger emphasized that the takeover would not threaten Pixar's culture, and Iger was quoted in the *New York Times* saying, "It is important that the Pixar culture be protected and allowed to continue."[13] John Lasseter became chief creative officer of both Disney Animation and Pixar Animation, and principal creative adviser to Disney's theme parks. Ed Catmull became president of both studios.

In the ensuing years, the acquisition of Pixar by Disney proved to be one of the most successful corporate acquisitions of its time. Disney's businesses soared in valuation, almost quadrupling the value of Disney's stock a few years later. Former stockholders of Pixar enjoyed all the benefits of this run-up in valuation, all the while enjoying diversification into Disney's range of businesses. Steve was now Disney's largest stockholder, and the value of his stock in Disney would eventually soar to over $13 billion, making his investment in Pixar by far the largest source of his personal wealth.

Almost overnight, Pixar restored Disney's dominance in animation, producing a string of hits including *Cars, Ratatouille, Wall-E, Up, Toy Story 3, Brave,* and *Inside Out.* Ed and John successfully turned

— —

13. Laura M. Holson, "Disney Agrees to Acquire Pixar in a $7.4 Billion Deal," *New York Times,* January 25, 2006, http://www.nytimes.com/2006/01/25/business/25disney. html?_r=1&adxnnl=1&pagewanted=print&adxnnlx=1436213533-POeVD0lfG4QX8v8Uu/ wY6g&.

around Disney Animation which, in 2013, released *Frozen,* which became the highest-grossing animated feature film of all time. Further, Steve, whose health tragically continued to decline, was freed of the burdens of running Pixar. He found in Ed, John, and Iger trusted friends and partners with whom he could share his ideas and advice and enjoy the triumphs that ensued. By every single measure, the acquisition could not have been more successful.

Every single measure, perhaps, except one.

"You seem like you're down," Hillary asked, about a week after the acquisition was announced.

"I dunno," I said. "Maybe a little."

"How do you feel?"

This was hard for me to admit. Every morsel of the lawyer, CFO, strategist, and board member in me told me the sale of Pixar was the right move, the fitting move, the best possible endgame in this phase of Pixar's history. Of this I had no doubt. But it also spelled the end of the road for Pixar and me. As soon as Disney bought Pixar, Pixar's board of directors dissolved, and all my formal ties to Pixar would come to an end. My journey with Pixar was over.

Almost twelve years had passed since that first phone call from Steve. Twelve years in which I hardly remember a day when I didn't feel responsible for Pixar's well-being. Even after I left my day-to-day duties, while I was a board member barely a week or two went by without some discussion with Steve that related to Pixar. Worrying about Pixar had been a big part of my life.

"Maybe letting go of Pixar is harder than I thought," I said.

I wasn't sure exactly why, though. After all, it was a business; it was a chessboard; it was about making the right moves. I had moved on from other endeavors before. But something about this one was lingering. I felt the way I did when I saw my children off to school for the first time, or went to their graduations. Why was I feeling this way?

Maybe it was because, in many ways, to me Pixar had been like a child: sweet, innocent, playful, and full of wonder and potential.

It took a certain amount of vulnerability, humility, and delicacy for Pixar to work. Ed, Steve, John, and I had watched over that. We had poured ourselves into it, pushing each other, learning from each other, helping each other. We had tried all we could to nurture and protect all that made Pixar great.

I remembered those years in Point Richmond, California, where the oil refinery across the street was the most notable way of identifying Pixar's unremarkable offices, a humble home that belied the wizardry within. I loved how Pixar had revealed itself to its visitors in a series of surprises that would awe them in ways they would not soon forget.

I recalled the challenges over Pixar's stock option plan, and worrying whether our best people would stay and see Pixar through. I remembered how excited my family had been to attend *Toy Story*'s premiere, and how we'd all anxiously waited at home for the phone calls that would reveal the opening weekend box office results of Pixar's films.

I could see myself at the desks of Pixar's creative and technical wizards for the first time, awestruck at their work. I looked back almost comically at our first meanderings into the entertainment industry and how we had cobbled together our first film financial model. I recalled the way Steve and I had debated every permutation of every possibility that bore on Pixar's strategy and business.

I remembered the triumph of Pixar's IPO, and the obstacle course we navigated to make it happen, and I recollected the long, protracted negotiation with Disney that set Pixar on the course of making real profits and becoming a worldwide brand.

Yet now it was all behind me. Pixar was in new hands, safe hands, hands that would take care of it from here on out. No doubt other adventures awaited me, but I guess I was taking one last look back as this one disappeared from my view.

I could not help but think of the way Nemo's dad, Marlin, felt in that exquisite scene in *Finding Nemo* when he cannot muster any more strength to continue the search for his son. Marlin's newfound companion, Dory, in her endearing, quirky, innocent way, says to Marlin, "When life gets you down, you know what you gotta do," and then in her sweet, rapturous manner she begins to sing:

"Just keep swimming.
Just keep swimming.
Just keep swimming, swimming, swimming."

That was exactly what I needed to do.

PART IV

25

FINDING MY DELI

AFTER THE SALE OF PIXAR TO DISNEY, I BEGAN TO POUR myself into a venture that had its origins several years before the sale. That venture had started back in late 1999, when I began to wonder if I should move on from my day-to-day responsibilities at Pixar. It grew into a new direction in my life that was perhaps wholly unexpected, one that would eventually bring me to see Pixar in a whole new light.

As 1999 came to an end, the strategic plan we had put in place at Pixar was working, and I had hired an extraordinary team to implement the business and financial details. I had no intention of dropping Pixar from my sights; it meant too much to me for that. But I just wasn't sure if I needed to continue as its CFO.

I had always found much to enjoy in my work. As an attorney, I had prided myself on crafting complex deals and then artfully expressing them in written contracts. As an executive, I loved the creativity and finesse involved with developing and implementing a strategy, the thrill of negotiation, the opportunity to be part of a team aiming for great things.

Yet something was missing.

I saw the world of business and finance as a game of sorts. Although I could play that game, I felt the restrictions of corporate life. I understood it was, in the end, about products, profits, market share, and competition. These all matter a lot; I well knew that. I had made a career around all of them. I could see, however, that these priorities also generated challenges around identity and meaning. It is easy to lose ourselves in corporate imperatives, to feel we are beholden to forces that might not be aligned with our personal aspirations and priorities, or with how we wish to give expression to our lives.

I had worked for some brilliant leaders—Steve Jobs, Efi Arazi— and some wonderful clients when I was a lawyer. I couldn't have asked for more, but I was still working at their behest. Now, I was beginning to wonder what it might feel like to spread my own wings.

After the 1999 release of *Toy Story 2,* Pixar's third film, I found myself reflecting a lot about this. I often thought about a story from my own family, harking all the way back to 1974 when I was a four-teen-year-old living in London. One of my first jobs had been as a dishwasher, working in a tiny deli that was owned by my grand-mother. My task was to gather the dishes from the counters—there was no room for tables—and load them into the small dishwasher that blasted me with boiling steam every time I opened it. I made a few shillings for my efforts and was allowed to sit at the counter for my lunch, staring out the window, gazing at the steady stream of passersby going about their business.

It was the origins of that deli that really stuck with me. Born in London in 1914, my grandmother Rose was the oldest daughter of five siblings, child to Jewish immigrants from Russia. She was petite, with auburn hair, a beautiful face, and deep blue eyes. Rose's father, Sam, my great-grandfather, was a tailor. The family scraped together the best china and finest clothes that they could afford and put much stock in good manners and proper etiquette. Rose grew up to be a proper Englishwoman. Her home was spic and span, she was always immaculately dressed, and if you paid her a visit, it would not take more than a few minutes for her to be serving you tea and biscuits on the finest British china. Rose spent most of her adult life taking care of the home and raising her family.

In her mid-fifties, however, Rose grew restless. She and my grand-father Mick, who had retired from his business, were looking for a way to make some extra money. Nobody had an inkling that Rose was bristling to do something about it.

"We'll open a deli," she announced to my grandfather one day.

"You must be crazy," my grandfather said dismissively.

It turned out she was.

That deli, called City Fare, was a tiny sliver of a shop in London's financial district. Rose and Mick woke up at 4:00 a.m. every day to buy food from the market and to open in time to serve breakfast. Rose treated all her customers as if they were close friends visiting for tea. She remembered their favorite lunches and would have their food prepared and ready to go before they even reached the front of the line. It wasn't long before those lines stretched out the door.

What always stuck with me about City Fare was how much Rose loved it. At just the moment when most people would have said she was an old housewife ready to retire, she jumped into something new. In that deli, Rose shed the mantle of traditional homemaker and doting grandmother and became alive in an entirely different way. Her years working there were clearly among the best of her life.

Now, I wondered what my deli might be.

Oddly, perhaps, the fire that was burning within me was the desire to learn more about religion and philosophy, particularly the Eastern varieties. For much of my adult life, I was fascinated by ideas that address human experience and enhancing our well-being. In what little spare time I had, I always enjoyed reading literature and philosophy that spoke to these issues. My favorite novel was *The Magic Mountain* by the Nobel Prize winner Thomas Mann, a literary masterpiece recounting the journey of its hero, Hans Castorp, to a tuberculosis sanatorium high in the Swiss Alps. I loved this book for its sweeping panorama of human experience—illness, love, death, philosophy—and its meandering tale of intellectual, emotional, and spiritual growth.

I also loved the words of Indian philosophers who wrote about our capacity to refine human experience. I was fascinated with ideas like those of Nagarjuna, who somewhere around the year 200 wrote, "There is no difference between samsara [suffering] and nirvana [contentment]." What did this cryptic idea mean? He seemed to be pointing to something that was really important.

I had also been inspired by these words from Annie Dillard's *The Writing Life*: "The life of sensation is the life of greed; it requires more and more. The life of the spirit requires less and less; time is ample and its passage sweet."[14]

Where time is ample and its passage sweet: this seemed the exact mirror opposite of corporate life. Was it a poetic cliché or something to which we could really aspire? I wanted to find out.

I felt embarrassed by my interests, however. What was a Harvard corporate guy doing thinking about philosophy? I was a business warrior, a corporate defender. I clearly knew how to play that role. But there lay the challenge. It *felt* like a role. For as much as I threw myself into that role, I still felt a bit like an actor on a stage. Deep down, something else was bubbling up.

Compounding these thoughts was an observation that Hillary and I had often made: For all the innovation and prosperity that modern economies generated, there seemed to be a corresponding increase in stress and anxiety. If knowledge and prosperity were the harbingers of the good life, we ought to be a race of enlightened beings by now. In our part of the world, education and material well-being had reached heights that had surely exceeded anything in history, yet we did not seem to have a particular advantage for gaining wisdom, joy, and peace of mind. On the contrary, stress levels and the drive to perform seemed more intense than ever. I also wondered, if the drive to succeed was so intense, what would eventually happen as illness, aging, or other reversals in life diminish one's capacities?

On this front, Hillary and I were doing our best to guide our own children through the pressure cooker that characterized modern child raising. One time I asked one of Sarah's teachers why there was so much homework in elementary school.

"This is what they'll have to deal with in middle school," was the answer.

"But they're in elementary school," I thought to myself.

— —

14. Annie Dillard, *The Writing Life* (Harper Perennial, 1989), p. 32.

I wanted to explore what we could do about the pressures and anxieties of contemporary life, and I hypothesized that there must be solutions in the words of the world's philosophers and spiritual thinkers.

So as things slowed down for me at Pixar, I sensed the time had come to say "enough," to take a break from corporate life, and to take time to search for answers to the questions I was passionate about. Pixar's success meant that I could now afford to take some time off, something I had never done before. Hillary and I had gone straight from college to graduate school to work to raising a family, without ever taking a breath. Through good fortune, I had come to a place where I could finally take one. Maybe I could put that time to good use.

I resolved to take a sabbatical to read, learn, and explore my interests more deeply. I thought I might take six months or a year to delve into it, and as the calendar turned from one century into the next, I decided to share my aspirations with Steve. I asked if we could meet at his house late one afternoon.

"It is hard for me to say this," I began, "but it's time for me to move on from my day-to-day duties at Pixar."

I don't think Steve was totally surprised. He knew Pixar was on a surer footing now, and that I had less on my plate.

"What do you want to do?" Steve asked.

"I want to explore philosophy and Eastern ideas for human well-being," I said, "and how these might integrate with modern life."

"How will you do that?" Steve wanted to know.

"I'm not really certain," I said. "I have a long reading list, and some ideas to get me started."

"Will you have a teacher?" Steve asked.

I knew Steve admired Zen Buddhist ideas and understood the importance of good teachers.

"I don't have one right now," I said. "I'll have to figure that out as I go."

Then Steve added something that stuck with me for a long time.

"I'm glad one of us is doing it," he said.

I've long pondered what Steve meant by those words; he had said them so sincerely. With the passage of time, I came to believe that Steve understood the possibilities of a life beyond corporate performance and product development, that beneath the corporate warrior was a sense that there were inner depths to plumb, and that—consciously or unconsciously—for him one had yielded to the other.

Steve explored some possibilities with me for staying on at Pixar, including becoming president. As flattering as that was, I felt it would not change much. Steve, Ed, and I would still work the same way. Nor would it help me figure what kind of deli I wanted. In the end, we agreed that I would join Pixar's board of directors, and I told him I would be around anytime to help if the company needed it.

"We'll miss you," Steve said, "more than you think. But I understand."

I felt very grateful for his support.

It was hard to clean out my office and say goodbye to Pixar. I wrote an e-mail to the entire company expressing how much I would miss everyone, how amazing everyone was, and how happy I was to be joining Pixar's board of directors. I ended the message with these words:

> I could not imagine a better working relationship than the one forged among Steve, Ed, and myself. I have learned so much from each of them and I have grown to love and respect them as partners, as leaders, and as humans.
>
> For those of you who take yoga, you know that at the end of each class it is common to place the hands together and utter the Indian greeting "Namaste." It means: "I honor the place in you of love, of truth, of peace. When you are in that place in you and I am in that place in me, we are one." Namaste.

The outpouring I received from this e-mail was extraordinary. From every corner of the company, from individuals I knew well, and even from individuals I didn't, came messages of gratitude, warmth, inspiration, and support. As I prepared to leave, Ed and John gave me a gift. It was a beautifully framed, hand-drawn picture of the characters in *Toy Story* and *A Bug's Life*. Above the image was a large **THANKS LAWRENCE**! and surrounding it were touching handwritten notes of thanks and support from many of my colleagues. I had never realized this was how people felt. For a person who had all but gone out of his way to keep his personal and business lives separate, I had utterly failed.

26

A HUNDRED YEARS

MY ENTHUSIASTIC LEAP INTO A NEW WORLD TURNED OUT to be more like a series of stumbles. It takes time to learn one's way in new terrain, and it is hard, maybe impossible, to do so without taking wrong turns and hitting dead ends. I was plunging into a world of Eastern philosophy and meditation I knew very little about.

I was drawn to Joseph Campbell's observation that "one of our problems today is that we are not well acquainted with the literature of the spirit."[15] *The literature of the spirit.* That seemed like a very good place to begin.

I assembled a collection of books, including a healthy dose of Western literature, mythology, philosophy, and contemporary physics and biology; books on Western religion and its mystical counterparts, Kabbala and Christian mysticism; as well as works by Hindu yogis, Sufi mystics, and Buddhist masters. Before long, I had many favorites.

Brian Greene's *The Elegant Universe* was a tour de force in modern physics. David Bohm's *Wholeness and the Implicate Order* brilliantly drew from physics to demonstrate important philosophical ideas. There was Herbert Guenther's *Ecstatic Spontaneity*, a tribute to the Buddhist sage Saraha, in which Guenther wrote, "We humans are fragmented and divided beings, at odds with ourselves and our surrounding world. We suffer from our ongoing fragmentation and

— —

15. Joseph Campbell, *The Power of Myth* (Anchor Books, 1991), p. 1.

yearn for wholeness."[16] This contrast of fragmentation and wholeness seemed to come up often.

I read T.R.V. Murti and Jay Garfield, two brilliant scholars whose expositions on Buddhist Middle Way philosophy were unprecedented in the English language; Aldous Huxley's groundbreaking *The Perennial Philosophy; Kabloona,* a riveting memoir of Gontran de Poncins's journey to live with the Inuit; Elisabeth Kübler-Ross's seminal *On Death and Dying,* which sparked an entire movement to humanize death; and Brenda Ueland's classic *If You Want to Write,* a monument to self-expression, written or otherwise. I read Nietzsche and Kafka, Camus and Wolfe, Pirsig and Didion, Heinlein and Clarke. I immersed myself in these and other works, excitedly following the threads from their footnotes and citations, making notes of the passages that most moved me, and generally giving myself the kind of education that I had never had time for earlier in my life.

One idea that strongly appealed to me was the Middle Way, an ancient Buddhist philosophy that has inspired and guided meditation masters for centuries. It is based on the insight that the mind cannot comprehend the full complexity of reality. Instead, in order to function, we rely on approximations of reality, usually in the form of images, templates, concepts, and stories that we hold in our minds. These approximations give us enough structure to get things done —*functional reality,* the Middle Way thinkers called it.

But because the approximations we use to function fall short of the way things truly are, we often suffer when reality conflicts with our perceptions. The Middle Way is about finding harmony between the *structure* that helps us function and the *fluidity* that opens us to experience more ease, richness, and connection in our lives.

One way to illustrate the ideas of the Middle Way is to imagine that there are two people inside of us. One is a bureaucrat; the other,

16. Herbert Guenther, *Ecstatic Spontaneity: Saraha's Three Cycles of Doha* (Asian Humanities Press, 1993), p. 16.

an artist or free spirit. The job of the bureaucrat is to get things done: wake up on time, pay the bills, earn good grades. The bureaucrat likes stability, rules, and values efficiency and performance. The artist or free spirit within us cares about joy, love, adventure, spontaneity, creativity, and feeling deeply connected and alive. The free spirit wants to break through the sea of convention and expectation in which we often find ourselves swimming.

The insight of the Middle Way is that becoming stuck in either of these states inevitably leads to frustration. If we are too focused on function, accumulation, and performance, we may wind up wondering if we have truly lived. If, on the other hand, we are so focused on living free and engaging our passions, we may become frustrated by lack of momentum or grounding. The Middle Way holds that the best outcomes arise from harmonizing these two sides—from harvesting our positive nature, spirit, and humanity without ignoring practicality. This invariably calls for finding the courage to look beyond the conventions that drive how we presently function.

Here was a philosophy—together with a system of meditation for realizing it—that I really wanted to study more. To do so, I would need a teacher, someone to help me navigate the terrain.

Although I met Western scholars and Tibetan lamas who understood this field, I felt a chasm between us. The Tibetan lamas had access to ideas I wanted to explore, but their monastic, Tibetan paradigms created an obstacle. I had a hard time connecting with their rituals, such as bowing to the ground and reciting in Tibetan. Instead of embracing the rituals, I kept asking myself, "Why do I have to do this?" I had too much resistance. On the other hand, the Western scholars were very learned, but I found myself too caught up in academic nuances rather than the pragmatic methods I had hoped to find.

All this made me quite skeptical about finding a teacher I could trust, and I searched for many months to find one. Then, one day in 2000, a scholar of Indian philosophy whom I had befriended introduced Hillary and me to his teacher, a Brazilian-born Tibetan Buddhist master named Segyu Choepel Rinpoche. He went by the honorary title Rinpoche.

We were invited to meet Rinpoche at his home in the rolling hills of Sebastopol, California, about an hour and a half north of San Francisco. Home would not be quite the way to describe it actually. It was a temple, a traditional Tibetan Buddhist meditation temple, full of ornate images and iconography—beautiful and authentic, but the kind I typically had a difficult time relating to. Meditation cushions lined the walls, and the smell of incense filled the air. When we arrived, Rinpoche was sitting comfortably on some cushions on one side of the room. Around fifty years old, he was of medium height, stocky, with a shaved head and a warm, magnetic smile. He spoke with a Portuguese accent, and he wore the dark red robes of a Tibetan Buddhist monk.

"Come in, come in," he said warmly. "Would you like some tea?"

With that, we sat down and described how we came to be there. Rinpoche listened attentively and shared a few details of his own story —his upbringing in Rio, his path through computer engineering, Brazilian healing, and Tibetan Buddhism. We were fascinated. He showed us around his simple but immaculately kept home. We enjoyed some tea. It could not have been more unassuming. Rinpoche seemed as well versed in Western news, culture, and technology as he was in Buddhist philosophy and meditation, and the conversation was warm and comfortable from the outset.

"There was such a positive feeling in there," Hillary noted on the drive home.

"It was very comfortable," I said. "I felt really at ease."

"I'd like to come back," Hillary added. "I think I can learn a lot from him."

I felt the same way. The ease and pleasantness of the conversation had made me drop my guard.

Over the next year, Hillary and I drove back and forth to Sebastopol to attend Rinpoche's classes and retreats. He brought a remarkable depth and vigor to meditation practices and their underlying philosophy. During this time, a friendship also began to blossom. Rinpoche had an infectious zest for life. He was a connoisseur with a taste for good coffee, artisan chocolate, and fine foods, and he loved to travel and ski. To Rinpoche there is a world of difference between insatiable craving and joyful indulgence.

Working with Rinpoche also helped me drop my skepticism about studying with a spiritual teacher. It helped that Rinpoche himself displayed enormous reverence for his own teachers. They were a source of deep connection for him, a feeling of being part of a profound lineage of insight. At the same time, he was as passionate about modern thought, science, and technology as he was about ancient meditation practices. I was inspired by this combination of respect for tradition and eagerness to embrace modern thought.

In late 2002, Hillary made an observation.

"He wants to change the way we engage with these practices, you know," she said. "He wants to make them more accessible for contemporary practitioners."

"Are you sure?" I replied. "His practices are quite traditional."

"They are traditional only because Rinpoche is using the tools available to him," Hillary said. "He wants us to help. He wants you to help him develop a strategy."

I understood that Rinpoche aspired to do more for Westerners. I was moved by that idea myself. I was just very skeptical about it. The Eastern traditions were designed for monastics in the Himalayas, not the tech-savvy go-getters of the cosmopolitan West. But Hillary would have none of it, and so one day I suggested to Rinpoche that we at least assess the challenge of what it would take to make the meditation tradition we were studying truly accessible in modern life.

Rinpoche was eager to do this assessment too, and so, beginning in January 2003, five of us gathered in the living room of a small house in Palo Alto, California, placed whiteboards all along the walls, and dove into the challenge. There was Rinpoche, Hillary, myself, and two other students of Rinpoche: Pam Moriarty and Christina Juskiewicz. Pam was a longtime meditator, grief counselor, and a wonderfully kind, gentle, and compassionate person. Christina was a Buddhist nun and Rinpoche's assistant. She was brimming with an unshakable, steadfast dedication to apply all she had learned to help others.

Every day for a month, we talked about how this brilliant method for refining human experience had become imprisoned in a cultural wrapper that made it hard to access. We examined the differences between ancient Eastern culture and the modern West, the impact of modern knowledge on spiritual traditions, and how Buddhist ideas for contentment and peace of mind had historically spread to different parts of the world.

At the end of thirty days, we had a plan, though perhaps *dream* was a better word. It called for making a long tradition of meditation practices accessible in our time, aligning those practices with modern discovery, and conforming them to contemporary social norms. It also acknowledged the importance of training individuals to be able to perpetuate that tradition.

As I looked at the plan, I was moved by the immensity of the challenge we were considering. It seemed beyond our capacity to take this on, certainly beyond my capacity. The fast pace, the pressures to perform, the onslaught of media and information that characterized contemporary life made it hard to slow down, hard to value the profundity of a deep tradition. Many seemed more interested in quick fixes to gain peace of mind—a book, a class, a weekend away—when it often takes much more to undo the habits that keep us stressed. Our task would not be an easy one.

"This will take five hundred years to achieve," I protested. "We're talking about the wholesale restatement of a two-thousand-year-old tradition."

"No," Rinpoche replied. "Just a hundred years."

"A hundred years!" I exclaimed. "Isn't that a little beyond our scope?"

"It's a big task," Rinpoche said calmly. "What else are you doing?"

Hillary, Pam, Christina, and I looked at each other. Was he serious? Who in their right mind takes on a hundred-year project? Four years or bust was my Silicon Valley mindset.

"How do we do it?" I asked Rinpoche. "Except for you, none of us has any qualifications."

"Think of me like a miner who has retrieved the gold in those Tibetan mountains," he said. "Each of you is in the New World. We have to build a bridge that links one to the other. Together we can do it."

"But where do we even begin?" I asked, still half in disbelief.

"Simple," he said. "We each put one foot in front of the other, then the other foot goes in front of the first one."

I looked at Pam, at Christina, at Hillary. I could tell on their faces. They were in.

And there it was. That same sparkle I'd felt when I'd first met Steve, Ed, and John. Once again, I felt that I was part of a group that was crazy enough to take on the near impossible. Only this time I probably wouldn't be around for the IPO.

So began a new chapter in my life. We named our organization Juniper, after the hearty tree that grows anywhere, including thirteen thousand feet high up in the Himalayas where many meditation masters long ago lived. Under Rinpoche's guidance, the five of us spent the next several years dissecting the works of those masters, carefully excising the essential practices from the cultural artifacts, engaging those practices, and putting them in a form suitable for contemporary meditators. We opened Juniper to the public in 2009 and established our first public meditation center in San Francisco in 2015.

We are off to a good start, but to fully realize this vision will take time. It is an investment in the idea that humanity has tremendous untapped potential, if only we can release it. This is the kind of change that occurs over generations. As such, it is a work in progress and will require many others to bring to fruition.

Juniper did not spell the end of my experience with Pixar, however. I would later realize that these endeavors were more connected than I thought, although it would take a highly unusual occurrence for me to see it.

27

THE MIDDLE WAY

I HEARD AN ENORMOUS EXPLOSION, AS THOUGH A METEOR had crashed into my car.

In an instant, I was no longer driving through the intersection. Everything was in slow motion as my mind tried to catch up with what was happening. In what seemed like minutes but could only have been seconds, I realized that I was in a major traffic accident. My car was spinning out of control.

The accident occurred one Tuesday evening in April 2014. Hillary and I were returning from a meditation and discussion at Rinpoche's house, now in Redwood City, about fifteen minutes from our home. By some small miracle, that night we had arrived there in separate cars, so Hillary was not in the car with me. She was a little ahead of me as I drove through the major intersection near our house where the accident occurred.

"If I can get out I'll be okay," I thought to myself as my car finally came to a stop. I opened the door and stumbled to the nearest street corner, where I sat down on the ground and looked back to see my utterly totaled car in the intersection. The rear door and wheel on the driver's side were completely smashed, and large pieces of the undercarriage were on the road. Two inches further up and the driver's door would have taken a direct hit.

I checked myself for physical damage. I had pain in my upper back and neck, and I was shaking uncontrollably, but everything seemed to be in the right place. I thought that if I could find one moment of calm amid this chaos, somehow it would help, so I shut my eyes and took one long, deep breath.

My next thought was about Hillary. I had to tell her what happened. I hadn't realized that the accident had been so loud that she had instinctively pulled her car over to see if anyone needed help, not thinking that I was involved. By now, she was walking back to the intersection and saw my car in the middle of it. After a horrifying moment of dread, she saw me sitting on the sidewalk, with some people around me checking if I was okay.

Thankfully, I was. I had been hit by a drunk driver in a Dodge Ram truck, driving with a suspended license due to a prior drunk driving conviction. He fled the scene and was later arrested. For the next few days I lay around with a neck and back so stiff I could hardly move.

Several weeks and much physical therapy later, Hillary and I went away for a few days to rest and recover. On one rainy day, we were sitting on a beach under an umbrella. Hillary was reading. I was just sitting there, mesmerized by the waves, wind, and rain, reflecting on what had happened. All of a sudden, I was struck by an insight.

"I just had a thought," I said to Hillary.

"What's that?" Hillary asked.

"It's about Pixar. I never realized it before. Pixar is a great metaphor for the ideas of the Middle Way."

"How do you make that connection?" Hillary asked, eager to discuss it.

"All those risks we took to balance artistry with business discipline," I went on, "they're an example of what the Middle Way is talking about."

As we sat there on the beach, with rain falling around us, I excitedly shared what I meant.

When I joined Pixar in 1994, it was full of artistic and creative wizardry. That is what mesmerized me when I sat in Pixar's ramshackle screening room watching scenes from *Toy Story* for the first time. But

I quickly learned that Pixar was stuck. For all its genius, it had no momentum. It was like a starving artist. Just as the Middle Way holds that if we are too ungrounded, we can be frustrated by lack of momentum, Pixar too was ungrounded and frustrated by lack of profitability, cash, stock options, and a business road map.

Pixar's entire success depended on developing enough strategy, order, and bureaucracy to give it momentum *without* killing the creative spirit. This is the entreaty of the Middle Way: to inspire us to give expression to our spirit, creativity, and humanity and still take care of day-to-day needs and responsibilities. The Middle Way is a dance between order and freedom, bureaucracy and spirit, efficiency and artistry. Every film that Pixar made struggled with this tension and ended up better for it.

The lessons of the Middle Way can apply to any organization wrestling with these forces. What we accomplished at Pixar was rare. Very rare perhaps. But it doesn't have to be. We can build extraordinary organizations that foster creativity, dignity, and humanity while respecting business disciplines. We just have to be tuned to it; we have to be willing to balance bureaucracy with the depth and subtlety of creative inspiration, and awareness of the human dimension of our endeavors. This won't make us weak or soft. Pixar was certainly neither of those. As it did for Pixar, it will simply make us better.

As I sat there in the gentle rain, I also reflected on the broader questions that inspired my journey beyond Pixar. I am convinced that we humans do better when we have something to ground us, a deep source from which we can draw wisdom, insight, and inspiration. The goal of that source is to empower us, to bring depth and fulfillment to our lives, to give us the means to soar. Myths, customs, and community rituals have long served these purposes—the Ohlone spoke to the sun each morning for good reason. What will serve us in these ways going forward? Unbridled efficiency, for all the prosperity it provides, can exact a heavy toll on our humanity if we are not careful. To truly soar, we need something from which we can push off, something to guide us.

For myself, I found in the Middle Way a solution that believes in the potential and possibilities of the mind and calls upon us to tap into that potential. It is a means to discover how what we take as truths are often merely paradigms that we can go beyond. I found this to be both a beautiful methodology and an inspiring way of thinking and being. This is why I wake up each morning and, before the rush of the day begins, take a few minutes to sit down, recollect the wisdom of the Middle Way masters, and enjoy my meditation.

The car accident gave me an unexpected chance to reflect on the different strands of my life. Looking back at Pixar all these years later, I felt immense pride at the way we transformed a struggling organization into a magnificent studio that mesmerized audiences the world over. Now, it was uncanny to observe how the threads of the Middle Way were woven through my different experiences, even when I was barely aware of it.

And so it was that I found myself sitting on the beach in the rain, recovering from the narrowest of escapes. In the quiet of that moment, as I took in the beauty that surrounded me, I could not help but marvel at seeing a shining example of my favorite philosophy in the story of a little company called Pixar.

EPILOGUE

"**I'M DELIGHTED TO INTRODUCE MY OLD FRIEND LAWRENCE** Levy," Ed announced. "Few people understood the strategic issues Pixar faced the way that Lawrence did. I'm quite sure we'll learn things today that we've long forgotten."

This is how Ed introduced me in May 2015, as I sat in the wings of the beautiful auditorium on Pixar's sparkling campus in Emeryville, California. The auditorium was a far cry from the old screening room in Point Richmond; it was a proper movie theater, with spacious velvet-covered seats, sophisticated lighting controls, and the quiet serenity of soundproofed walls. Ed had invited me to give a talk at Pixar a couple of months earlier, after we met for a walk in San Francisco one Saturday afternoon. We had forged a nice habit of meeting every so often for dinner or a walk. It was always great to reconnect with Ed, and we easily picked up our conversation right where we had left off.

"I developed this talk about Pixar," I told Ed during that walk. "It tells the strategic and business story behind the company and links it to bigger ideas about the Middle Way. I gave it recently at the Harvard Business and Law schools. They loved it."

"We should do it at Pixar," Ed said immediately. "I want people to understand Pixar's history. This is a really important part of it."

"That would be wonderful," I said. "It would be very meaningful for me to do that."

That is exactly how I felt when I got in my car a couple of hours earlier to make the drive to Pixar. I didn't have to drive as far as Point

Richmond anymore. Years earlier Steve had orchestrated the building of Pixar's campus in Emeryville, just across the Bay Bridge, tucked to the south of the Berkeley Hills. It had been a couple of years since I had visited Pixar, but I never tired of seeing the film posters that lined the walls. *The Incredibles, Cars, Wall-E, Finding Nemo, Monsters, Inc., Up, Ratatouille, Brave*—who could have imagined such a legacy from Pixar's humble beginnings?

Pixar's campus was not the only thing that had changed.

Jenna, our *Toy Story* baby, was now nineteen, a sophomore at the University of Washington in Seattle, majoring in psychology and communications. Sarah, our gleeful seven-year-old playing with Lite-Brite at *Toy Story*'s premiere, was twenty-six. She had studied psychology and neuroscience as an undergraduate at the University of Southern California and was now at the Massachusetts Eye and Ear Infirmary in Boston, finishing a clinical doctorate degree in audiology from the University of Washington. She had connected with Stanford Medical Center about a possible position there. Jason, now twenty-nine, had studied economics and creative writing, also at USC, and earned an MBA from Stanford. He was passionate about developing high-quality story experiences and was producing his first one for Pocket Gems, a mobile gaming company in San Francisco. Hillary and I remained engaged in our work at Juniper.

There had been one other change too.

My drive to Pixar took me past Steve's house, still just a few blocks from mine. It had been three and a half years since he died. Three and a half years. How could so much time have passed? My memory of our time together was as vivid as if I had seen him the day before. I could only imagine the things we might have discussed had he still been here: the political infighting in Washington, trends in blockbuster film releases, Pixar's and Apple's newest quests, the latest adventures of our children. Or maybe we would have said few words. Just sat and enjoyed a few moments of quiet.

On this day, as I headed to Pixar for the first time in a few years, I slowed down as I drove by Steve's house. I felt moved by a mixture of sadness and nostalgia. How nice it would have been to pull over just one more time and see if he was home. How good it would have felt to enter through the side gate, admire the great variety of vegetables growing in his garden, and walk through the kitchen door; to say hello to the chef working quietly in the kitchen and enjoy the delicious smells of the day's foods; to walk down the hallway to Steve's office and knock gently on the door; to peer inside and check if he was there; and then, just one more time, to see him look up, smile, and say to me:

"Hey, Lawrence. You up for a walk?"

ACKNOWLEDGMENTS

This project would never have come to fruition were it not for the invaluable efforts of some extraordinary individuals.

Jamie Malinowski has been all I can hope for in a writing coach. At one moment during the project, I told Hillary, "Forget the book; all I want is a gold star from Jamie." Jamie's unrelenting, critical eye and heartfelt concern for every part of the book made for a potent if not humbling source of guidance.

If a literary agent is meant to be a steady, guiding hand and a staunch defender of an author's interests, then I can testify that David McCormick and the staff at McCormick Literary are amazing at what they do. The same would go for my editor, Rick Wolff, at Houghton Mifflin Harcourt. He believed unwaveringly in the book from day one and has been a steady, grounding force behind the scenes the whole way. Many thanks also to the entire team at Houghton Mifflin Harcourt; I am very fortunate to have been in their very capable and dedicated hands.

One of my favorite parts of writing this book was reconnecting with the people in it. It proved to be a wonderful opportunity for reminiscing with old friends and hearing their insights on the story. I remain immensely grateful to Ed Catmull, John Lasseter, Larry Sonsini, Skip Brittenham, Sam Fischer, Todd Carter, and Hal Vogel for their contributions, friendship, and support.

Many thanks to my dear friend Lisa Brennan-Jobs, who helped me believe I could turn this story into a book even when I doubted it. I am deeply grateful for her encouragement and support.

Much gratitude also to my great friend Peter Glassman. From long walks along the seawalls of Vancouver to our inspiring correspondence, Peter's encouragement spurred me on more than I think he knows.

Very special thanks to Christina Juskiewicz, Pam Moriarty, Terry Moriarty, Will Pierog, and David Pirko, each of whom took much time and care to read the manuscript and share their many thoughtful insights.

If there were a living example of what it means to embody the Middle Way, it would be Segyu Rinpoche. The vitality and energy of life course through him, and he is a tribute to selfless action. He has taught me what it means to enjoy simultaneously a beautiful friendship and a profound teacher.

Which brings me to my immediate family, Hillary, Jason, Sarah, and Jenna.

Jason has blossomed into a wonderful creative leader. His penetrating critiques of each chapter, sensitivity to story structure, and willingness to patiently talk through any detail helped me every step of the way.

Sarah has long brought the highest standards of excellence to all she does. I have now discovered that this includes an uncanny eye for editing. The book benefited tremendously from her discerning comments and many thoughtful ideas.

Jenna has insight way beyond her years. She took to playfully using smiley faces and sad faces on her reviews of the manuscript. Although the moment in the story when she was born received the biggest smiley face, ignoring the sad faces would have made for a far lesser book.

Hillary is my partner in life. She has always skillfully encouraged me to be my best while remaining my staunchest defender. Her keen critical eye watched over the evolution of the book, making sure it reflected what happened to the best of her, and my, memory. The story reveals a good part of our adventure together. I am ever thankful that after more than thirty years, we are still on that adventure.

At the end of Jason's review of the final draft he wrote:

"You wrote a book. Yay!"

We all did it together.

INDEX

ABOUT THE AUTHOR

Lawrence Levy is a former Silicon Valley attorney and business executive who was personally recruited by Steve Jobs in 1994 as CFO and member of the Office of the President of Pixar Animation Studios. Levy was responsible for Pixar's business strategy and IPO and guided Pixar's transformation from a money-losing graphics company into a multibillion-dollar entertainment studio. He later joined Pixar's board of directors.

Levy left corporate life to study Eastern philosophy and meditation and their relevance to modern life. He now writes and teaches on this topic and cofounded Juniper Foundation (www.juniperpath .org) to pursue this work. Originally from London, Levy earned degrees from Indiana University and Harvard Law School. He lives with his wife, Hillary, in Palo Alto, California.

For more information please visit www.lawrencelevy.com.